THE POLITICAL LIVES OF VICTORIAN ANIMALS

During the Victorian era, animals were increasingly viewed not as property or utility, but as thinking, feeling subjects worthy of inclusion within a political community. This book reexamines the nineteenth-century British animal welfare movement and animal characters in the Victorian novel in light of liberal thought, and argues that liberalism was a decisive factor in determining the cultural, ideological, and material makeup of animal–human relationships. While the animal welfare movement often represented animals as desiring submission to the human, animal characters in the Victorian novel critiqued the liberal norms that led to the oppression of both animals and humans. Through readings of animal rights legislation, animal welfare texts, and writings by Charles Dickens, Lewis Carroll, Thomas Hardy, and Olive Schreiner, Anna Feuerstein outlines the remarkably powerful political role animals played in the Victorian novel, as they offer ways to move beyond the exclusionary and contradictory strategies of liberal thought.

ANNA FEUERSTEIN is an assistant professor at the University of Hawai'i at Mānoa.

CAMBRIDGE STUDIES IN NINETEENTH-CENTURY
LITERATURE AND CULTURE

General Editor
GILLIAN BEER, *University of Cambridge*

Editorial Board
ISOBEL ARMSTRONG, *Birkbeck, University of London*
KATE FLINT, *University of Southern California*
CATHERINE GALLAGHER, *University of California, Berkeley*
D. A. MILLER, *University of California, Berkeley*
J. HILLIS MILLER, *University of California, Irvine*
DANIEL PICK, *Birkbeck, University of London*
MARY POOVEY, *New York University*
SALLY SHUTTLEWORTH, *University of Oxford*
HERBERT TUCKER, *University of Virginia*

Nineteenth-century British literature and culture have been rich fields for interdisciplinary studies. Since the turn of the twentieth century, scholars and critics have tracked the intersections and tensions between Victorian literature and the visual arts, politics, social organization, economic life, technical innovations, scientific thought – in short, culture in its broadest sense. In recent years, theoretical challenges and historiographical shifts have unsettled the assumptions of previous scholarly synthesis and called into question the terms of older debates. Whereas the tendency in much past literary critical interpretation was to use the metaphor of culture as 'background', feminist, Foucauldian, and other analyses have employed more dynamic models that raise questions of power and of circulation. Such developments have reanimated the field. This series aims to accommodate and promote the most interesting work being undertaken on the frontiers of the field of nineteenth-century literary studies: work which intersects fruitfully with other fields of study such as history, or literary theory, or the history of science. Comparative as well as interdisciplinary approaches are welcomed.

A complete list of titles published will be found at the end of the book.

THE POLITICAL LIVES OF VICTORIAN ANIMALS

Liberal Creatures in Literature and Culture

ANNA FEUERSTEIN

University of Hawai'i at Mānoa

CAMBRIDGE
UNIVERSITY PRESS

University Printing House, Cambridge CB2 8BS, United Kingdom

One Liberty Plaza, 20th Floor, New York, NY 10006, USA

477 Williamstown Road, Port Melbourne, VIC 3207, Australia

314-321, 3rd Floor, Plot 3, Splendor Forum, Jasola District Centre, New Delhi - 110025, India

79 Anson Road, #06-04/06, Singapore 079906

Cambridge University Press is part of the University of Cambridge.

It furthers the University's mission by disseminating knowledge in the pursuit of education, learning and research at the highest international levels of excellence.

www.cambridge.org
Information on this title: www.cambridge.org/9781108730211
DOI: 10.1017/9781108632096

© Anna Feuerstein 2019

This publication is in copyright. Subject to statutory exception and to the provisions of relevant collective licensing agreements, no reproduction of any part may take place without the written permission of Cambridge University Press.

First published 2019
First paperback edition 2021

A catalogue record for this publication is available from the British Library

Library of Congress Cataloging in Publication data
NAMES: Feuerstein, Anna, author.
TITLE: The political lives of Victorian animals : liberal creatures in literature and culture / Anna Feuerstein, University of Hawaii, Manoa.
DESCRIPTION: Cambridge, United Kingdom ; New York, NY : Cambridge University Press, 2019. | SERIES: Cambridge studies in nineteenth-century literature and culture | Includes bibliographical references and index.
IDENTIFIERS: LCCN 2019001954 | ISBN 9781108492966 (hardback)
SUBJECTS: LCSH: Animal rights–Great Britain. | Animal welfare–Great Britain. | Animals in literature. | Human-animal relationships in literature.
CLASSIFICATION: LCC HV4805.A3 F48 2019 | DDC 179/.3094109034–dc23
LC record available at https://lccn.loc.gov/2019001954

ISBN 978-1-108-49296-6 Hardback
ISBN 978-1-108-73021-1 Paperback

Cambridge University Press has no responsibility for the persistence or accuracy of URLs for external or third-party internet websites referred to in this publication, and does not guarantee that any content on such websites is, or will remain, accurate or appropriate.

*Mostly for Jack, but also for Eliot and Oliver,
my little friends*

As we can see, the model for the art of government is that of God imposing his laws upon his creatures.
— Michel Foucault, "Omnes et Singulatim"

Contents

List of Figures	*page* ix
Acknowledgments	x

Introduction: The Political Lives of Victorian Animals   1

PART I ANTI-CRUELTY LEGISLATION AND ANIMAL WELFARE   29

1 The Government of Animals: Anti-Cruelty Legislation and the Making of Liberal Creatures   31

2 The Incessant Care of the Victorian Shepherd: Animal Welfare's Pastoral Power   63

PART II DEMOCRACY, EDUCATION, AND ALTERNATIVE SUBJECTIVITY   93

3 'Tame submission to injustice is unworthy of a Raven': Charles Dickens's Animal Character   95

4 *Alice in Wonderland*'s Animal Pedagogy: Democracy and Alternative Subjectivity in Mid-Victorian Liberal Education   134

PART III THE BIOPOLITICS OF ANIMAL CAPITAL   161

5 Animal Capital and the Lives of Sheep: Thomas Hardy's Biopolitical Realism   163

6 The Political Lives of Animals in Victorian Empire: Olive
   Schreiner's Anti-Colonial Animal Politics   198

Coda   227
Works Cited   229
Index   247

Figures

1.1 "Birds without Friends in Parliament. – No. 3" *page* 56
1.2 "Birds without Friends in Parliament. – No. 4" 56
2.1 "Toby. – A Portrait by Harrison Weir" 81
6.1 "Attacked by an Ostrich." Frontispiece to R. M. Ballantyne, *The Settler and the Savage* 210

Acknowledgments

This book began as a dissertation in the English department at Michigan State University, where it flourished under the formal guidance of Zarena Aslami, Justus Nieland, Stephen Rachman, and Judith Stoddard. I thank them for their support and intellectual guidance. I also thank the less formal support of many other colleagues from MSU, especially Hannah Allen, Erin Beard, Kate Birdsall, Mike Blouin, Megan Charley, Cajetan Iheka, Neal Klomp, Elizabeth Pellerito, and Morgan Shipley. My earliest mentors were at the University of Washington. Lana Dalley, the first to teach me the intricacies of the triple-decker novel, nourished my love for Victorian literature and showed me how to teach it well. While Doug Collins may be disappointed I never ended up in a French department, I think he will be happy to see both animals and Foucault in the following pages. Many conversations with Jonathan Crimmins and Charles LaPorte helped develop my thinking as a Victorianist.

What luck to end up in the English department at the University of Hawai'i-Mānoa! While the weather does not align with my ideas of paradise (too much sun!), my amazing colleagues across the UH system make this a wonderful place to be. Not only did I receive the kindest possible welcome, but the political energy of this department continually inspires me to ground my teaching and scholarship in social justice. Thank you to everyone in the English department, and others across the UH system, especially Sarah Allen, Cristina Bacchilega, Nandini Chandra, Cynthia Franklin, Monica Ghosh, Kristine Kotecki, Jesse Knutson, J. Vera Lee, Laura Lyons, Njoroge Njoroge, Georganne Nordstrom, Nandi Odhiambo, Suzanna Reiss, Yasmine Romero (the best cat sitter ever!), Shawna Yang Ryan, Susan Schultz, Subramanian Shankar, and John Zuern. Special thanks go to Carmen Nolte-Odhiambo, an amazing co-editor and a dear friend. Carmen taught me the joys of developing scholarship collectively, and helped me grow as a thinker and a writer. Paul Lyons, who passed away while this book was under review, was a true role model. He was an incredible colleague, beloved teacher, brilliant scholar, and constant ally. We miss him dearly. My students, undergrad and graduate, continually educate me. I thank them for their generosity and patience as I learn about Hawaiian history and culture. A special thanks to Veronica Freeman, Kalei Galarita, Joseph Han, Brittney Holt, Sam Ikehara, Scott Kaalele, Caryn Lesuma, Mike Pak, and Tina Togafau.

I presented parts of this book at conferences across the country and at the University of Hawai'i, where I received much helpful feedback. Thank you to everyone who offered suggestions for development. My colleagues in Charles Lawrence's junior faculty seminar helped me see this project from many angles, and especially pushed my thinking on Olive Schreiner. Thank you to the lovely folks at the Vegetarian Society in Manchester, who were so kind to me in the time I spent there. I especially thank them for making my research possible by giving me a space heater to warm the weak constitution I've developed while living in Hawai'i. Thanks also to the librarians at the British Library, and David Allen at the RSPCA, who allowed me to go through their archives.

Many thanks to the generous people at Cambridge University Press. I spoke with Linda Bree at NAVSA back in 2014 when this project was in its early stages, and her encouragement and excitement inspired me to keep going. Her advice helped me develop the project in productive ways. I also thank Gillian Beer, Bethany Thomas, Carrie Parkinson, and the anonymous reviewers.

A very early version of Chapter 2 was published as "'I promise to protect Dumb creatures': Pastoral Power and the Limits of Victorian Animal Protection," in *Society and Animals*, vol. 23, no. 2, 2015, pp. 148–165, while a version of Chapter 4 was published as "*Alice in Wonderland*'s Animal Pedagogy: Governmentality and Alternative Subjectivity in Mid-Victorian Liberal Education," *Victorian Review*, vol. 44, no. 2, fall 2018.

Obvious thanks go to family and other friends who have supported me academically and non-academically: Katharine Beutner, Rebecca Evans, Lydia Feuerstein, Shelly Feuerstein, Stacy Hagiya, Rachel Skibo, Jack Taylor II, Janet Taylor, Phil Tobin, and Leah Woldman. Nicole Harrison and Dan Landon first encouraged me to become an English major, and taught me how to talk about literature. Tony Feuerstein was skeptical of my choice to major in English, but supported me nonetheless. Thank you for letting me pursue my own desires, and encouraging me to do so.

Jack Taylor – my best friend, favorite colleague, and husband – has made life better in every way. Ever since we met in graduate school, he has supported me in ways that are too numerous to list here. This book has emerged from our many conversations over the years; he has read nearly every word, and his feedback has been invaluable. I thank him for his kindness, generosity, patience, forgiveness, humor, and, of course, his love.

Introduction
The Political Lives of Victorian Animals

> And being furnished with like Faculties, sharing all in one Community of Nature, there cannot be supposed any such *Subordination* among us, that may Authorize us to destroy one another, as if we were made for one another's uses, as the inferior ranks of Creatures are for ours.
> – John Locke, *Second Treatise on Government*

> Human beings are not like sheep; and even sheep are not undistinguishably alike.
> – John Stuart Mill, *On Liberty*

> All animals, particularly those whose services are most required, as if conscious that they were ordained to be subject to man's dominion yield to it without reluctance, asking in return only to be treated with humanity.
> – William Drummond, *The Rights of Animals and Man's Obligation to Treat Them with Humanity*

This is a story about the political lives of animals in Victorian Britain. It seeks to show how mostly domestic animals were increasingly incorporated into a liberal political community, and how Victorian novels were fundamentally engaged with their politicization. *The Political Lives of Victorian Animals* reads animals outside of a symbolic and metaphoric framework to show how the rise of animal welfare discourses and anti-cruelty laws shifted how Victorians understood, related to, and imagined animals and animal subjectivity, especially within the novel. Not only did the rise of Victorian liberal thought and its regulatory strategies influence conceptions of and relationships with animals, but these new understandings of animals also affected the development of Victorian liberalism's most foundational categories: character, individualism, education, property, and self-government. Representations of animals throughout Victorian culture were increasingly liberalized and politicized, as animals were imagined as both having liberal qualities and challenging them.

The Political Lives of Victorian Animals argues that while nineteenth-century British animal welfare discourse aimed to give animals political representation, and profoundly challenged how animals were conceptualized, it largely positioned animals within pastoral power, a power of care regulating their conduct through representing them as desiring subjection. The Victorian novel, I suggest, gave animals an alternate form of political representation that destabilized liberal categories governing animal subjectivity, and through more expansive representational strategies included animals into demands for democracy. Novels by Charles Dickens, Lewis Carroll, Thomas Hardy, and Olive Schreiner, among many other writers and thinkers, demonstrate the influence of Victorian liberalism on animals while working through the problems animals posed to liberal thought as Victorians sought to represent them literarily and politically.

Animals did not always fit easily into the confines of Victorian liberalism, and movements to incorporate them into a political community highlight the limitations of liberal thought and tensions within its claims of inclusivity. I adopt the capaciousness of the term "liberalism," and use it to signify a set of ideas, discourses, and practices inspired by and inspiring legislation, social reform movements, and political philosophy, constituting an often regulatory set of habits, or "way of being in the world" (Vernon 304). L. T. Hobhouse's definition of liberalism as "an all-penetrating element of the life-structure of the modern world" (22) emphasizes the pervasive nature of liberal thought as I understand it throughout this book. More specifically, Victorian liberalism promoted progress, freedom, and equality, while guiding economic thought and the movement of capital. It inspired democratic movements while also providing rationales for imperial expansion and the subjection of non-Western peoples.[1] Victorian liberalism cultivated the liberal individual, who had reason, character, the ability to consent to governmental rule, and the capacity to transform nature into property and move up economically. For Elaine Hadley, the liberal subject is "one who originates in a private sphere that predates the public sphere of civic duty but whose status as private property owner enables his disinterested participation in the privileged, deliberative exchanges of civil society" (*Living* 67). By the

---

[1] Lauren Goodlad notes the difficulty of this term, in part because of the many ways it can be defined: "as a democratic political philosophy; a theory of progress, freedom, equality, or tolerance; a universalizing perspective; a cosmopolitan ethics; a procedural ethics rooted in theories of democratic consent; an economic doctrine; or a basis for either promoting or rejecting imperial pursuits" (*Geopolitical Aesthetic* 4). Throughout, I engage with Victorian liberalism in nearly all of these senses.

mid-nineteenth century, Hadley argues, liberalism cultivated liberal cognition, which she defines as

> a wide range of strikingly formalized mental attitudes ... such as disinterestedness, objectivity, reticence, conviction, impersonality, and sincerity, all of which carried with them a moral valence. Included under this category of cognition are also what seemed to them [the Victorians] quite specific techniques of thought production and judgment, such as "free thought," reflection, abstraction, logical reasoning, and internal deliberation. Such attitudes and techniques produced liberalized ideas in the individual, whose ideas then entered the political domain as "opinion" – liberalism's version of political agency. (*Living* 9)

The animal, by contrast, was property, irrational, or too wild for inclusion in a political community. Indeed, as Locke stresses, "inferior" animals were made for humans, and thus lack political autonomy (*Second Treatise* 271). What were considered animal qualities such as instinct, wildness, appetite, and brutality were also attributed to racialized subjects and the lower class. Mel Chen's claim that "animality is coarticulated with humanity in ways that are soundly implicated in regimes of race, nation, and gender, disrupting clear divisions and categories that have profound implications ramifying from the linguistic to the biopolitical" (159) highlights the construction and regulation of animality in both animals and humans. Animals deserved political inclusion only if they obeyed the rules of a hierarchical and civilized liberal thought.

In order to include animals in a political community, Victorian animal welfare discourse constructed animals to adhere to liberal norms: they had reason, were civilized, consented to domestication, and obeyed an animal–human hierarchy. Most often in Victorian discourses of the law, animal welfare, social reform, and education, animals were imagined as internalizing an animal–human hierarchy. Treat us well, these animals said, and we will obey your authority, as Unitarian minister William Drummond suggested in 1839: "All animals, particularly those whose services are most required, as if conscious that they were ordained to be subject to man's dominion yield to it without reluctance, asking in return only to be treated with humanity" (82–83). Throughout animal welfare discourse especially, animals showed a striking similarity to liberal individuals, as they were constructed with liberal cognition. Yet shared qualities have the opportunity for disruption; the fact that liberal discourses strove to suppress non-liberal animal qualities suggests animals had the ability to challenge the very discourses that struggled to maintain them. For alongside the inclusion of animals into the regulatory strategies of Victorian liberalism there was a counter animal politics that challenged and disrupted liberalism's central tenets and philosophies.

This disruption happens most forcefully in Victorian novels, where representations of animals register tensions within liberal discourses and offer an alternative politics. Indeed, I argue that animals in the novel should be read more politically, as they frequently advance an animal politics that destabilizes the primacy of liberal thought and its regulatory strategies. That is, rather than just projecting liberal politics onto the animal sphere, some Victorians brought animals into the political sphere, privileging animal qualities and showing how non-hegemonic forms of animality challenge liberal discourses and offer alternate forms of community and political agency. As Derrida emphasizes, one cannot assume animals are pre-political; rather, "the animal is already political, and exhibit, as is easy to do, in many examples of what are called animal societies, the appearance of refined, complicated organizations, with hierarchical structures, attributes of authority and power ... so many things that are so often attributed to and so naïvely reserved for so-called human *culture*, in opposition to *nature*" (*Beast* 14–15). More recently, Brian Massumi calls for "a different politics, one that is not a human politics of the animal, but an integrally animal politics, freed from the traditional paradigms of the nasty state of nature and the accompanying presuppositions about instinct permeating so many facets of modern thought" (2). For Massumi, animal politics asks us to rethink how we value instinct and animal epistemologies, "animality itself" (3), for "to think the animal is to think instinct. Would it even be possible to conceive of an animal without instinct? Why, then, the widespread embarrassment at the term? Why must it always be played down, like some beastly Victorian secret best left unsaid?" (54). Massumi's reference to the Victorian era is telling, for the period saw a fundamental shift in how animals were conceptualized. Yet the multiple ways Victorians imagined animality shows the reductive nature of Massumi's characterization of animality. For the Victorians, animality signified a wide array of qualities and epistemologies, both positive and negative. Cultivating an animal politics informs and challenges an anthropocentric human politics, especially the destructive yet unstable hierarchies that posit reason above instinct, civilization above nature, the human above the animal.

The Political Lives of Victorian Animals traces the rise of liberalized animal subjects and their counterpart, the animal offering alternatives to the confines of Victorian liberalism. Representations of animals can disrupt animal–human hierarchies and put pressure on animacies often reserved for the human. Understanding "language as animated, as a means of embodied condensation of social, cultural, and political life," resulting in an "*animacy hierarchy*, which conceptually arranges human life, disabled life, animal life, plant life, and forms of nonliving material in orders of value and priority" (Chen 13), suggests that language and representation can also reorder such hierarchies. This happens through rethinking conceptions of animality, for as Chen rightly explains, "animality must be considered as a complex thing, material, plastic, and imaginary, at least in conformation with other concepts such as wildness, monstrosity, bestiality, barbarity, and tribality, as well as what it is to be human" (122). In order to avoid watered-down conceptions of animality, I examine different ways animal subjectivity – and by extension notions of animality – were represented by Victorians across numerous discourses: animal welfare, the law, popular culture, economics, natural history, political philosophy, and the novel. I demonstrate how liberalism influences representations of animals throughout the Victorian novel, complicating readings that reduce animals to metaphors or symbols. Although Mary Sanders Pollock has suggested that "the conventions of literary realism (like those of modernism) exclude the representation of nonhuman subjectivity, and hence, the exploration of a biotic and social community which includes nonhuman animal subjects" (137), I show how mostly realist novelists took pains to imagine animals as subjects within a multi-species social and political community. Indeed, representing animals in ways that veer from their dominant representations in animal welfare discourse registers a desire to examine all the possible realities of animal lives.

I begin with an analysis of nineteenth-century anti-cruelty and animal welfare movements, which constitute turning points in the inclusion of animals into the political sphere. The first anti-cruelty law was passed in 1822, which protected cattle from "wanton cruelty," and the Society for the Prevention of Cruelty to Animals (SPCA) was formed two years later to help enforce the new law and push for more legislation. The period continued to witness a massive influx of publications promoting kindness toward animals, pushes for more legislation, and a revision of appropriate animal–human relationships. Through this, animals were increasingly incorporated into juridical structures, and regulated under what Foucault calls governmentality, that is:

> the tendency, the line of force, that for a long time, and throughout the West, has constantly led towards the pre-eminence over all other types of power – sovereignty, discipline, and so on – of the type of power that we can call "government" and which has led to the development of a series of specific

governmental apparatuses (*appareils*) on the one hand, [and, on the other] to the development of a series of knowledges (*savoirs*). ("Security" 108)

Governmentality is the mentality of governing, the extended power networks that govern a population rather than a territory. The term emphasizes both the juridical *and* extra-juridical strategies humans use to govern, manage, and control animals, often under the guise of reform and protection. It results in what I call the government of animals: a movement away from individual human sovereignty over animals toward their incorporation into the regulatory strategies of liberal governmentality and its extended power networks. The government of animals works in part by regulating subjectivity. Beginning in the nineteenth century, alongside the rise of anti-cruelty legislation, certain animals – mostly domestic – were increasingly *liberalized*; not only were they viewed as subjects with thought and feeling, but they were frequently represented with liberal qualities such as reason, character, and disinterest. While Hadley identifies the importance of liberal cognition for the mid-Victorian human, I suggest there was a simultaneous liberal animal cognition, not confined to the second half of the period, but present from the beginning of the nineteenth century.

This is not to suggest that animals were never conceptualized politically before the nineteenth century. Tobias Menely has shown how in eighteenth-century England "publics, advocates, representatives, and positive law itself" suggest animals were not the "exception" to "modern political community" (12). While Menely shows how poets of sensibility spoke for animals within the public sphere, I argue that in the nineteenth century animals were brought under the government of humans through cultural representations more broadly, and that this resulted in the increasing liberalization of animal subjectivity. While animal populations were affected by a biopolitics that controlled and enhanced biological life, animal subjectivity was often constructed within pastoral power, strategies of cultivation and protection that resulted in subjection. Biopower and pastoral power were central to the political lives of Victorian animals, as they were increasingly taken under the stretching arms of liberal expansion.

After an analysis of anti-cruelty legislation and animal welfare discourse, I transition to Victorian novels and demonstrate how they often countered dominant liberal discourses of animal subjectivity, thus complicating the government of animals. Ian Watt, Nancy Armstrong, and Alex Woloch have demonstrated how the British novel was fundamental to the rise of liberal subjectivity and political inclusion, and I suggest animals are included in these politics even as they challenge them. While Watt describes

Introduction

how, beginning with *Robinson Crusoe*, realist novels represented white male individualism, or *homo economicus*, in *Desire and Domestic Fiction*, Armstrong focuses on the novel's role in crafting female middle-class subjectivity. She further locates two types of individuals in the realist novel: an individual who allowed him- or herself to be subjected to the social contract and was inscribed in a narrative of social movement, and an Althusserian "bad subject," who "take[s] the ideology of free subjectivity too much to heart and do[es] not freely consent to their subjection" (*Novels* 29). The realist novel's incorporation of minor characters, Alex Woloch argues, represents the field of democracy. He explains that the

> asymmetric structure of characterization – in which many are represented but attention flows toward a delimited center ... registers the competing pull of inequality and democracy within the nineteenth-century bourgeois imagination ... a dialectical literary form is generated out of the relationship between inequality and democracy ... the *claims* of minor characters on the reader's attention – and the resultant tension between characters and their functions – are generated by the democratic impulse that forms a horizon of nineteenth-century politics. (30–31)

Woloch never suggests that animals are minor characters, yet they proliferate throughout the Victorian novel, often as individualized characters who jostle for space with protagonists in significant ways.

Following these claims, I argue that qualities of the Victorian novel – such as the valorization of individualism, delineation of subjectivity, the proliferation of minor characters – and its reflection of democratic concerns, make it an ideal space for exploring how Victorians constructed animal subjectivity and brought animals into a liberal political community. Within the novel, animals often function as the "bad subject" Armstrong identifies: they resist human subjection, challenge human representational strategies, and disrupt liberalism's hierarchical ideologies that contribute to the oppression of animals and other non-bourgeois subjects, such as working-class and colonized subjects. Animal characters and epistemologies in the Victorian novel demonstrate how alternative subjectivities existed alongside and often challenged the individualism of liberal subjectivity. Indeed, as Pam Morris argues, Victorian novels "are undoubtedly complicit with the shaping and legitimizing of a perception of subjectivity" and "provide alternative and, at times, even utopian perceptions of inclusiveness as genuine community and democracy. In turn, this multifaceted dialogic participation in processes of imagining mass society produced intrinsic innovations to the formal structures and verbal codes of the novel as a genre" (6). I suggest that animals are included in these novelistic efforts, even as they undo them; for the inclusion of animals in the Victorian novel is itself a formal innovation that expands political inclusion. Indeed, conceptualizing animals as minor characters nuances how we read them more generally.

Animals populate the pages of Victorian fiction widely and diversely: from the dogs of Charles Dickens and George Eliot, *Black Beauty*'s beaten and exhausted horses, to the hunted elephants and tigers of late-century adventure fiction, Victorian novels portray the many ways animals are entwined with humans, often through individualized animal characters. George Levine posits realism as an important genre for representing animal otherness, suggesting that "Animals are almost the perfect test of the possibility of achieving the kind of imaginative self-transference that the ideal of Victorian moral realism implies" (*Realism* 250). Yet for Levine, Victorian texts most often end up "assimilating the animal to human purposes" (*Realism* 250), foreclosing the productive engagement with otherness realism aims for. In this reading, animals in realist texts, as in Victorian society, are at best projections of human ideologies, as Harriet Ritvo outlines in *The Animal Estate*. For Ivan Kreilkamp, this does not prohibit the production of sympathy, as he claims that narratives of animal suffering permeate domestic fiction and cultivate the sympathetic middle-class reader, linking "real" animals to strategies of the Victorian novel ("Petted"). Theresa Magnum notes how even anthropomorphic animals have the potential for disruption:

> Penned in by the conventions of character and plot that organize genres, animals cannot escape the binary opposition that separates humans from non-human animals. Still, the increasingly scientific approach to observation over the course of the eighteenth and nineteenth centuries and the emphasis on imagined thoughts and feelings, quotidian life, and detailed, localized settings often led to productive tensions with anthropomorphic representations of animals in popular literature and art. The great power of the best of these texts is that in their sheer alien otherness, in the quiet yet shocking details of a being's not-human-ness, the animal characters sometimes baffle conventions of representation, if only via the startling details of their particularity caught by an observant artist's brush, chisel, camera, or pen. These moments of animal intractability sometimes launch an "animal" commentary on "the human" as a category. (156)

Animals in Victorian fiction are mostly anthropomorphized, but this does not mean they cannot be taken on their own terms. Anthropomorphic animals frequently register moments of alterity, and analyzing them more closely illuminates how Victorians attempted to imagine animal lives. Taking these representations seriously helps show that Victorian novels may be more posthuman than has been recognized, and that Victorian animal representations may be more radical than has been previously believed.

Like liberalism, the "Victorian novel" is a capacious term, and I do not mean to suggest that *all* Victorian novels and genres offer a radical animal politics. For example, John Miller's *Empire and the Animal Body* demonstrates how late-century adventure novels glorify animal death. Animal autobiographies such as *Black Beauty* are often the product of an animal welfare discourse in which claims for animal protection rest on their acceptance of human authority. Even children's literature, which prominently features talking animals, often reinforces an animal–human hierarchy through its anti-cruelty message, religious discourse, and engagement with natural history, as Tess Cosslett shows. With the exception of *Alice's Adventures in Wonderland*, I focus on realist novels for their detailed portrayal of subjectivity and multi-species communities. I am interested in novels that purport to represent quotidian life, as they highlight how animals were imagined in the everyday lives of Victorians. Particularly in the realist novel, representations of animal subjects focus less on the subjected nature of animals and more on their status as subjects with interiority and their imbrication within daily life. Animals in the Victorian realist novel are both part of the tradition of interiority linked to Victorian individualism and a radical departure from it. As I have shown elsewhere, the incorporation of animals into the realist novel extends its examination of alterity and highlights its limitations.[2] Here, I expand this to show the political nature of animals and their connections to liberal strategies of governmentality.

Within Victorian culture, animals are often represented as liberalized creatures yet also exude forms of character and subjectivity that challenge the more typical liberal emphasis on moral character and a well-articulated subjectivity. By using the term "creature," I gesture toward the differences humans project onto animals, as Locke does when he calls them "inferior creatures" "made for another's uses" (*Second Treatise* 271), and the similarities and sympathetic connections that arise from understanding both animals and humans as "fellow creatures," as Thomas Hardy does throughout his fiction.[3] In *On Liberty*, J. S. Mill frequently writes of a political

---

[2] See "The Realism of Animal Life: The Seashore, *Adam Bede*, and George Eliot's Animal Alterity."
[3] Anna West and Elisha Cohn give extensive readings of the term "creature" in Thomas Hardy's work. For West, "the word 'creature' encourages readers to consider the liminal ground between the human and the animal, the juxtaposition of kinship and alterity, and the compounding of (at times

community composed of fellow creatures, thus the term gestures toward a political sphere constituted by otherness and inclusion. Anat Pick has more recently employed the term "creaturely" to signify a bodily vulnerability shared by animals and humans. More significantly for my purposes, she claims that "Reading through a creaturely prism consigns culture to contexts that are not exclusively human, contexts beyond an anthropocentric perspective" (5). In this sense, a discourse of the creature encourages us to examine multi-species cultural contexts that de-privilege the human. Although reading the creature in relationship to humanity rather than animality, Eric Santner's definition of "creaturely life" as "the peculiar proximity of the human to the animal at the very point of their radical difference" (12) is useful to emphasize the animal–human similarities *and* differences that the term "creature" implies. A liberal creature is thus an animal holding qualities of the liberal subject, who at the same time has the ability to highlight the radical differences between animals and humans, and put pressure on the very culture from which liberal discourse emerges. Thus *The Political Lives of Victorian Animals* highlights how the inclusion of animals into a political community both reifies the distance between animals and humans and includes them under similar strategies of care and control.

Victorian Liberalism and Victorian Animal Studies

Considering the large body of work on Victorian liberalism, and the influence of animal studies on Victorian studies, it is striking there are only rare mentions of how animals too were regulated by liberal strategies. Bringing animals into studies of Victorian liberalism can show a less anthropocentric liberalism and highlight liberalism's limitations in dealing with otherness. Critics from Lauren Goodlad and Elaine Hadley to Uday Singh Mehta and Lisa Lowe have recently detailed Victorian liberalism's exclusions and contradictions, providing more nuanced accounts of its regulatory practices. Such studies have come from calls to understand how liberalism was challenged "from below" (McWilliam 110) and to examine popular culture, social movements, and key terms such as "character" and "the liberal subject," associated with Victorian liberalism. Goodlad's

---

contradictory) connotations that together gesture toward the unknowability of the individual" (*Hardy* 11). Cohn emphasizes the term's connection with power as she argues, "in *Tess*, the word 'creature' links humans to the natural world through vulnerability to suffering caused by intentional manipulation, rather than by mindless natural processes ... To be a creature is to be shaped by external forces and to be unable to change them" (169).

suggestion in *Victorian Literature and the Victorian State* that Victorianists apply Foucault's work on pastorship and governmentality rather than on discipline opened a space for detailed accounts of how Victorians internalized state power. For Goodlad, pastorship describes the indirect power relationships influenced by the state and enacted by British citizens. Descriptive notions of "character," for example, regulated British subjects. In Hadley's examination of "how liberal politics in the mid-century imagined its liberalized political subjects to operate" (*Living* 3), she analyzes the category of the liberal individual and the cultivation of liberal cognition through forms such as the signed opinion piece and the ballot box. More recently, Amanda Anderson nuances critiques of liberalism by suggesting that Victorians were cognizant of the challenges facing liberal thought. These manifested in what she calls a bleak liberalism, one aware of its shortcomings and the difficulties facing its central tenets of inclusion, freedom, and liberty. I intervene in these conversations and argue that animals too were often imagined as liberalized subjects, and their ways of being in the world were regulated by the liberal thought these scholars outline. That is, liberalism's obsession with cognition and its regulation extended to the animal world. At times animal representations offered their own versions of bleak liberalism, and at others afforded alternate ways to conceptualize ideas of individualism, freedom, liberty, and character.

These recent analyses have given Victorianists a larger framework for understanding the logics of liberalism as a political philosophy influencing how citizens think, a constellation of principles regulating one's daily actions and beliefs, and a project struggling to live up to its ideals. Relatedly, scholars such as Uday Singh Mehta, Lisa Lowe, and Andrew Sartori have examined how the British empire exposes inconsistencies within liberal philosophy's engagement with alterity. Liberalism's love for reason, civilization, and progress, Mehta argues, posits colonized subjects as childlike and in need of Western domination (*Empire*). Instead of trying to reconcile how a politics ostensibly about liberty and individual freedom could justify empire, Mehta and Lowe suggest that such violence is part of its rationality. As Lowe argues, liberalism was "a project that includes at once both the universal promises of rights, emancipation, wage labor, and free trade, as well as the global divisions and asymmetries on which the liberal tradition depends, and according to which such liberties are reserved for some and wholly denied to others" (3). Andrew Sartori's argument that colonial contexts could "extend" and "radicalize" liberal commitments further calls for the need to examine liberalism within specific contexts and look for "a reception of liberal ideas in social spaces in which one might not readily expect to find them – without thereby succumbing to a naïve conception of the transparent universality of the appeal of liberal norms" (5–6). Cultural and political representations of animals offer another such site for nuancing the workings of liberalism.

Representations of animals and relationships with them have long been a part of liberal strategies, and as Colleen Glenny Boggs argues, animals are "integral to liberalism, as a structuring force that destabilizes the liberal subject at its core" (9–10). In *Some Thoughts Concerning Education*, John Locke posits stories about and pictures of animals as an effective way to teach children social norms and organization. Locke stressed the importance of kindness toward animals for creating a liberal subject, a belief carried over into Victorian social reform movements. Sir William Pulteney first introduced animal welfare legislation in 1800 when he called for an end to bull-baiting, igniting decades-long debates about the role of governmental intervention in animal–human relationships.[4] Debates over the government's role in regulating the treatment of animals challenged liberal ideology and embraced its strongest principles: while opponents of animal welfare legislation decried the regulation of private property and its infringement on individual liberty, others saw the kind treatment of animals as a way to educate the lower class in middle-class morality and cultivate civilization around the globe. Organizations such as the Royal Society for the Prevention of Cruelty to Animals (RSPCA)[5] asked citizens to see certain animals as thinking, feeling, and even rational subjects, yet posited animals as subjects who internalized an animal–human hierarchy. Animals were thus employed in social reform movements while representations of them were affected by the effects of governmentality Goodlad posits as foundational to Victorian liberalism. Indeed, it is no surprise that in the same period that liberalism strove to regulate human subjectivity through its obsession with character, individualism, and liberal cognition, there was a drive to represent animal cognition and interiority as well. From animal welfare discourses to scientific texts, there was a large interest in speculating about and representing the inner lives of animals.[6]

---

[4] While legislation was not brought before parliament until 1800, animal rights advocates published calls for justice for animals much earlier. See Menely, *The Animal Claim*, for an analysis of the long eighteenth-century's engagement with animal rights rhetoric, and David Perkins, *Romanticism and Animal Rights*, for a discussion of the development of animal rights in Romantic literature and culture.

[5] The SPCA received its "Royal" designation in 1840, yet for sake of clarity I refer to it as the RSPCA before 1840.

[6] Texts focusing on animal minds emerged in the 1850s, and comparative psychology originated in the late Victorian era. While early animal welfare tracts discussed the cognitive capabilities of animals

Indeed, scholars have mapped out a vast terrain of the ways animals existed in Victorian society and culture. Harriet Ritvo inaugurated such work with *The Animal Estate: The English and Other Creatures in the Victorian Age*. Focusing on how "animals became significant primarily as the objects of human manipulation" (2), Ritvo shows how animal–human relations reflected larger social ideologies of class, gender, science, and empire. Deborah Deneholz Morse and Martin Danahay's collection *Victorian Animal Dreams: Representations of Animals in Victorian Literature and Culture* built on Ritvo's work by expanding its scope: contributors analyze representations of animals within cultural productions (paintings and the novel) and sociocultural practices (such as fashion, pet mourning practices, and hunting). *Victorian Animal Dreams* productively expands our knowledge of the multiple ways animals existed within Victorian culture and society. Yet these essays often circle back to the human, as they "examine questions of symbolic and rhetorical uses of animal imagery that both code and illuminate the subject of human identity in Western culture" (3). Work by Sarah Amato, Keridiana Chez, Ann Colley, Monica Flegel, Philip Howell, Ivan Kreilkamp, John Miller, and Shefali Rajamannar further highlights the ideological makeup of Victorian animal–human relationships. While Flegel's work examines intersections between child and animal cruelty, and more recently pets and domesticity, Howell's perspective as a geographer leads him to claim that "the dog question" in the Victorian period – the question about "the dog's *place* in British society" – was much more complicated than previous analyses suggest (3). Chez also analyzes dog–human relationships to argue that pet-keeping "enhanced" human affective capacities and "completed" humanity (2). Kreilkamp argues that animals and animality within Victorian texts by writers such as Emily Brontë and Thomas Hardy promote sympathy, while Amato examines how animals circulated as commodities throughout the period. Similarly, Colley focuses on the circulation of animal skins to not only suggest that the project of empire was perhaps as messy as it was about control, but to analyze the various meanings attributed to animal skins throughout the Victorian period. Relatedly, John Miller shows that within imperial discourses wild animals did not have a stable meaning, and often destabilized animal–human boundaries, while Rajamannar argues

and made the popular argument that instinct is a type of reason, texts such as Edward Pett Thompson's *The Passions of Animals* (1851), Charles Darwin's *The Descent of Man* (1871) and *The Expression of the Emotions in Man and Animals* (1872), William Lauder Lindsay's *Mind in the Lower Animals in Health and Disease* (1880), and George Romanes's *Animal Intelligence* (1881) all discuss animal minds extensively.

conceptions of animals – from "brute" beast to docile creature – were foundational to British conceptions of Indians and the Raj.[7] These texts have built a solid foundation of the myriad roles animals played in Victorian society and culture, and demonstrate the many possible avenues for analyzing Victorian animal–human relationships.

However, more work is needed on the political role of animals found throughout Victorian literature and culture, as there is little analysis of how animals were influenced by and pressured Victorian liberalism, and how the animal welfare movement exerted troubling forms of power over animals even as it sought to gain them protection. There is a large body of work that discusses the animal welfare movement; Brian Harrison and Hilda Kean analyze how it fit into the trajectory of Victorian politics more broadly, while Kathleen Kete asks that we "de-couple animal protection from the history of social liberation which we intuitively, or Whiggishly, or romantically, wish to uphold" ("Animals" 21).[8] Howell examines the dog's liminal status between companion and citizen, arguing that dogs were political actors and "interpellated as political subjects of a particular kind" (178). In his reading of late-century debates over dog muzzling, Howell calls the move from muzzle to leash one from disciplinarity to governmentality, and argues that the leash functioned as a form of canine emancipation. Further explaining that the leash signified "a newly domesticated public sphere," Howell claims we can "make a space for the dog not just as a sort of quasi-enfranchised, liberal political subject, conditionally allowed into public space, but also as an agent in its own right" (171). While Howell productively deepens our knowledge of dog–human relationships, other animals were also affected by governmentality. And while Howell ends with such provocative claims, I begin with them, as I argue not only that mostly domesticated animals were often liberalized political subjects, but that attempts to bring them into the political sphere put pressure on liberal thought more generally.

Recent work on Victorian science has also proven productive for examining the political nature of arguments regarding evolution and instinct, two concepts that changed how Victorians understood and related to animals. For example, Piers Hale demonstrates how Darwinian evolution was employed by liberal discourse in often contradictory ways, from

---

[7] Other analyses of animals in Victorian literature and culture include Kathleen Kete, ed., *A Cultural History of Animals in the Age of Empire*, and Larry Mazzeno and Ronald Morrison's collection *Animals in Victorian Literature and Culture*.

[8] See also Richard French, *Antivivisection and Medical Science in Victorian Society*; Carol Lansbury, *The Old Brown Dog*; and James Turner, *Reckoning with the Beast*.

evidence for individualism and laissez-faire economics, to social welfare programs and collectivist forms of governance. Relatedly, Kathleen Frederickson argues that instinct was a significant category within Victorian liberalism that offers ways out from disciplined subjectivity (8), yet she focuses on instinct as a human quality.[9]

I expand the scope of such analyses and emphasize the politics behind conceptions of Victorian animals and qualities associated with them, examining how understandings of animals as subjects of political concern were intertwined with liberal discourse and articulated in the Victorian novel. Thinking politically about where animals fit in the history of Victorian liberalism invites us to understand the workings of governmentality in delineating alternative subjectivity and alterity. By alternative subjectivity I mean a way of thinking beyond liberal cognition, a nonnormative subjectivity that attempts to resist the individualizing effects of governmentality and may veer from techniques of reason, character, and disinterestedness. Looking at how Victorians envisioned animal subjectivity allows for further investigation into how liberalism imagined and regulated its subjects, and adds to the growing body of work concerned with liberal subjectivity. *The Political Lives of Victorian Animals* thus makes significant claims about how animals were figured within Victorian political discourse as well as figured *by* political discourse. That is, I do not solely look for moments where animals appear in political writings, although this forms a significant entry point into understanding how animals were liberalized. I rather illuminate how Victorian political thought influenced representations of animal subjects, and vice versa. Indeed, I suggest that liberalism, a fundamentally anthropocentric set of ideologies and strategies, was not disconnected from the Victorian posthuman, as it consistently attempted to bring more subjects under its fold.

Beginning with Locke, liberal political theory formulates animals as property, a means to produce capital. He highlights how animal subordination is inherent in liberal thought: "And being furnished with like Faculties, sharing all in one Community of Nature, there cannot be supposed any such *Subordination* among us, that may Authorize us to destroy one another, as if we were made for one another's uses, as the inferior ranks of Creatures are for ours" (*Second Treatise* 271). Locke emphasizes the common belief that animals were put on earth by God

---

[9] For an analysis of Darwinian thought on animal–human representations within the novel, see Virginia Richter, *Literature after Darwin*.

for human use, a claim widely propagated by animal welfare discourse. For Locke, the purpose of government is the protection of property, and this is why one should treat animals well. Even in suggesting that children be taught animal welfare, as I discuss in Chapter 4, Locke treats animals as a form of educational capital to help advance liberal human society. One hundred years later, Jeremy Bentham famously argued for anti-cruelty legislation on the grounds of sentience, bringing animals beyond the realm of property only. He asked that humans take seriously animal suffering, even if animals cannot talk or reason; their ability to feel pain should encourage their protection. Bentham posits this in specifically liberal language, suggesting that "The day *may* come, when the rest of the animal creation may acquire those rights which never could have been withholden from them but by the hand of tyranny" (*Principles* 311).

As liberal thought develops, most notably with John Stuart Mill, its purpose is less protection of property and more about educating citizens and helping them progress toward what was understood as a more civilized state of being. Indeed, in his statements about animals – of which there are not many – Mill challenges Locke's views toward animals and property. In his chapter on laissez-faire economics in *Principles of Political Economy*, for example, Mill claims anti-cruelty legislation is not government interference. He writes, "It is by the grossest misunderstanding of the principles of liberty, that the infliction of exemplary punishment on ruffianism practiced towards these defenceless creatures, has been treated as a meddling by government with things beyond its province" (344). Mill moves beyond Locke's arguments that animals are property, instead promoting animal liberty. Mill's push for animal welfare in the context of claims *against* government interference is not about regulating human morals and behavior, but "the intrinsic merits of the case itself" (344). As such, Mill suggests that incorporating animals into a political community actually challenges liberal notions of property, liberty, and the role of government more generally.[10] His comments show how contentious debates were about anti-cruelty legislation throughout the nineteenth century, as many believed animal welfare could come only at the loss of human liberties. Instead, Mill suggests a space for animals in a liberal political community; he includes them in the "Greatest Happiness Principle," asking that "the

---

[10] Although animals can be protected as part of a liberal political community, Mill's comments in *Utilitarianism* suggests they could not participate in it or form their own. He argues that one of the differences between animals and humans is that humans, with their "more developed intelligence," are "capable of apprehending a community of interest between himself and the human society of which he forms a part" (187).

whole sentient creation" be allowed to lead "an existence exempt as far as possible from pain, and as rich as possible in enjoyments" (*Utilitarianism* 142–143). Mill's incorporation of animals into a liberal political community extends beyond protection from physical suffering, as he projects individuality onto the animal world. "Human beings are not like sheep," he argues in *On Liberty*, "and even sheep are not undistinguishably alike" (75). This claim rejects animal–human similarities at the same time it accepts them. No longer understood as a homogeneous group, sheep are individuals with thoughts, desires, opinions, and personalities. Placed in his larger argument about the necessity of individualism for a healthy public sphere, sheep become liberal subjects even though their subject status remains ambiguous. Thus with the rise of anti-cruelty legislation and animal welfare advocacy – both liberal projects of social reform – animals gained a form of political representation in which they were understood as liberalized individual subjects.

Throughout this book I follow Foucault's definition of the subject as "subject to someone else by control and dependence, and tied to his own identity by a conscience or self knowledge" ("Subject" 331), as it illuminates how representations of animal identity, conscience, or self-knowledge function as a form of power. Within many representations of animal subjectivity Foucault's two aspects of the subject collapse together, thus subjecting animals to systems of human knowledge. I rely on Foucauldian categories because they highlight the undiscussed dimensions of liberalism in relation to animals, and help extend Goodlad's analysis of pastoral power and governmentality to the animal world. Even further, the fact that Foucault locates pastoral power – one of the most pervasive power structures he identifies – within an animal–human relationship emphasizes the productiveness of his thought for analyzing animal representations. Matthew Chrulew and Dinesh Joseph Wadiwel's 2017 collection *Foucault and Animals* is evidence that his categories of discipline and biopower especially are useful for negotiating the status of animals today.[11] As Alex Mackintosh argues, "nonhuman animals are strongly implicated in the

---

[11] See especially Clare Palmer, "'Taming the Wild Profusion of Existing Things'? A Study of Foucault, Power, and Human/Animal Relationships"; Matthew Chrulew, "Animals as Biopolitical Subjects"; and Alex Mackintosh, "Foucault's Menagerie: Cock Fighting, Bear Baiting, and the Genealogy of Human–Animal Power." While I focus mostly on discourse, Palmer examines the ways animals can or cannot resist human power, and Chrulew analyzes how animal subjectivity is affected by animal–human relationships in spaces such as zoos. Mackintosh astutely shows how the movement from sovereign power to discipline was influenced by shifting views toward animal fighting in the seventeenth and eighteenth centuries.

history of human power structures, and our relationship to other species has shaped the forms of power that operate on the bodies and 'souls' both of human and nonhuman animals" (184–185). I suggest Foucault helps politicize animal studies work beyond an animal rights framework, as his categories expose how care – so essential to many animal–human relationships – can also control and subjugate. By understanding the different forms of power relations humans have with animals, we can more productively move beyond them to cultivate alternative animal–human relations, and grasp the potentialities of animal agencies and animal politics.

Conceptualizing liberalism as a strategy of governmentality and understanding how animal welfare operated through pastoral power and biopower elucidates how although animal welfare discourse importantly posits animals as subjects, it largely encloses them within a regulatory liberal framework that reifies their exploitation and oppression. Yet the very fact of animal welfare advocates seeking political representation on behalf of animals, and their inclusion in a wide array of cultural artifacts, from paintings and periodicals to the novel, gives them a prominent voice within the public sphere. I thus claim that like the unenfranchised working class, women, and colonized subjects, animals too were present in nineteenth-century demands for political inclusion. Not only were they represented within parliament, but their representation within spaces such as the novel gave them a voice within a larger political community.

In *Vibrant Matter*, Jane Bennett imagines a democracy in which the nonhuman – a term I avoid as it groups animals with objects and centers the human through its negation – can be viewed with political agency. She writes,

> If human culture is inextricably enmeshed with vibrant, nonhuman agencies, and if human intentionality can be agentic only if accompanied by a vast entourage of nonhumans, then it seems that the appropriate unit of analysis for democratic theory is neither the individual human nor an exclusively human collective but the (ontologically heterogeneous) "public" coalescing around a problem. (108)

While not specifically focused on animals, Bennett's envisioning of a democratic sphere that incorporates nonhuman political agency invites us to imagine how animals can affect political change and influence the development of political thought. As Bennett argues, "surely the scope of democratization can be broadened to acknowledge more nonhumans in more ways, in something like the ways in which we have come to hear the political voices of other humans formerly on the outs" (109). I suggest that in the Victorian era the political voices of animals and the problem of how to incorporate them into a political community intensified in ways that brought animals into liberal thought, in turn affecting key categories of liberalism. In this way, Victorian demands for democracy that include animals can be understood as the kind of radical and plural democracy articulated by Chantal Mouffe: "Radical democracy demands that we acknowledge difference – the particular, the multiple, the heterogeneous – in effect, everything that has been excluded by the concept of Man in the abstract" (13). Indeed, Mouffe's understanding of "the individual" as male – "We are all taught that the 'individual' is a universal category that applies to anyone or everyone, but this is not the case. 'The individual' is a man" (13) – certainly holds true in the Victorian era. At the same time, many animals were increasingly seen as individuals with character, reason, and disinterestedness. Yet overall, when applied to animals "the individual" was a regulatory concept keeping them within systems of exploitation. The novel, however, often represents animals who challenge their objectified status while moving beyond liberal individualism. Such representations offer an animal politics that shows the political potential of alterity, animal epistemologies, and alternative subjectivities, thus destabilizing the primacy of liberal human thought.

Beyond the Victorian Human Subject

As a project that puts animal lives at the center of its analysis, *The Political Lives of Victorian Animals* is informed by recent work in animal studies and posthumanism. Instead of uncovering what representations of animals tell us about humans, I seek to show how Victorians imagined animals and their inner lives. Although I often analyze anthropomorphic representations, my analyses demonstrate how our conceptualizations of animals take place within unequal power structures, and affect how we relate with them. Animal studies asks us to explore the possibilities of seeing animals as autonomous subjects, read animals *as animals*, and uncover their material and cultural histories. Colleen Glenny Boggs explains that "At its core, animal studies asks what happens when we include other species in our understanding of subjectivity" (3), while Cary Wolfe similarly explains that animal studies requires "fundamentally rethinking the question of what knowledge is, how it is limited by the overdeterminations and partialities of our 'species-being'... in excavating and examining our assumptions about who the knowing subject can be; and in embodying that confrontation in its own disciplinary practices and protocols" ("Human" 571).

Largely, the goal of animal studies is to challenge categories that create an oppressive animal–human divide keeping animals within systems of exploitation, even those that seem relatively benign, such as pet-keeping and animal welfare.

Jacques Derrida's work on animal–human relationships, animal subjectivity, vegetarianism, and animality is foundational to theoretical animal studies and has influenced this book from its earliest conceptions. His set of lectures gathered under the title *The Animal That Therefore I Am* examines how Western philosophy has largely used animals as a negative against which to define the human. Derrida demonstrates the inability of the Western philosophical tradition to responsibly think about animals as subjects in their own right. The now famous phenomenological reading of his cat's gaze upon his naked body underscores the importance of animal perspectives and their power to disrupt human knowledge and, by extension, human exceptionalism. Derrida explains that this gaze allows one to "*see and be seen*," for "As with every bottomless gaze, as with the eyes of the other, the gaze called 'animal' offers to my sight the abyssal limit of the human" (12). For Derrida, recognizing that animals have a "point of view regarding me" – a response – is a major ethical imperative of animal–human relationships (11). He explains that "nothing will have ever given me more food for thinking through this absolute alterity of the neighbor or of the next (-door) than these moments when I see myself seen naked under the gaze of a cat" (11). The cat's gaze signals his own limitations, as he realizes it signifies subjectivity and a point of view, and that he is restricted in his ability to understand, comprehend, or read such subjectivity. *The Political Lives of Victorian Animals* examines how Victorians imagined this animal point of view.

Derrida's analysis of the violence enacted when we group all animals under the term "the animal" also informs this project. As a term, "the animal" erases profound differences across species, grouping animals together as a homogenous group. Rather, we need to "envisage the existence of 'living creatures,' whose plurality cannot be assembled within the single figure of an animality that is simply opposed to humanity" (*Animal* 47). Derrida emphasizes multiplicity rather than singularity:

> I repeat that it is rather a matter of taking into account a multiplicity of heterogeneous structures and limits: among nonhumans, and separate from nonhumans, there is an immense multiplicity of other living things that cannot in any way be homogenized, except by means of violence and willful ignorance, within the category of what is called the animal or animality in general. (48)

While I frequently use the term "animal" throughout this book for the sake of brevity, I stress specific differences among animals, often using them as the base of my analyses.[12] For example, it is certainly not true that all animals were liberalized throughout the period. Early anti-cruelty legislation was geared toward working domestic animals grouped under the umbrella of cattle, such as horses, sheep, and donkeys. It was not until later in the period that legislation extended to cats, birds, and – at the end of Victoria's reign – wild animals in captivity.[13] Groups such as the RSPCA rarely spoke out against the violence and genocide facing wild animals across the empire, and at times promoted their killing.[14] Yet even if certain animals were not always conceptualized as liberal animals, such as tigers, they were still regulated by liberal governmentality through the rationale for excluding them. Placing specific animals in their cultural context, as I do with ostriches in Chapter 6 or sheep in Chapter 5, allows for a deeper analysis of how animals functioned historically, culturally, and politically. It also provides a more nuanced understanding of the larger ideologies in which representations of animal functioned.

As should be clear, animal studies critiques humanism and the Enlightenment subjectivity that still shapes animals and humans. For this reason, animal studies shares many goals with posthumanism, a project Rosi Braidotti characterizes as "an opportunity to empower the pursuit of alternative schemes of thought, knowledge and self-representation" (12), by in part moving away from a nature–culture dualism and acknowledging nonhuman actors in the creation of knowledge. A posthuman analysis of Victorian liberalism offers numerous opportunities for the disruption of Enlightenment thought, given that it is foundational for both liberal political philosophy *and* early animal welfare movements. Indeed, in *Staying with the Trouble*, Donna Haraway argues we must think against the dominance of individualism in relation to shifting multi-species relationships. She claims that "bounded individualism in its many flavors in

---

[12] Within animal studies work, scholars often favor the term "nonhuman" or "nonhuman animal" over "animal," and "companion species" over "pet." I prefer the term "animal," as "nonhuman" posits animals as a negative against the human and collapses them in the same category as plants and objects. I attempt to privilege animals by using the modifier "animal–human" instead of "human–animal." I also use the term "pet" over "companion species" to recognize the unequal power structures of this relationship. See Andrew Linzey and Priscilla Cohen, "Terms of Discourse," for a discussion of how the language we use to talk about animals is linked to their oppression.
[13] Cats and dogs were not named specifically until the 1849 Cruelty to Animals Act, while legislation protecting birds did not appear until 1869. Wild animals in captivity were not protected until 1900.
[14] An 1874 article in *Animal World* titled "The Cruelty of Preserving Ferocious Wild Animals" claims that in India "All tigers should be killed, without inquiring into character" (41).

science, politics, and philosophy has finally become unavailable to think with, truly no longer thinkable, technically or any other way" (5). Looking back at the Victorian era, with its obsession with individualism, reason, and progressive civilization, helps illuminate how individualism limits attempts to bring animals into political communities. We can also find moments where animals destabilize "bounded individualism." As such, posthumanism privileges alternate ways of thinking. As Haraway emphasizes, "It matters what thoughts think thoughts. It matters what knowledges know knowledges. It matters what relations relate relations. It matters what worlds world worlds. It matters what stories tell stories" (*Staying* 35). Continuing to conceptualize animal subjects within the style of thought and oppressive knowledge structures perpetuated by the legacy of Victorian liberalism reifies animals into positions of exploitation.

I suggest that the Victorian novel, however, frequently attempts to imagine alternate ways of thinking about animals beyond the confines of Victorian liberal ideology. Even if the writers I examine here cannot fully remove themselves from liberal categories, I suggest that animal representations offer telling moments of the limitations of liberal thought for animality and alterity. Alterity is not necessarily just difference; rather, I use the term to refer to unknowability. Derrida's frequent modifications of animal otherness in *The Animal That Therefore I Am* – "absolute alterity" and "wholly other" (11) – suggest that animal interiority is something humans cannot easily conceptualize or understand. Throughout my analyses, I look for moments when Victorians were aware of their limitations in articulating animal subjectivity, and find that alterity often functions as a way out from the more oppressive articulations influenced by liberal thought.

Indeed, critics such as Timothy Morton and Jane Bennett have found the Victorian period a productive moment for posthuman thought. In *The Ecological Thought*, Timothy Morton locates the Victorian period as an originary moment in conceptualizing "the mesh" – interconnections and entanglements with nonhumans – and "strange strangers" – the unfamiliar, those whom we do not expect, alterity in its most unknowable form. For Morton, "Darwin brings ecological interconnectedness and thinking together" (29). Jane Bennett also classifies Darwin as a posthuman thinker, seen in his claims that worms "inaugurate human culture" (96). Although I do not engage much with Darwin throughout this project, it does not mean he was not influential for the articulations of animal subjectivity I discuss. Darwin pushed Victorians to reconsider the animal–human divide in ways that made them uncomfortable, and forced them to reconceptualize their relationships with animals and other humans they saw as animal-like.

It may seem like my engagement with anthropomorphic representations of animals conflicts with posthumanism's call for alterity and alternative ways of thinking. Yet not only is there much to learn from how we imagine animal minds, but reconsidering how we think about anthropomorphism is itself a posthuman move. As Bennett suggests, "Maybe it is worth running the risks associated with anthropomorphizing ... because it, oddly enough, works against anthropocentrism: a chord is struck between person and thing, and I am no longer above or outside a nonhuman 'environment'" (120). Massumi similarly critiques rejections of anthropomorphism, asking, "Is it not the height of human arrogance to suppose that animals do *not* have thought, emotion, desire, creativity, or subjectivity? Is that not to consign animals yet again to the status of automatons?" (51). Thus, anthropomorphism registers similarities between animals and humans; to reject anthropomorphism is to claim that humans are the sole bearers of qualities such as emotion, intelligence, and desire. Throughout this project I am invested in the politics behind anthropomorphic representations, especially as they posit animals as members of a political community. I argue that anthropomorphic representations of animals often show the limitations of incorporating animals into human political frameworks, such as rights and legislation; emphasize that how we envision animal interiority is a human construction, bound up in human power networks; and demonstrate how animals can be considered historical, social, and political actors. Examining the Victorian period with today's theoretical lenses offers new readings of the past and informs the legacies that shape our contemporary moment. While Victorian liberalism and drives for democracy were highly exclusionary, looking back with the concepts posthuman theory offers helps nuance the exclusionary nature of democratic thought in the Victorian era. As Lisa Lowe argues, "it is possible to conceive the past, not as fixed or settled, not as inaugurating the temporality into which our present falls, but as a configuration of multiple contingent possibilities, all present, yet none inevitable. ... It is a space of reckoning that allows us ... to consider alternatives that may have been *unthought* in those times" (175). She continues, "We are left with the project of imagining, mourning, and reckoning 'other humanities' within the received genealogy of 'the human'" (175). I suggest that examining the co-constitution of Victorian animal–human relationships and Victorian liberalism with the tools of animal studies and posthuman theory presents new ways to think about the Victorian period, helps us reconsider our relationships with animals today, and encourages us to imagine other humanities and non-humanities.

Chapter Summaries

In order to understand how animals were increasingly brought into a juridical-political community throughout the Victorian period, this book opens with parliamentary debates over anti-cruelty legislation from 1809 to the 1880s. In Chapter 1, "The Government of Animals: Anti-Cruelty Legislation and the Making of Liberal Creatures," I argue that while attempts to bring animals into a liberal political community challenged notions of the law, government, property, and human sovereignty, they often reinscribed animals into an anthropocentric framework predicated on animal subjection. While the early debates have been discussed in detail, I use the lens of governmentality to understand how they project regulatory liberal strategies onto the animal world, and show how these laws were often less liberating than has been previously discussed. As the century progresses, with anti-cruelty legislation becoming more common, legislators remain unable to understand animal subjects outside of anthropocentrism, as seen within debates over wild bird legislation in the late 1860s and through the 1880s. Although proponents of anti-cruelty legislation adopted liberal philosophical ideals in their arguments for animal protection, and tried to craft a liberalized animal subject, most often they were unable to conceptualize animal subjects outside of human rights and freedoms. At the same time, however, drives for more legislation led to new understandings of the law, and conceptualizations of certain animals as political subjects challenged major aspects of liberal politics, such as understandings of property, the role of government, and laissez-faire philosophy. These debates within the public sphere constructed a liberalized animal subject with character, simultaneously reinforcing and reinventing the liberal subject. Examining anti-cruelty legislation in the context of liberal governmentality demonstrates how animals were increasingly brought out from under human sovereignty and into governmentality, or what I call the government of animals.

While Chapter 1 focuses on how animal subjects were constructed and regulated through legislation, Chapter 2, "The Incessant Care of the Victorian Shepherd: Animal Welfare's Pastoral Power," examines the animal welfare discourse of the RSPCA, formed in 1824 as a response to the 1822 anti-cruelty bill. In an effort to supplement legislation with moral education and policing, the RSPCA represented animal subjects within forms of pastoral power that would solicit care and sympathy for them. At the same time, the organization's construction of animals as subjects with thoughts, feelings, character, and individuality cultivated a striking liberalized animal subject who challenged *and* reinforced the anthropocentric logic structuring Victorian liberalism. To illustrate these claims, I read a selection of animal welfare texts published by or connected with the RSPCA from 1838 and 1839, and articles from the RSPCA's journal *Animal World*, first published in 1869. I end with a brief discussion of the Vegetarian Society, formed in 1847, and the London Vegetarian Society (LVS), formed in 1888. While the Vegetarian Society began as a temperance movement concerned with public health, the LVS split from the national organization over its more radical socialist politics. Both organizations throw into relief the conservatism behind the RSPCA and its reliance on liberal capitalism. Not only did the Vegetarian Society critique the RSPCA for neglecting to advocate for the abolishment of meat-eating, but the LVS, seen especially through its associations with socialism, posits animals as part of a universal brotherhood, articulating a radical equality lacking in RSPCA discourse. Taken together, all three organizations demonstrate the extent to which animals were influenced by nineteenth-century political thought and affected by governmentality, yet at times succeeded in challenging the primacy of a liberal human subject and the dominance of Victorian liberalism.

The first two chapters present a broad yet nuanced understanding of how animals were conceptualized by the discourses that most fully incorporated them into a political community. With this grounding, I transition to a selection of Victorian novels that present alternate ways of conceptualizing animals politically, and revise the often oppressive animal subjectivity perpetuated by animal welfare discourses. Through examining work by four different Victorian novelists, I show how liberal discourses of character, education, democracy, capitalism, biopolitics, and imperialism were engaged with animal lives and subjectivity. This examination begins with Charles Dickens, whose novels contain some of the most widely discussed animal characters in Victorian fiction. In Chapter 3, "'Tame submission to injustice is unworthy of a Raven': Charles Dickens's Animal Character," I examine *Hard Times*, *Oliver Twist*, and *Barnaby Rudge* to show how the Dickensian novel incorporates animals into its political critiques, questions human access to animal subjectivity, and cultivates an alternate form of animal character. Although Dickens rarely removes himself from pastoral power, his animals often function outside it. Dickens's animal characters critique dominant notions of liberal character and the character of government, offering a way out from animalizing discourses of both animal and working-class character. I first give a brief analysis of *Hard Times* to show how Dickens posits animal epistemologies – in fiction especially – as privileged sites of resistance to governmentality. Although written after *Oliver Twist* and *Barnaby Rudge*, *Hard Times*'s engagement with animal subjects offers a lens through which to examine Dickens's earlier animal characters. *Hard Times* suggests that imagining animals outside of governmentality and pastoral power offers alternate ways to incorporate alterity into a political community. I then analyze *Oliver Twist* in the context of pastoral power and the New Poor Law to show how Bill Sikes's dog Bull's-eye offers a radical animal politics that registers character outside the regulatory logic of pastoral power. As a working-class animal, Bull's-eye refuses the faithful and loyal bourgeois animality middle- and upper-class Victorians desired in both animals and the working class. Reading *Oliver Twist* by way of its more radical animal politics offers alternate forms of freedom and character than those encouraged by liberal governmentality.

Chapter 3 ends with a discussion of Dickens's *Barnaby Rudge*, a historical novel about the 1780 Gordon Riots. Written during the height of the Chartist movement, the novel shows a deep engagement with worries over working-class political participation. I place the novel in this historical context to demonstrate how its animal character Grip, a raven, challenges dominant constructions of animality, especially when used as a reason against political representation for the working class. Grip exudes a striking amount of alterity that highlights limitations in constructing another's subjectivity. Examining the novel's animal character in the context of cultural assumptions about ravens and misreadings of Grip as an evil omen illuminates Dickens's critique of how governmentality animalizes its subjects in ways that prohibit political participation. Grip offers alterity as a site of resistance to the regulatory effects of state institutions *and* provides alternate forms of animal subjectivity that veer from animal welfare discourse. Grip's role as a minor character is dual: to refigure animal and working-class character and to expose political forces that cultivate negative forms of animality prohibiting political participation. Significantly, Grip also works politically to highlight the constructed nature of animality in its relationship to liberal democracy. Grip thus enters into the political horizons of the novel to show the limitations of representative democracy: the people should speak for themselves without influence from a self-interested political system. Taken together, these three novels highlight the radical nature of Dickens's animal politics, as they challenge constructions of liberal character and posit alternate animal subjectivities within a more democratic political community.

In Chapter 4, "*Alice in Wonderland*'s Animal Pedagogy: Democracy and Alternative Subjectivity in Mid-Victorian Liberal Education," I move away from novels written for adults and examine the political uses of animals in children's literature, and connect them to understandings of alterity in mid-Victorian demands for democracy and debates over national education. I begin by examining John Locke's discussion of animals in children's literature and education in *Some Thoughts Concerning Education*, to show how the inclusion of animals in children's education positions them as educational and financial capital. I argue that although scholars suggest Locke presents an early form of animal welfare, this is self-serving: children are instructed to practice animal welfare so they can translate this kindness to the human sphere and respect property. The positive potentialities of Locke's theory, I suggest, come through his valuation of literature for illustrating a political animal subjectivity. I then discuss mid-Victorian debates about education in relationship to demands for democracy, and show how philosophers such as John Stuart Mill similarly brought excluded others into the political sphere only to reject their otherness. As with animals, the role of working-class men and colonized subjects in educational theories was to conform them to liberal subjectivity. Lewis Carroll's novel *Alice's Adventures in Wonderland*, however, revises the role of animals in children's literature and of alternative subjectivity in the political sphere. Instead of instructing children to conform to liberal ideology, Carroll's unconventional animals educate Alice in undoing liberal subjectivity and appreciating the political potential of alterity. Alice's ultimate disruption of Wonderland's political sphere comes, I argue, from the education in alternative subjectivity she receives from the novel's animal characters. The novel's radical animal politics, however, is ultimately undercut by Carroll's emphasis on the disrupting effects of a democracy composed of alternative subjectivities. The novel thus teaches readers that alterity is excluded from the political sphere due to its ability to disrupt liberal ideology.

The Political Lives of Victorian Animals then shifts back to the realist novel and animal welfare discourse to examine how animals raised as capital were figured as subjects of biopolitical concern. While Chapter 3 shows how Dickens revises animal character, and Chapter 4 analyzes how animal pedagogy can disrupt the regulatory nature of liberal education, Chapter 5, "Animal Capital and the Lives of Sheep: Thomas Hardy's Biopolitical Realism," explores intersections between animals produced for human consumption, liberal inclusion, and biopolitics. I first examine mid-century cattle industry reform and concerns over the treatment of animals raised for human consumption. By embracing notions of animal capital and profit to better regulate animal lives, animal welfare discourse showed how animal bodies can negatively or positively affect the wealth of the nation, depending on their treatment. I contrast this biopolitical discourse with Thomas Hardy's concerns over the treatment of cattle, and his desire for animal justice and equality. After briefly examining his own animal welfare, especially concerns about the cattle industry, I analyze his novel about shepherding and pastoral power, *Far from the Madding Crowd*, which presents what I call an affirmative biopolitical realism. Through focusing on the lives of sheep and enhancing them with his biopolitical realist techniques, Hardy offers an alternative ethic for relating with animals that values them outside of capitalist discourses of profit, ultimately positing a liberal inclusion that welcomes animals. As seen through his views on animals, Hardy's politics emphasizes a multi-species interdependence and cooperation that cultivates life not for death but for justice.

The final chapter, Chapter 6, "The Political Lives of Animals in Victorian Empire: Olive Schreiner's Anti-Colonial Animal Politics," takes us outside of England and into empire to examine how Indigenous South African animals, especially those used for capital, reinforced or rejected liberal imperial ideologies. While scholars most often focus on animal death and capture across the empire, and argue that exotic animals represent British domination over their colonies, I examine living domestic animals to show how they functioned in both pro- and anti-colonial discourses. I focus on the ostrich, native to southern Africa and first domesticated by British colonists in the 1860s, and argue that even though ostriches were seen as ungovernable, colonists fostered their lives; as such both animal minds and bodies were controlled by liberal imperialism. I then turn to British South African writer and activist Oliver Schreiner, and show how her political writings and best-selling novel *The Story of an African Farm* conceptualizes animals outside of liberal imperial discourses and suggests that animality offers alternate political models for human relationships within the space of empire especially. Through her portrayal of ostriches, meerkats, and birds, Schreiner offers an animal politics that invites readers to rethink negative conceptions of animality and, by extension, liberal imperial discourses that operate within a speciesist logic.

PART I

Anti-Cruelty Legislation and Animal Welfare

CHAPTER I

The Government of Animals
Anti-Cruelty Legislation and the Making of Liberal Creatures

> This form of power so typical of the West, and unique, I think, in the entire history of civilizations, was born, or at least took its model from the fold, from politics seen as a matter of the sheep-fold.
> – Michel Foucault, *Security, Territory, Population*

> The modern concept of rights depends massively on this Cartesian moment of the *cogito*, of subjectivity, freedom, sovereignty, etc. . . . Consequently, to confer or to recognize rights for "animals" is a surreptitious or implicit way of confirming a certain interpretation of the human subject, which itself will have been the very lever of the worst violence carried out against nonhuman living beings.
> – Jacques Derrida, *For What Tomorrow*

> Meanwhile let us bear in mind that the responsibility is now fairly on the Government (for which it cannot escape, if it would), and that a population of living, sensitive beings, five times more numerous than that of human beings, are having their plea for justice heard by the Government.
> – "Contagious Diseases (Animals) Act, 1869," *Animal World*

In February 1870, *Animal World*, the new journal of the Royal Society for the Prevention of Cruelty to Animals (RSPCA), printed a poem by Lord Thomas Erskine, the first legislator to bring anti-cruelty bills into parliament on the grounds of animal rights. Titled "The Liberated Robins," the poem had been written in 1798, on the occasion of Erskine freeing seven robins after purchasing them from a boy who held them in a cage. The poem asks the robins to enjoy their new liberty; yet by the end of the poem, the birds explicitly become Erskine's own:

> Now, harmless songsters, ye are free!
> Yet stay awhile and sing to me;
> And make these sheltered bounds your home,
> Nor toward yon dangerous meadow roam.
> Your ruddy bosoms pant with fear,

> But no dark snare awaits you here.
> No artful note of tame decoy
> Shall lure you from your native joy.
> These blossomed shrubs are all your own,
> And lawns with sweetest berries strewn;
> And when bleak winter thins your store,
> This friendly hand shall furnish more;
> Nor shall my window-shutters fold
> Against my robins numbed with cold.

While in the last line Erskine claims the robins as his, there is a contradictory relationship between liberty, captivity, and property early in the poem. Although the birds are free, Erskine asks them to stay and sing to him, the "yet" signaling hesitation about their freedom. This freedom is "sheltered," suggesting that the best natural and free state for the birds is under human protection, rather than in a "dangerous" meadow. Erskine's home is where the birds can be free, yet this freedom is dependent on his human power. As the human governor, Erskine grants the birds protection and freedom, yet they become his property in the last line.

The next issue of *Animal World*, March 1870, contains a direct reply to Erskine from the liberated robins. In "The Robins' Reply to their Benefactor (Lord Erskine) at Hampstead," written by Erskine's daughter Mrs. Holland, the robins extend their gratitude to Erskine, and "promise" to stay at Hampstead and remain his:

> We happy robins, here set free,
> With grateful hearts will sing to thee;
> Henceforward this shall be our home,
> We promise never far to roam,
> But rest, devoid of every fear,
> Since no dark snare awaits us here;
> Nor hazard these our peaceful joys
> By answering to tame decoys.
> We'll eat thy berries thickly sown,
> And look upon them as our own.
> We thank thee for our promised store –
> What can poor robins give thee more?
> And when we're numb'd with winter's cold
> To us thy shutters shall unfold.
> For this thou art already blest,
> And great's the joy within thy breast –
> We see it in thy face expressed!
> And oh! may thou who set us free
> Enjoy in peace, sweet liberty.

> We'll sing to thee all day, till death
> Deprives us of our little breath.
> And then our sons shall sing to thee,
> For thou hast given them liberty.
> If they, like us, should be trepanned,
> Once more stretch out thy friendly hand
> And snatch them from their hapless fate –
> Restore them to their native state,
> And feed and shelter them from ill,
> And be their guardian angel still.

The robins' reply contains similar themes to Erskine's poem, yet they are now imagined from the robins' own point of view. As in Erskine's poem, freedom here comes at the hand of human governance, and the robins promise to stay within the bounds of his home. Their task of daily singing will be passed down through generations, as if pleasing the human becomes an inherited trait. Erskine gives liberty to generations of robins, yet this results in a contractual relationship of debt, whereby future generations will stay and sing to him. Indeed, the fact that the robins will "sing to thee all day, till death / Deprives us of our little breath" (21–22) is strikingly similar to the idealized loyal dogs popular throughout the Victorian period, portrayed as so loyal they will die for their owner. Even further, the birds suggest that it is not they who will enjoy liberty, but Erskine: "And oh! may thou who set us free / Enjoy in peace, sweet liberty" (19–20). Finally, the birds' description of Erskine as a "guardian angel" posits him as divine, miraculous, and their constant protector. The relationship between liberty and human governance, protection and power, has been internalized by the robins, as they enter into a social contract with Erskine as a good governor, and themselves as loyal subjects.

These poems demonstrate how historical conceptions of animal subjectivity were envisioned in relationship to human power and the state, and how they shifted throughout the nineteenth century. The publication of these poems in *Animal World* places them in the context of social reform, connected as it was with the cultivation of character and its ascription to animal subjects. The fact that one poem was written by Lord Erskine, a radical member of parliament with an eccentric love of pets, and the other was addressed to him, posits animals with political representation.[1] The first poem, written by a legislator who would in 1809 decry the fact that

---

[1] Kathryn Shevelow discusses how Erskine kept two leeches as pets, Home and Cline, who he claims saved his life after bleeding him when he was ill (231). He also kept two dogs, a macaw, and "a goose that followed him wherever he went" (233).

"Animals are considered as property only ... the law regards them not substantively; they have no rights!" (*Cobbett's* XIV: 554), positions animals in a contractual relationship similar to what Locke describes as the removal of humans from nature and into a political community of governmental protection. By remaining in a sheltered space of the human, the birds gain protection and security. In the second poem, written more than seventy years later, the birds are represented with their own voice, as individuals, making a sincere promise to remain within human bounds and sing for human pleasure. Their ability to reason and express moral character and feeling posits them as liberalized subjects, with qualities similar to those prized throughout Victorian society and located mostly in middle- and upper-class white men. Taken together, these poems place animals within pastoral power and highlight the themes I will discuss throughout this chapter and the next. In both poems, the robins' freedom is a technique of governmentality, as it occurs only within the domain of human power. The poems contain familiar themes of nineteenth-century liberal thought, such as freedom, liberty, and property, along with the more specific strategies of Victorian liberalism: individualism, social reform, character, and liberal cognition. The liberated robins are thinking, feeling individuals who willingly submit to the human in exchange for protection and security.

In a drive to gain more legislation to protect certain animals from cruelty, animals were increasingly politicized and liberalized throughout the nineteenth century. They were envisioned as subjects deserving of rights, liberty, and freedom, with qualities exemplary of the liberal subject. Mostly domesticated animals and wild birds were constructed as reasoning individuals with character and idealized moral qualities; they were represented with an awareness of nineteenth-century moral norms, and were often illustrated with striking amounts of sincerity, disinterestedness, and objectivity. In fact, often certain animals were imagined as an ideal liberal subject, even though liberalism was predicated on white male human exceptionalism. If, as Jacques Derrida suggests, animal rights reinforce "a certain interpretation of the human subject, which itself will have been the very lever of the worst violence carried out against nonhuman living beings" (*For What Tomorrow* 65), in the Victorian context anti-cruelty and animal welfare discourses reinforce an idealized liberal subject that perpetuates speciesist, classist, gendered, and racist violence. At the same time, these discourses decentered the white male human; if animals can be liberal subjects, then the human exceptionalism at liberalism's core is threatened and rendered unstable. While liberalism's influence on animal welfare demonstrates the wide reach of liberal thought throughout the period, and challenges some of our deepest assumptions about the logics of Victorian liberalism, it also shows us liberalism's limitations in regard to political inclusion and alternative subjectivity. Even further, it elucidates a key feature of Victorian liberalism: a desire for expansion beyond the human, and the incorporation of those previously outside its power networks.

In this chapter and the next I examine the strategies used within anti-cruelty legislation and animal welfare discourses to bring animals under liberal governance, and delineate how they fit within nineteenth-century liberal thought and modes of governmentality. I demonstrate how animals increasingly became *liberalized* political subjects – or liberal creatures – by which I mean those who are envisioned as part of a liberal political community, and conceptualized as individuals with qualities similar to those of liberal subjects and prized by liberal discourses. Yet although some animals were increasingly understood as self-conscious subjects, they were still subjected to humans both physically and through constructions of their subjectivity. Liberalized animals are governed by regulatory strategies emerging from state power and culture, rather than ruled by an individual human sovereign. Governmentality, I argue, is the defining political apparatus of animal–human relationships in the nineteenth century. I focus on anti-cruelty legislation and social reform discourse about animals, as these were the two major modes by which animals were increasingly incorporated into a political community and envisioned as liberalized subjects. Anti-cruelty legislation and animal welfare set up two different yet interconnected forms of power over animals: state power, through legislative discourse, and cultural power, through animal welfare discourse. Through examining legislative discourse in this chapter, and the discourse of the RSPCA and the vegetarian societies in the next, I present an overview of how animals were increasingly imagined as liberalized subjects, often with notable amounts of political representation. While Derrida asks us to reexamine the history of human rights to look for its "presuppositions" in regard to animal rights, I demonstrate how interrogating Victorian animal protection discourses brings "this problematic concerning the relations between humans and animals into the *existing* juridical framework" (*Tomorrow* 74). Indeed, my analysis largely shows the limitations of incorporating animals into a liberal framework, which rests on human exceptionalism and a suppression of animality.

The history of anti-cruelty legislation has been discussed in detail elsewhere, thus my goal in this chapter is not to rehash the many bills brought up for consideration.[2] Rather, I analyze a selection of debates and the discourse surrounding them to argue that anti-cruelty legislation signals a tension between human sovereignty over animals and the strategies of governmentality that result in the government of animals. That is, these debates center around whether or not the government – and, by extension, social reform strategies – should become the protector of animals, rather than the individual human as sovereign. While transferring a limited amount of power to the government created a new set of standards that citizens had to follow in their treatment of animals, the incorporation of animals into governmentality inaugurated new power structures that regulated not just animal–human relationships, but animals themselves, and how they were conceptualized by humans. I argue that although attempts to bring animals into a liberal political community challenged notions of the law, government, and property, they often reinscribed animals into an anthropocentric framework that rests on animal subjection. Although proponents of anti-cruelty legislation adopted liberal philosophical ideals in their arguments for animal protection, and tried to craft a liberal animal subject, most often they were unable to conceptualize animals outside of human rights and freedoms. Through examining early debates about the protection of domestic animals, and later debates about wild birds, I show how both domestic and wild animals were regulated by liberal governmentality. At the same time, drives for more legislation led to new understandings of the law, suggesting that conceptualizations of certain animals as political subjects affected understandings of property, the role of the government, and laissez-faire philosophy. Through constructing a liberalized animal subject with character, anti-cruelty debates simultaneously reinforced and reinvented the liberal subject. Although liberal thought most often constrains how humans conceptualize animals, they sometimes escape its bounds, forcing us to rethink its goals, logic, and strategies.

Animal Governmentality in Early Anti-Cruelty Debates

Lord Thomas Erskine's famous May 5, 1809, anti-cruelty speech to the House of Lords opens by aligning the political aims of animal protection

---

[2] For overviews of nineteenth-century British animal rights legislation, see Dix Harwood, *Love for Animals and How It Developed in Great Britain*; Hilda Kean, *Animal Rights*; Christine Kenyon-Jones, *Kindred Brutes*; David Perkins, *Romanticism and Animal Rights*; Harriet Ritvo, *The Animal Estate*; Kathryn Shevelow, *For the Love of Animals*; and James Turner, *Reckoning with the Beast*.

with moral feeling and human dominion.³ This speech, which circulated in pamphlet form and was used by early animal rights advocates, registers tensions between individual human sovereignty over animals and a regulation of animals through governmental strategies.⁴ Presenting to the House of Lords his Cruelty to Animals bill, which would make cruelty to all domestic animals an "indictable offence," Erskine claims that the subject is "very near my heart," and asks the House of Lords "in the name of that God who gave to man his dominion over the lower world, to acknowledge and recognize that dominion to be a moral trust" (*Cobbett's* XIV: 553–554). Erskine admits that "the subject of the bill is most peculiar and unusual," explaining he is trying to "produce, perhaps, more than the effect of law, where the ordinary sanctions of law were wanting" (557–558). Erskine desires a new regulatory ethics toward animals influenced by legislation, yet first a fundamental reconceptualization of animal–human relationships must take place. To properly govern animals, individual human sovereignty must transition to governmental strategies that can influence society's overall conduct toward animals. Yet as domestic animals were property under the law, this relinquishment of power presented a problem: to what extent should government regulate one's relationship to one's own property, when the larger goal of government is to protect it? Erskine thus assures his listeners that his bill will not interfere with individual property, but rather protect it: "all its provisions protect them [animals], as property, from the abuses of those to whose care and government their owners are obliged to commit them" (560–561). Finally, to reinforce how deeply humans are indebted to domestic animals that are, in his view, specifically constructed for human use, Erskine emphasizes "the helpless condition of man with all his god-like faculties, when stripped of the aids which he receives from the numerous classes of

---

³ Erskine's bill was not the first piece of legislation concerning the treatment of animals. Sir William Pulteney and John Dent introduced bills in 1800 and 1802, respectively, to ban the practice of bull-baiting. Erskine's bill, however, specifically identified the need for animals to have rights protected and guaranteed by the law, whereas Pulteney and Dent's arguments against bull-baiting rested on social management and lower-class regulation. See Kathryn Shevelow for the best introduction to these bills, and Alex Mackintosh, who discusses bull-baiting as an expression of human sovereignty over animals. Kathleen Kete discusses an even earlier law – a 1654 ordinance against cockfighting and cock-throwing – as well as England's game laws, which regulated hunting ("Animals and Ideology").

⁴ Erskine's speech was published and much admired by animal welfare advocates (Shevelow 242–243), and at one of their earliest meetings in 1824, the RSPCA voted to publish the speech at their own expense (Moss 22). Timothy Morton notes that Erskine's speech was also published by Richard Phillips, the vegetarian printer imprisoned for selling Thomas Paine's *The Rights of Man* in 1793 (*Shelley* 33).

inferior beings, whose qualities, and powers, and instincts, are admirably and wonderfully constructed for his use" (554–555), and notes domestic animals "are most wonderfully organized to assist man in the cultivation of the earth, and by their superior activity and strength to lessen his labor" (560). The "god-like faculties" of the human are augmented by the domination of animals, thus imbricating animals in a capitalist system that keeps them subjected to the human. Indeed, such subjection rests in their very bodies, tailored for assisting human labor. Treating these laboring animals more kindly, Erskine suggests, will keep them in a position to be better workers.

Erskine's speech highlights three major issues at stake for both proponents and opponents of anti-cruelty legislation, and demonstrates the political implications of envisioning animals as both subjects *and* property protected by the law. First, Erskine's speech registers the fundamental aspect of governmentality: the "conduct of conducts" (Foucault, "Subject" 341), which Colin Gordon describes as "a form of activity aiming to shape, guide or affect the conduct of some person or persons" (2). In this sense, Erskine asks for legislation to guide private animal–human relationships, believing it will encourage citizens to self-regulate their conduct toward animals. Erskine argues that the cause of his bill is not simply indirect duty, which would "obscure" the bill's larger principle, but more so

> a spontaneous rule in the mind of every man who reads it – which will make every human bosom a sanctuary against cruelty – which will extend the influence of a British statue beyond even the vast bounds of British jurisdiction, and consecrate, perhaps, in all nations ... that just and eternal principle which binds the whole living world in one harmonious chain, under the dominion of enlightened man, the lord and governor of all. (*Cobbett's* XIV: 557)

A "spontaneous rule in the mind of every man" could not be a better description of liberalism's self-regulating behavior. And not only does legislation here function as a regulatory mechanism that influences how humans treat animals, but it also guides behavior beyond Britain as part of a larger civilizing mission. Erskine's belief that British legislation can influence other countries to self-regulate as Britons do shows a remarkable confidence in the importance of animal–human relationships as a civilizing mission, a confidence extended throughout the period, as seen in an 1875 letter to the editor of *Animal World*: "Wherever the English flag is hoisted, there likewise should a Royal Society for the Prevention of Cruelty be in full operation" (Jesse). Erskine's bill would not just monitor the conduct of animal–human relationships and inspire a new set of morals in relation to animals, but would also influence the ways humans conduct themselves toward one another. Erskine explains, "The humanity you shall extend to the lower creation will come abundantly round in its consequences to the whole human race. The moral sense which this law will awaken and inculcate, cannot but have a most powerful effect upon our feelings and sympathies for one another" (*Cobbett's* XIV: 556). Such morals are class-based, as "The violences and outrages committed by the lower orders of the people are offences more owing to want of thought and reflection, than to any malignant principle" (556). Anything that "sets them a thinking upon the duties of humanity" will influence more proper behavior (556). For Erskine, this is not the full-fledged indirect duty Kant articulates, in which he argues that "we have no immediate duties to animals; our duties toward them are indirect duties to humanity" (212). As a regulatory mechanism directing not just human–human relationships, but also animal–human relationships, Erskine's speech suggests legislation will function as pastoral power, which "involves a permanent intervention in everyday conduct (*conduite*), in the management of lives, as well as in goods, wealth, and things" (Foucault, *Security* 154). A new legislative realm over animals can conduct the population to become better liberal subjects; it would "produce, perhaps, more than the effect of law, where the ordinary sanctions of law were wanting" (*Cobbett's* XIV: 557–558).

The second issue Erskine raises is a tension between animals as property and animals as subjects of the law, as he removes domestic animals from the power of an individual human sovereign and places them into the hands of the government. Especially when framed in terms of property, Erskine exposes the limitations of individual human sovereignty and the reluctance citizens had in relinquishing it. Indeed, in his drive to bring animals under the government Erskine never refigures Locke's hegemonic formulation of government as the protection of property, but rather emphasizes that some property may have natural rights and need legal protection. Locke's influential notions of property emphasize how important the subjection of animals is to notions of the liberal individual and the self-interest of *homo economicus*. As he explains in *Second Treatise on Government*, all natural materials, animals included, belong to the community. Once an individual transforms this material through labor, it becomes that individual's property. As far as animals are concerned, this proprietorship comes through taming (domestication), or gathering them. Once one transforms these natural products through labor, property becomes an extension of oneself. Locke explains, "From all which it is evident, that though the things of Nature are given in common, yet Man, (by being Master of himself, and *Proprietor of his own Person*, and the Actions or *Labor* of it), had still in himself *the great Foundation of Property*; and that which made up the great part of what he applied to the Support or Comfort of his being … was perfectly his own" (298–299). Because materials have been transformed into property through labor, property takes on immense importance to the individual. The regulation of one's animal property thus threatens the individual sovereignty of *homo economicus*, and signifies too much governmental power over humans. To counter this threat, Erskine emphasizes that abusing animals is not in one's self-interest – "I defy any man to point out any abuse of a brute which is property, by its owner, which is not directly against his own interest" (*Cobbett's* XIV: 555) – positing kindness toward animals as essential to the economic sphere. To work toward one's own interest, they must be kind to animals, even if this means certain relationships will be state regulated.

Significantly, this tension between animals as property belonging to an individual and as subjects with rights under the law registers a more radical understanding of animals as subjects with agency, thoughts, feelings, and desires, as *more than* property. Erskine's statement that "Almost every sense bestowed upon man is equally bestowed upon them … the sense of pain and pleasure; the passions of love and anger; sensibility to kindness, and pangs from unkindness and neglect, are inseparable characteristics of their natures as much as of our own" (*Cobbett's* XIV: 555) suggests animals exceed the objectifying logic of property, even though his bill is based on protecting it. Although this conceptualization of animals risks destabilizing the agency of individuals over their property, it gives animals subject status under the law. It registers not only subjectivity, but a subjectivity used as evidence for better treatment. Such understandings of animals are foundational to demands for more legislation throughout the period, and to the RSPCA's own regulation of animal and human populations. The belief that animals have thoughts, feelings, and desires will become essential to constructing their subjectivity in ways that influence kind treatment, without too fully disrupting the animal–human hierarchy.

The third issue Erskine's speech raises is a tension between an inherent subjection of animals to humankind and a desire to give them more freedom. While anti-cruelty logic may not blatantly be about freedom, as domestic animals are always constrained by their human owners, the reasoning behind it seeks to allow for more beneficial animal–human relationships; ideally, if animals are treated better, they can exert more agency, and will recognize the importance of staying in their position as laborers. Indeed, later in the period animal welfare texts like *Black Beauty* reinforce this idea, as when Ginger explains, "I was willing to work, and ready to work hard too; but to be tormented for nothing but their fancies angered me" (37), and Black Beauty's comment that "We horses do not mind hard work if we are treated reasonably" (213). Not only does this inherent subjection happen on physical and mental levels – as animal bodies are described as innately tailored for labor, and they themselves desire to work – but it also occurs through a religious discourse that posits humans above animals and grants them dominion over the animal population. Claims for animal welfare throughout the period will rest on this supposed God-given human superiority. Such knowledge of animal bodies, and later, of their minds, works as a form of security, as it ensures Britain's financial well-being through the exploitation of animals, adds to British prosperity, and reifies human superiority. This tension between animal freedom and animal subjection sits, I argue, at the core of animal welfare discourse.

While Foucault would take issue with working animals having freedom – he explains, after all, that "Power is exercised over free subjects ... individual or collective subjects who are faced with a field of possibilities in which several kinds of conduct, several ways of reacting and modes of behavior are available" ("Subject" 342) – animal protection discourses will imagine animals enacting a voluntary servitude in their relationships with humans. For Foucault, servitude, slavery, and physical power do not compose power relationships; "how could we seek to be slaves?" (342) he asks. Yet when placed in the context of early animal welfare I claim servitude – more particularly, a *voluntary* servitude – is an essential strategy of governmentality. Anti-cruelty legislation can be understood as a negative freedom from violence and mistreatment, a core element of liberal political thought, and this freedom results in a range of "possibilities" for animals: some can choose to take part in labor and servitude, while others may choose to revolt against it. Thus, translating Foucault's theories of power to animal–human relationships requires us to take seriously constructions of animal subjectivity and how they were used to imagine animal freedoms and reify human power.

The themes Erskine raises – animals as property, the scope of the law, innate animal subjection, and a well-developed animal subjectivity – are the foundation of many debates regarding animal welfare and anti-cruelty legislation throughout the nineteenth century. The tensions raised by these themes, I argue, signal the beginning of a movement from animals under the protection of a human sovereign, to the government of animals by a larger set of regulatory frameworks that affect new animal–human relationships and alter how humans conceptualize animals as subjects.

Erskine's bill passed unanimously in the House of Lords on June 9, 1809, yet failed in the House of Commons. Opponents of the bill saw animal protection, especially if grounded in morality, as beyond the scope of legislation. The bill's most outspoken opponent, William Windham, stressed that "In no country had it ever yet been attempted to regulate by law the conduct of men towards brute animals," and that "The province of criminal legislation had hitherto been confined to the injuries sustained by men" (*Cobbett's* XIV: 1030). Further, he argues, the "masters" should regulate the treatment of their animals, not the state: "Why do not these masters and owners exert themselves in earnest, in punishing such offences whenever they come within their cognizance?" (1037). Through a reinforcement of class power, alongside the cultivation of character and conduct, animals will be treated well. "It must at all events," Windham argues, "be more by manners than by laws that any good could be done upon this subject" (1027). To govern animals is thus in part to govern humans; when animals are granted more freedom from cruelty, humans lose previously held freedoms yet are cultivated as better subjects. The triangle between sovereignty, discipline, and governmental management Foucault maps (*Security* 107) manifests here in debates over animal–human relationships, specifically regarding which kind of regulation should have the guiding hand in governing such relationships. And while Windham suggests that manners rather than laws should regulate animal–human relationships, within the next few decades, both will ultimately work to reify animal protection and human power.

Arguments against Erskine's bill were also founded on class politics, as opponents believed it unfairly discriminated against the lower classes. Animal rights risked undermining upper-class supremacy and the hierarchy of social privilege in which liberal politics was grounded. If the state began to regulate animal fighting, for example, and monitored how the lower class treated the animals with which they worked, then the government would have to legislate against upper-class sports such as fox hunting. As novels such as Anthony Trollope's *Phineas Finn* will show later in the period, hunting helped define aristocratic masculinity, especially as connected to state power.[5] Those against anti-cruelty legislation thus sought to

---

[5] For example, Lady Laura tells Phineas, "I mean you to be very intimate with Mr. Kennedy, and to shoot his grouse, and to stalk his deer, and to help keep him in progress as a liberal member of parliament" (76). Anthony Trollope famously loved and defended hunting. For a history of the

reinforce the power of the ruling class and make sure state power reinforced it as well. Indeed, in this instance, a regulation of conduct would destabilize class divides, as it would expose that all classes had a similar behavior that must be conducted toward better animal–human relationships. Further, as David Perkins explains, granting animals natural rights would by implication grant those same rights to other human subjects, such as the lower class. "You could not grant a right to animals," he argues, "that you denied to subordinate classes of humans" (43). These debates thus expose a lingering fear of disrupting traditional notions of the liberal subject – white males with property, similar to Derrida's formulation of the *carnophallogocentric* subject – and taking away property rights and liberties of the upper classes.[6] Thus as parliament concluded in 1809, anti-cruelty legislation interfered with state protection of human individuals and their property, and destabilized individual human sovereignty over animals.

In his account of animals, sensibility, and political rhetoric in the long eighteenth century, Tobias Menely claims that the 1809 debate is about the "potential personhood of animals" and liberalism's rejection of sensibility (173). As Menely rightly notes, liberal principles are at the heart of these debates on both sides of the aisle. He explains, "While advocates invoked a liberal rhetoric of inherent interest and progressive reform, their adversaries called upon the liberal principle of moral pluralism, according to which our duties toward animals are a matter of voluntary choice rather than political justice" (173). Yet these debates also challenge core tenets of early nineteenth-century liberal thought, for concerns regarding the role of law and the political status of property risked redefining the human subject and the very purpose of liberal government itself. For example, Erskine's emphasis on morality, and his admission that his bill was "peculiar," was followed by Windham's claim that animal rights would redefine legislation and "form a new era of legislation!" (*Cobbett's* XIV: 1030). In this understanding, bringing animals into the scope of legislation destabilizes traditional notions of the law, and, perhaps more frighteningly for opponents,

---

association between British masculinity and hunting, and an overview of Trollope's defenses of hunting, see Rob Boddice, "Manliness and the Morality of Field Sports: E. A. Freeman and Anthony Trollope, 1869–1871."

[6] In "Eating Well," Derrida defines carnophallogocentrism as the "dominant *schema*" of patriarchy, logocentrism, and "carnivorous virility" (113). In other words, for Derrida, the normalized subject is human, male, and meat-eating: "Authority and autonomy ... are, through this schema, attributed to the man (*homo* and *vir*) rather than to the woman, and to the woman rather than to the animal" (114).

challenges the primacy of the carnophallogocentric liberal subject and its sovereign power over animals. Following Agamben's formulation of *zoē* and bios – natural or "bare life" versus life under the law or as part of a political community – this moment of decrying the lack of animal rights moves animals toward bios and more fully within a political community. Agamben explains, "Declarations of rights represent the originary figure of the inscription of natural life [*zoē*] in the juridico-political order of the nation-state" (*Homo* 127). Thus Erskine's declaration that "the animals themselves are without protection; the law regards them not substantively; they have no rights!" (*Cobbett's* XIV 554) registers a desire to bring certain animals within the juridico-political sphere, and ultimately, under liberal strategies of governmentality.

Erskine's speech and the debates that followed exemplify tensions between sovereign power – of the human rather than a king – and governmentality, where a specific set of strategies inspired by legislation and animal welfare discourse guides animal–human relationships. Erskine's attempt to bring those who were previously excluded from the realm of the law into the juridico-political community further marks the incorporation of animal–human relationships into biopower's regulatory strategies. Foucault describes biopower as the government and management of a population, which seeks to enhance life; it results in the government of humans, or governmentality. As opposed to sovereign power, whose specific target is territory, governmentality works through an extended series of power networks, whose goal is to manage and foster a population. This often works through pastoral power, which regulates conduct under the guise of care. Foucault explains that "government is not related to the territory, but to a sort of complex of men and things" (*Security* 96). "Things" can mean anything from wealth and resources, climate and the fertility of the soil, to misfortunes, famines, and death (96). Governmentality thus signals a wider reach of political power into daily life, working through "apparatuses of security," one of which is freedom. Freedom, in this sense, is "no longer the exemptions and privileges attached to a person, but the possibility of movement, change of place, and processes of circulation of both people and things" (48–49). In nineteenth-century Britain, this population management enters the dynamics of animal–human relationships, in part through envisioning animals as subjects under the law and removed from individual human sovereignty. Nineteenth-century anti-cruelty debates expose how governmentality was concerned not only with the government of humans but with the government of animals as well. Indeed, Mario Ortiz-Robles reads nineteenth-century anti-cruelty legislation as making "the rhetoric of biopolitics visible," as "animals become an over-determined stand-in for life itself." While Ortiz-Robles emphasizes how a move from disciplinarity to biopower destabilizes the animal–human divide, I stress that the incorporation of animals into the legislative realm marks both an extended form of power over animals and a new understanding of them as liberalized subjects. Given Lauren Goodlad's emphasis on how the Victorian state worked through governmentality, we can here both confirm and expand her understanding of Victorian power structures as they move to the animal world.

The 1809 debates reflect the tensions that will occupy arguments regarding animal protection legislation throughout the nineteenth century. Although early debates brought up notions of rights, they were also deeply concerned with the strategies used to govern both animals and humans. They further elucidate the extent to which the ruling class legislated on its own behalf even within animal–human relationships. The religious discourse framing animal–human relationships, and the conceptualization of animals as property, encourages yet is in tension with the movement toward governing animals and understandings of animals that challenge human exceptionalism and inaugurate a new liberalized status of animals. If Erskine is trying to "produce, perhaps, more than the effect of law," such production is a self-regulating conduct of animal–human relationships that aligns with liberal strategies. Understanding anti-cruelty legislation as part of bringing animals into governmentality, shaped by biopower and pastoral power, nuances how animals were treated and constructed under liberal thought. Debates about animal protection legislation were not just about whether or not animals had natural rights, or about their potential personhood, but more about how to govern animals and animal–human relationships especially. The triangulation of sovereign power, discipline, and governmentality involved a refiguration of human power over animals. As the effects of governmentality intensified, human power over animals was more often than not imagined as benevolent, and animals were increasingly imagined as desiring such benevolence.

England's first anti-cruelty act, the "Act to Prevent the Cruel and Improper Treatment of Cattle," was introduced by Richard Martin and passed on June 7, 1822. The act confined itself to domestic animals, and only protected working animals who fell under the definition of cattle: "Horses, Mare, Gelding, Mule, Ass, Ox, Cow, Heifer, Steer, Sheep, or other Cattle." The act's focus on cattle suggests the extent to which legislators were willing to protect only those animals who worked for humans and reinforced their own position of power, and emphasizes how badly these animals were subject to violent treatment. Derrida, for example, emphasizes that cattle signifies "an animality not domesticated ... but already defined and dominated by man *in view of man*, an animality that is already destined, in its reproduction organized by man, to become either an enslaved instrument of work or else animal nourishment" (*Beast* 12). Without diminishing the ground-breaking importance of such legislation, I argue that this first act emphasizes the extent to which early animal welfare was fundamentally anthropocentric, more about controlling animals than protecting them. An MP from Ireland with a "rowdy sense of humor," Martin had previously argued on behalf of Irish Catholics, wanted to end the death penalty for forgery, and sought to give public defenders to poor people who had been accused of crimes but could not afford a lawyer (Shevelow 245). Martin tried to pass the bill one year earlier, and although it passed in the Commons, it failed in the House of Lords, in part due to the ridicule it received. A *Times* report of the bill's reading and debate notes the audience's laughter, especially after descriptions of animal fights ("Cruelty").[7] After it passed, Martin continued to bring in anti-cruelty bills, particularly against bull-baiting. Although he brought in nine anti-cruelty bills over the next four years, none of them passed. Whereas Erskine was unable to reconcile animal rights, property, and human freedoms, Martin relied on the need to cultivate human conduct. Martin's arguments suggest a concern for a population that includes both animals and humans but is focused on humans, rather than animals. For example, in 1824, Martin moved to appoint a committee to investigate cruel sports, yet the goal was "to inquire how far cruel sports, if persevered in, tended to deteriorate and corrupt the morals of the people" (*Parliamentary Debates* X: 487). He emphasized that "the sports which were the object of his motion ought to be suppressed, as tending to corrupt morals and endanger good order; and it was on this ground that he particularly founded his motion" (487). While Martin's logic in these debates is strategically grounded in indirect duty – that kindness toward animals is good only insofar as it prohibits cruelty toward humankind – it also posits pastoral power as central to

---

[7] Ivan Kreilkamp discusses the ridicule surrounding Martin's bill in "The Ass Got a Verdict: Martin's Act and the Founding of the Society for the Prevention of Cruelty to Animals, 1822." He argues that the bill passed, in part, due to Martin's "facing up to and rerouting the quality of ludicrousness, humour, and disbelieving laughter that had always accompanied any efforts to change the standing of animals." See also Stefan Bargheer's "The Fools of the Leisure Class," which discusses ridicule in early anti-cruelty legislation.

legislative efforts. For Martin sidesteps notions of rights to proclaim that animals deserve kindness because they are under human protection:

> It might be said, that animals were not possessed of those rights which man possessed; but he should contend, that though they could not be said to possess rights in the same degree as men, yet that being placed under the protection of man, they were entitled, so far as was consistent with the use which was given to man over the brute creation, to be treated with kindness and humanity. (487)

As in Erskine's arguments, anti-cruelty ideology is grounded in an assumed animal–human hierarchy. This should not be surprising, for the human is always the end result of liberalism. This assertion demonstrates, however, the limitations of bringing animals into the *human* political sphere, for it only results in alternate forms of subjection.

Animal welfare falls under the purview of social reform, which Goodlad identifies as a key strategy of pastorship, and highlights the extent to which governing animals took place within the state, through law, and within indirect forms of state power, such as the RSPCA. Understanding animal protection as pastoral power emphasizes the animal–human hierarchy at the heart of anti-cruelty efforts and reshapes our thinking about animal welfare and animal–human relationships in the Victorian era. Foucault locates the origin of pastoral power in the sheep-fold, in the relationship between sheep and their shepherd. Foucault claims this is "fundamentally a beneficent power" (*Security* 126), concerned with the conduct and salvation of the sheep: "It looks after the flock, it looks after the individuals of the flock, it sees to it that the sheep do not suffer, it goes in search of those that have strayed off course, and it treats those that are injured" (127). Within early parliamentary debates, animals and humans converge under pastoral power, as the goal is simultaneously to protect animals and regulate human conduct. While the RSPCA will more forcefully take up animal conduct in their constructions of animal subjectivity, here the rationale for anti-cruelty legislation is based on the belief that animals were given to humans by God. If pastoral power is "essentially the relationship of God to men ... a religious type of power that God exercises over his people" (124–125), then when taken more literally as a power of humans over animals, this human–God hierarchy is mirrored in the animal–human hierarchy. Although Foucault claims there is no hierarchy in pastoral power, when understood as a human power over animals, there is indeed a hierarchical logic that reaffirms the dominant belief that humans reign sovereign over animals, and they must therefore protect and treat them well.

For opponents of anti-cruelty legislation, placing animal protection under government control rather than individual human sovereignty conflicted with early liberalism's laissez-faire philosophy. Sir Peel, a die-hard opponent, for example, "called upon the House not to allow themselves to legislate upon such subjects. The evils complained of would be done away with, by the growing intelligence and refinement of the country" (*Parliamentary Debates* XII: 1005), and exclaimed that banning animal fighting "would open a door to the practice of a wanton and oppressive tyranny" in regard to humans (1004). Indeed, many opponents shared similar beliefs, as they saw their human freedoms at stake. As the country begins to realize that animal cruelty is uncivilized behavior, they claimed, citizens will self-regulate and cease treating animals cruelly through their own agency. While both Erskine and Martin believe that government regulation is needed to encourage proper conduct, others saw the incorporation of animals into the political as a deep rejection of individual liberty, and most importantly, as a negation of human sovereignty.

The first animal welfare act and early anti-cruelty debates are important moments in nineteenth-century political history, as they highlight the beginning of pastoral power's regulation of animals. Keeping in mind that the animals included in the first anti-cruelty act were cattle, including sheep, Foucault's claim that pastoral power, a "form of power so typical of the West ... was born, or at least took its model from the fold, from politics seen as a matter of the sheep-fold" (*Security* 130), invites us to take more literally how animals influenced and were influenced by nineteenth-century governmentality. In her call to de-metaphorize the sheep in formulations of pastoral power, Nicole Shukin claims that to assume pastoral power is only about human–human relationships "is to underestimate just how contingent governmentality may be on the production and ordering of 'species' as a play of similarity and difference" ("Tense" 152). While metaphorization is necessary to understand how pastoral power works in other arenas, we should take seriously Foucault's marking of this power within animal–human relationships. Anti-cruelty legislation demonstrates how animals and relationships with them were influenced by governmentality, as both proponents and opponents discussed the role of the government – indeed, its mentality – in conducting citizens and their animals. The arrival of animals into the juridico-political sphere coincided with the centrality of pastoral power to the workings of Victorian liberalism. This understanding illuminates how deeply human exceptionalism and anthropocentrism were part of the strategies of governmentality, and how the incorporation of animals into a liberal political community began to challenge them.

Wild Bird Legislation and the Protection of Animal Populations

At the 1871 annual meeting of the RSPCA, the chairman emphasized how fully animal populations have been taken under the protection of both the government and the human population. He explains,

> The time is much changed since Martin, with great difficulty, and amidst shouts of mockery in the legislature, attempted to interpose the law in the protection of the animal creation. That time has gone by. It is now a popular subject. Magistrates are no longer reluctant to put the laws in force; public opinion supports them; and ministers of religion take their stand ready to promote every feeling of humanity. ("Annual Meeting" 174)

By the 1870s animal fighting had been banned; dog carts were illegal; dog stealing became an official crime; the slaughter of horses and the transit of animals for slaughter became more regulated; more domestic animals were covered under the Prevention of Cruelty to Animals Bill, including dogs and cats; a committee was investigating the foreign trade in animals; and wild birds were seen as worthy of protection.[8] While the large number of new laws suggests Britain viewed itself as the forerunner in humane animal–human relationships, and that both the government and the public were more comfortable with anti-cruelty legislation, the discourse surrounding such legislation had not evolved very far.[9] Legislation still emphasized property, targeted the working class, and upheld a conduct of social order and middle-class morality; rarely was the ethical impetus focused on the good of animal lives. Yet as animal protection legislation became more common throughout the century, animal–human relationships were not only disciplined, but contained within numerous mechanisms that governed the animal population at large. Although citizens could be punished under the law, animal–human relationships were policed and influenced by animal autobiographies, journals such as the RSPCA's *Animal World* and *Band of Mercy*, public lectures, animal welfare tracts, sermons, and paintings. Together they instilled in the population a more humane view toward animal–human relationships and a conceptualization

---

[8] See the Cruelty to Animals Acts of 1835, 1849, and 1854; the 1845 Dog-Stealing Bill; and the Seabirds Preservation Act of 1869. The revisions of the Cruelty to Animals Acts generally incorporated other acts, such as the 1839 Metropolitan Police Act, which banned dog carts in London, prohibited places used for animal fighting, and punished people caught cruelly driving cattle; and the Extension of Metropolitan Police Act in 1854, which banned dog carts in England.

[9] Anti-cruelty legislation after 1870 includes the Wild Bird's Protection Act of 1872, the 1876 Anti-Vivisection Act, more wild bird legislation in 1880, 1881, and 1894; the Injured Animals Act of 1894; and the 1900 Wild Animals in Captivity Act.

of animals as subjects with emotions, thoughts, and desires. Such relationships frequently operated within an indirect form of governance, which Goodlad describes as a desire "to implement parliamentary power in ways that encouraged self-help, philanthropy, voluntarism, and local government" (*Victorian Literature* 14). That is, the legal sphere works in tandem with public opinion, liberal discourses of character, and religion to protect not just individual animals, but the entire animal creation. Indeed, an 1872 article in *Animal World* titled "What Shall I Do to Help the Animals?" suggests all citizens should take it upon themselves to regulate animal–human relationships and supplement the law where it is lacking. From writing, preaching, or donating money, to monitoring servants and workmen, it is up to middle- and upper-class citizens to help cultivate better treatment toward animals (241). Notions of humanity are redefined to include a conception of animals that veers from utility and sovereign power to care and protection – the cultivation of life. Thus, while anti-cruelty discourse still relied on liberal notions of property and class hierarchy, the regulatory strategies of protecting animals expanded throughout both animal and human populations.

If the Victorian period stands as an era of burgeoning democracy, however limited in scope, the incorporation of animals into the political sphere suggests they too were worthy of political inclusion and representation. Relationships with them were even politically charged with educating the new groups of men included in the franchise under the 1867 Reform Act. An 1871 article about Richard Martin from *Animal World* explains,

> Civilisation now demands talent and education, even in our handicraftsmen; therefore, and that this nation may not be left behind, we are giving our people knowledge. They have demanded and obtained political power; we fear the consequences of ignorance – and, therefore, we are now in earnest in giving them knowledge. Now that our international policy is not aggressive, there is no danger in cultivating in their minds the principles of this journal – mercy, compassion, justice – and, therefore, there will be no objection. ("Richard Martin" 194–193)

With an expanded franchise indirect duty may now matter more than ever. The importance this passage places on animal welfare suggests that treating animals well had larger political implications, as their treatment indirectly secured the proper functioning of society and the state. In this conceptualization of indirect duty, animals gain political power, as they are seen as subjects whose proper treatment affects a larger liberal political order. Animals do not necessarily reinforce individual human sovereignty, but rather state sovereignty and the workings of governmentality. This does not mean, however, that humans so easily relinquished their individual sovereignty over animals. Debates about wild bird legislation in the late 1860s through the 1880s highlight the extent to which animal protection aimed to keep animals within a hierarchical framework, as even wild animals were brought within the scope of governmentality. Arguments for bird protection emphasize animal conduct and character, at the same time they show a striking move to construct avian subjects outside of a linear ordering of animals and humans. As the period progresses, individual human sovereignty was increasingly in tension with governmentality, especially in its concern for animal populations. However, an emphasis on the utility of animals keeps even wild animals, or those wild animals with moral character, within an anthropocentric framework. Human exceptionalism and the economic utility of animals remain strong strategies of governmentality, showing how deeply anti-cruelty legislation was tied to the workings of capitalism.

Many scholars who discuss anti-cruelty legislation in the second half of the Victorian period focus on the anti-vivisection movement that took place between the 1860s and 1880s; scholars rarely discuss the simultaneous movement to protect birds.[10] While the anti-vivisection movement focused on domestic animals such as cats and dogs who were undergoing cruel experiments, within wild bird protection discourse the problem of cruelty took a back seat to worries over extinction and an acknowledgment of ecological relationships. Jeremy Gaskell, for example, suggests that the extinction of the great auk in the mid-nineteenth century spurred the push for wild bird legislation and governmental concern with animal populations. Humans recognized the economic and aesthetic benefits they would lose through the loss of bird life. Inspired by a Darwinian discourse that emphasized inter-species dependency, wild bird advocates acknowledged the benefits from small creatures. Indeed, James Turner has marked the mid- to late-century concern with wild birds as the ushering in of a new "ecological ethic: the feeling that, when human beings abused nature, they not merely damaged their own long-term interests but perpetrated a morally vicious act" (127). With today's posthumanist language, we can

---

[10] Most often analyses about wild birds focus on connections between women and the plumage trade, and emphasize the period after 1880. See Robin Doughty, *Feather Fashions and Bird Preservation*; Kean, chapter 5; R. J. Moore-Coyler, "Feathered Women and Persecuted Birds: The Struggle against the Plumage Trade, c. 1860–1922"; Tony Samstag, *For Love of Birds*; Turner, chapter 7; and Robert Welker, *Birds and Men*. Scholars have also discussed the practice of keeping birds in cages. See, for example, Nigel Rothfels, "How the Caged Bird Sings: Animals and Entertainment," and Sarah Amato, *Beastly Possessions*, chapter 1.

read the ecological relationships between birds, insects, plants, and humans as a multi-species one, or what Donna Haraway would label a "sympoietic" relationship, in which individualism loses prominence for "collectively-producing systems that do not have self-defined spatial or temporal boundaries" (Dempster qtd. in Haraway, *Staying* 33). In *Staying with the Trouble*, Haraway argues that rejecting "bounded" human individualism (30) acknowledges all the "mortal critters entwined in myriad unfinished configurations of places, times, matters, meanings" (1). To think ecologically, sympoietically, or in terms of multi-species relationships decenters humans and destabilizes the great chain of being. Thinking ecologically, for the Victorians, is a radical and striking departure from earlier debates that refuse to "stay with the trouble" and make kin with the nonhuman "in lines of inventive connection as a practice of learning to live and die well with each other in a thick present" (1). However, traces of liberal anthropocentrism remain, most especially within constructions of avian subjectivity. Victorians could stay with the trouble for only so long, before they again reified animal lives into a biopolitical framework that controlled not just their lives, but also the construction of their minds.

In between the years 1869 and 1881, parliament passed four acts to protect wild birds, whom many feared were rapidly becoming extinct due to shooting and trapping. These acts enforced a closed time during breeding season, making it illegal to kill, wound, or trap wild birds during certain months. As such, debates about wild bird legislation generally focused on avian liberty and often, although not always, a destabilization of human sovereignty over animals. The discourses surrounding these debates demonstrate the extent to which governmentality spread beyond the domestic sphere and brought select wild animals under its fold. These debates also highlight how strategies of governmentality functioned by way of a biopower that regulated bird populations – indeed, bird life itself – in order to benefit human economies. Debates over how to regulate bird life emphasize that the strategies used to regulate animal populations – not just legislation but social reform and education – result in a state power operating directly and indirectly, deciding when and how birds will die while simultaneously seeking to foster their lives. The control of wild birds results in a freedom Foucault characterizes as security, which bolsters the British economy. This is not a classic liberal definition of freedom, he argues, "but the possibility of movement, change of place, and processes of circulation of both people and things" (*Security* 48–49). Animal freedom, in this instance, keeps animals within a framework that protects property and the nation's wealth, under the guise of protecting animal life.

Like most anti-cruelty legislation, wild bird legislation was, at its core, a capitalist enterprise; most wild bird discourse focuses on utility, especially in relationship to capital and the economy. While wild birds were not property like the cattle discussed in earlier debates, they were seen as essential to securing property nonetheless. Christopher Sykes, the writer of the 1869 Sea Birds Preservation bill, first introduced it by emphasizing that there "were no mere sentimental or humanitarian grounds" to the bill, "though these were strong enough" (*Hansard's* CXCIV: 405). Rather, he explained that the bill was in the interest of "the farmers, the merchant seamen, and the deep-sea fishers" (405). Birds "afforded warning of the proximity of a rocky shore" and helped deep-sea fishers know where to cast their nets (405). If cattle were brought under governmental protection on grounds of humanitarianism and social order, wild birds emphasize the extent to which the government of animals still reinforced the protection of property and economic relationships.

Soon after the bill's passage, constituents and MPs complained it did not go far enough in protecting birds. Their critiques emphasize both utility and an ecological ethic that showcases the interconnectedness of animal and human life. Auberon Herbert, for example, explains, "There was scarcely a tree or plant which had not its enemies in certain insects or worms . . . there was also an army of protection in the shape of the small birds, which had been well called the police or the soldiery of nature . . . . the principal part of the work of destroying these hurtful insects was done by the birds" (*Hansard's* CCXI: 1648–1649). He continues to note that "the act of shooting sparrows had been compared by one who knew the value of these small birds, to the act of shooting down our own soldiers at the moment of invasion by an enemy" (1651). The comparison of birds to police and soldiers suggests birds are so useful they function as a governing apparatus that protects human citizens and the nation at large. Indeed, it directs their daily actions and means of survival toward the human. Valued for their usefulness, the birds solidify human superiority and protect human property. Such discourse privileges the human economy, even though birds are increasingly viewed as political subjects with moral character and domestic qualities.

Although wild birds benefit economic security, the rationale for legislation is often animal freedom. Indeed, MPs emphasized how freedom of movement benefits both birds and humans. Discussing birds who come to England's shores to breed, Mr. Johnson emphasizes that they were

> rapidly becoming extinct, owing to the inordinate and exterminating persecution to which they were subjected. Not only that, but he also thought

> that with the increase of feathered visitors which must inevitability arise under the Bill, when they found that persecution no longer awaited them, would be found, along perhaps with some new, the once familiar forms and agreeable songs. (*Handsard's* CCXI: 1646–1647)

Johnson's use of the term "persecution" characterizes birds as subjects needing political protection. Considering that such birds come from outside British jurisdiction, Johnson describes them as welcome others due to the diversity they bring to England. Herbert similarly constructs birds as political subjects when he emphasizes that

> we ought to give a refuge to birds of every kind, and certainly to those curious ones which were now shot down on their first appearance in England, but which, with a little encouragement, would either breed with us or pay us future visits ... for by doing so we should endow our parks and the face of the country generally with a greater charm of interest and variety. (*Hansard's* CCXI: 1651–1652)

While Herbert's argument has human interests at its core – more birds give the country "a greater charm of interest and variety" – it posits birds as agents deserving political protection. The language of persecution does not grant birds rights, but registers them as political subjects under the law, subjects who can be unfairly oppressed merely for their difference. In other words, it attempts to reject speciesism. Such moments register the tension between animal and human sovereignty common in earlier debates; these arguments expose how the incorporation of animals into the political sphere results in a weakening of individual human sovereignty and strengthens animal liberties and freedoms. Both, it turns out, benefit the human population.

Those in favor of bird protection often debated which birds deserved to live based on their character and conduct, demonstrating a heightened emphasis on animal character as a rationale for political protection. For example, Herbert explained in the 1872 debates that "There was a large class of birds, such as the swallow, the swift, the marten, the wagtail, the cuckoo, the wryneck, the goat-sucker, the white owl, the shrike, the stone chatterer, and the three warblers, which did nothing but good, though there were other birds with characters of a more doubtful description" (*Hansard's* CCXI: 1649–1650). One MP commented in the 1873 debates that "he thought the Act required amendment because it was founded on a wrong principle – namely, that birds should be destroyed unless it could be shown that they were harmless; whereas the true principle should be that no birds should be destroyed in the breeding season unless it could be shown that they were mischievous" (*Hansard's* CCXV: 1189). Animal character was further constructed through emphasizing maternal qualities, as when Herbert explains,

> No one could have observed birds in the breeding season without noticing the entire devotion which they had for their young, and the courage which that attachment gave them in the face of all enemies – even in the face of man himself . . . though they had no power of agitating in their own behalf, yet did us good service, and possessed many of the qualities the presence of which we so much respected in men and women. (*Hansard's* CCXI: 1652)

Birds are constructed with idealized moral qualities, such as devotion and courage; envisioning animals with qualities of the liberal subject brings them under governmentality and affects how the state regulates their lives. Thus if birds with a "doubtful" character are not deserving of protection – indeed, of life itself – then the presence of moral animal character becomes a necessity for government protection.

Through their journal *Animal World*, the RSPCA helped this effort and emphasized avian character in relationship to animal–human relationships and legislation. Their May 1871 issue, for example, notes, "It will be seen that prominence has been given in this number of our journal to the interests of small wild birds, though caged birds are scarcely alluded to; and it will be obvious that such omission is designed to act more forcibly on public opinion in favour of further legislation for the protection of such feathered friends of man" ("Occasional Notes"). The journal published bird autobiographies, wrote about the benefits humans gain from birds, published poems about birds and from their point of view, included articles on pet birds, and urged parliament to go further in the kinds of birds the bills protect. For the focus on protecting individual species and not *all* birds created a debate over why certain birds were left out, or why they had no "friends" in parliament. Images of the bullfinch and the yellowhammer, for example, "without friends in parliament," cultivate sympathy and rationalize the need for state protection through showing their maternal devotion (Figures 1.1 and 1.2). An article on pet birds similarly constructs avian character through alignments with nationality. In "Our Pets – III. 'Oberon' and 'Titania,'" the author describes the process of choosing a pet bird, stating it ultimately came down to avian character: "After divers discussions about love-birds, parroquets, and so forth, we decided to get a bullfinch, not an artificially-reared, conceited, and unnatural piping bullfinch, but an honest, common English bird" (E.A.W. 51). This discourse around character and conduct functions as an

Figure 1.1 "Birds without Friends in Parliament. – No. 3." *Animal World*, vol. 4, no. 46, July 1873, p. 100.

Figure 1.2 "Birds without Friends in Parliament. – No. 4." *Animal World*, vol. 4, no. 46, July 1873, p. 101.

individualizing power, one of the features of pastoral power, through focusing on individual types of birds rather than *all* birds, and constructs them in relation to their perceived conduct. A racialist discourse that equates external characteristics with internal moral qualities is projected onto the animal world, and becomes grounds for legislation and political protection. Ultimately, animal character conducts humans on the basis of how birds are perceived to conduct themselves in relationship to the human.

On one level, this anthropomorphic construction of animal character lessens the gap between animals and humans and, if only to a certain extent, destabilizes human sovereignty. By attributing to animals capacities that were for centuries denied them, wild bird and anti-cruelty discourse challenges the very grounds of the animal–human hierarchy. Indeed, the rejection of animal capacities undergirds Derrida's formulation of human sovereignty, which imposes itself by way of *logos*, or rather, a certain interpretation of *logos* as reason, or even carnophallogocentrism. Michael Naas explains that "In all his work on the animal, we see Derrida questioning the confidence with which humans attribute certain capacities to themselves while denying them to animals, all in the name of a certain conception of human sovereignty that so often results in aggression and violence against the animal world and in a pervasive denial or denegation of this violence" (8). In *The Open*, Agamben describes this split between animals and humans as the "anthropological machine," which separates animality and humanity based on capacities reserved for the human. For Agamben, this split is the foundation of biopolitics, in which natural life becomes the stakes of the political. It is no surprise that in the era of evolution, with science and psychology locating cognitive similarities between animals and humans, the state expands toward animal life. Within Victorian anti-cruelty and animal welfare discourse, the anthropological machine continues to grind; even when humans recognize shared capacities with animals, they result from power structures that control the lives of animal populations. Indeed, these capacities are consistently directed toward the human. The construction of some birds with conduct and some without encourages the exclusion of birds from the cultivation of life. Those who are included are brought under governmental strategies for the benefit of human economies, which can result in their death, as the government legislates when they may be killed. That is, life is fostered only to the extent that the natural lives of birds – daily activities such as eating or singing – benefit the human. As seen at the beginning of this chapter, Derrida critiques animal rights discourse because it prizes the human subject, language, and reason. This way of thinking is specifically liberal: It values moral conduct, character, and individualism, all central to the liberal human subject. Liberal governmentality thus regulates animal life through its construction of animal conduct.

This is not to suggest that members of parliament did not recognize the violence resulting from human power. Indeed, birds are often imagined as agents and subjects who recognize not the authority of humans, but their danger. Herbert acknowledges this and critiques unchecked human power: "it would be a good thing for us, and have a good effect upon our national character, if we were willing to give up just one little bit of the power we possessed over the life and freedom of this part of surrounding creation. Where anything lay absolutely in our power it was a bad thing for us not to restrict ourselves in the use of that power" (*Hansard's* CCXI: 1652). Noting the detriment of rampant human power, proponents of bird protection argued that birds would be more helpful if left alone. This laissez-faire attitude toward animals brings them further under the scope of governmentality for the benefit of their liberty; like the robins in Erskine's poems, avian freedom comes from the regulation of animal populations, their character, and conduct. To return to Foucault, freedom works in tandem with governmentality, allowing for "the possibility of movement, change of place, and processes of circulation of both people and things" (*Security* 48–49). Governmentality, especially in its construction and regulation of character, permits the immigration of birds and their protection on England's shores, *if* they contribute to the British economy and an aesthetically pleasing countryside. As Michael Freeden illustrates, laissez-faire philosophy had a contentious relationship with late Victorian liberalism, and in the later decades of the Victorian period conflicted with social reform ideologies. Indeed, L. T. Hobhouse explains that regulation is necessary for greater freedom, and that only restraint can guarantee social freedom: "The liberty which is good is not the liberty of one gained at the expense of others, but the liberty which can be enjoyed by all who dwell together, and this liberty depends on and is measured by the completeness with which by law, custom, or their own feelings they are restrained from mutual injury" (44–45). In a reversal from the laissez-faire of early anti-cruelty opponents, who did not want to regulate animal–human relationships, supporters of wild bird legislation such as Herbert relied on legislation to produce the effects of laissez-faire. Even J. S. Mill critiqued the belief that animal legislation conflicted with ideals of human liberty, when he claimed, "It is by the grossest misunderstanding of the principles of liberty, that the infliction of exemplary punishment on ruffianism practiced towards these defenceless creatures, has been treated as a meddling by government with things beyond its province" (*Principles* 344). The government of animals is also affected by the expanding role of the welfare state as it regulates humans in order to secure animal liberties.

Thus while earlier legislators wanted individual morality rather than legislation to guide animal–human interactions, MPs such as Herbert believed legislation was necessary for letting animals be. In a surprising move, Herbert – a staunch libertarian who believed government should function only to protect individual liberty, and saw the use of force and power as "antiprogressive" (44) – places animal liberty above individual human liberty. While earlier anti-cruelty supporters believed government should regulate morals, Herbert would later argue that such "interferences of government in the affairs of the people, however benevolent or philanthropic may be the cloak you throw over them," are unjustified (49). His strong support for wild bird legislation, then, suggests a passionate belief in animal liberty, so much so that it would cause him to argue for a restraint on human liberties. The human, however, benefits economically and aesthetically from such liberty, while avian freedoms remain reliant on constructions of their character and conduct. In a reversal from the laissez-faire arguments of early anti-cruelty opponents, who believed the regulation of animal–human relationships was outside the scope of government and hindered individual sovereignty, Herbert relies on legislation to produce effects of laissez-faire that cultivate avian freedom. Yet such logic rests on the benefits human economies receive from animals left alone. For "they had no power of agitating in their own behalf, yet did us good service, and possessed many of the qualities the presence of which we so much respected in men and women" (*Hansard's* CCXI: 1652). Avian freedom is conditional, left up to the whims of the state and an interpretation of animal behavior that aligns with qualities of the liberal subject. Humans are regulated for the good of animal lives, while the regulation of animal lives benefits the human.

As the expansion of legislation covers more animals, many of the issues raised with Erskine's first bill remain present. Given the vast differences between cattle and wild birds, and the amount of time between Erskine's attempt at legislation, Martin's first bill, and wild bird debates, it is surprising how anti-cruelty discourse recognizes animal difference yet still regulates animals by similar strategies. The treatment of animals reflects national character, and functions as a way for humans to become better liberal subjects. Wild bird discourse emphasizes property even though the birds under protection are not owned by humans. Birds are subjects constructed with agency, character, and individualism. They are liberal creatures who, while not necessarily constructed as inherently submitting to humankind, are viewed as working to protect human property. As the period progresses, the animals who need governmental protection are more frequently constructed with liberal notions of conduct and character, yet at times this destabilizes the animal–human hierarchy. Citizens of England desired to extend legislation to an entire population of certain animals and made arguments based on a biopolitical discourse that regulated avian bodies and subjectivities. The focus on reproduction, the fostering of life, the protection of entire populations, and the benefits to humans – the health of the nation, the economy, and a beautiful countryside – posits animals within what Mel Chen labels a "human–animal biopolitics, which is at once linguistic, discursive, state-directed, and sometimes directed toward 'health'" (134). This animal–human biopolitics regulates animal bodies *and* minds through state power and strategies of liberal governmentality. While Chen analyzes the practice of neutering pet animals, and thus the regulation of animal sexuality within a relationship of care and affection, I contend we can locate a similar relationship within anti-cruelty and animal welfare discourse. Care and protection become a means of regulating animal minds and bodies, controlling who lives and dies, and when. Legislating around avian reproduction *and* constructing birds within conceptions of liberal character and motherhood demonstrates the extent to which governmentality brought animals under its scope and subjected them to the whims of state power.

Legislation for animals continued throughout the period, and included claims for wild animals and a broad range of domestic animals, from pets and animals slaughtered for food, to working animals in the streets. From the regulation of vivisection, worries over the spread of rabies, to the care of wild animals in zoos, biopolitics fostered animal and human lives while encouraging citizens to self-regulate their own relationships with animals. Philip Howell suggests that late-century debates over rabies and dog muzzles imagined dogs as "political subjects of a particular kind" (178) and were "addressed via the arts and practices of a more-than-human 'governmentality'" (179). Howell's claims follow an analysis of debates from the 1870s and 1880s over whether or not muzzling dogs in public could lessen the spread of rabies. For Howell, the government's regulation of dogs signaled they were "increasingly recognized by the state as beings to be *governed*" (179). He argues that the 1891 decision that allows dogs to be leashed in public rather than muzzled shows a movement from disciplinarity to governmentality in regard to animals, even characterized by some Victorians as "'emancipation' for dogs" (165). Howell's analysis demonstrates that reconsidering the ways animals were affected by liberal governmentality puts pressure on anthropocentric notions of governmentality more generally. As discussed earlier, however, animals were brought under strategies of governmentality well before debates about dog muzzling, and there are various ways to understand what it means to be governed. While both muzzling and leashes seek to physically control dogs for the benefit of human health, for example, other forms of governing function as a means of care and protection. While governmentality expands to animals, the logic behind the government of animals privileges human economies, epistemologies, and anthropocentric interpretations of the subject. The wide variety of animals incorporated into the political sphere suggests that the politicization of animal subjects worked differently depending on the species, even though the governing logic often remained the same. Seeing animals as political subjects to govern invites us to expand the meaning of political subjectivity beyond the human, and to locate a liberalized animal political subject imagined as holding agency while submitting to the human, who is constructed within strategies of governmentality that remain mostly anthropocentric yet at times destabilize human sovereignty. For if animal character was a determining factor in how animals were governed, we must think beyond the confines of a human liberal subject to see how liberal thought influenced constructions of animal character in arguments for animal welfare. Such is the focus of Chapter 2.

The bird poems that opened this chapter demonstrate how governmentality regulated animal life for the good of humans, and we can locate such strategies within anti-cruelty debates spanning the century. The animal liberty Erskine grants the robins, similar to the liberty Herbert hopes to enforce, results in human benefits. Erskine himself, in granting birds liberty and freedom, represents the hand of government allowing such freedom. The birds' gratefulness to Erskine reflects the avian character legislators constructed in an effort to bring birds under governmental protection. Indeed, the protective space of Erskine's home mirrors the protective space of England's shores, where birds can seek freedom and refuge from persecution. Both early and later debates demonstrate the extent to which liberal animal subjectivity, utility, and human sovereignty are core aspects of the government of animals, a new way of policing animal–human relationships that intensified at the beginning of the nineteenth century. Yet, as the debates examined in this chapter demonstrate, the government of animals results in a tension between individual human sovereignty and state power. Conceptualizing animals as part of a liberal political community forced humans to rethink the extent of their power, and the government's role more broadly. The government of animals shifts understandings of both animals and humans; animals are newly liberalized political subjects, a population over whom humans must rethink the scope of their power.

CHAPTER 2

The Incessant Care of the Victorian Shepherd
Animal Welfare's Pastoral Power

> All the creatures with which man is surrounded, feel instinctively that he is their sovereign.
> – John Styles, *The Animal Creation*

> At all events, brutes cannot speak for themselves; and as man stands at the head of nature, the lord of creation, with powers of articulate expression, should not the inheritance of the whole race and every portion of it enlist his sympathy and engage his tongue ... As king having dominion, should he not protect his subject?
> – "Our Object," *Animal World*

> Consequently, to want absolutely to grant, not to animals but to a certain category of animals, rights equivalent to human rights would be a disastrous contradiction. It would reproduce the philosophical and juridical machine thanks to which the exploitation of animal material for food, work, experimentation, etc., has been practiced (and tyrannically so, that is, through an abuse of power).
> – Jacques Derrida, *For What Tomorrow*

In 1837, the RSPCA announced an essay competition for the best essay illustrating humankind's moral obligation to the animal world. With the opportunity to win one hundred pounds, the winning essay

> shall morally illustrate, and religiously enforce, the obligation of man towards the inferior and dependent creatures – their protection and security from abuse, more especially as regards those engaged in the service, and for the use and benefit of mankind ... [It will show] humanity to the brute as harmonious with the spirit and doctrines of Christianity, and the duty of man as a rational and accountable creature. (qtd. in Mushet xi–xii)

Anglican minister John Styles's winning essay, *The Animal Creation: Its Claims on Our Humanity Stated and Enforced*, reflects the Christian discourse of the RSPCA, its strategies of pastoral power, and its striking construction of animal subjectivity. Dedicated to Queen Victoria and published in 1839, the text exposes the RSPCA's ideologies at the beginning of the Victorian era. While Styles bases his arguments on Christian principles and morality, argues that animals feel pain and suffering as humans do, and claims that civilization breeds animal cruelty, his most pervasive argument is that because humans have God-given dominion over animals, they should treat them with mercy and benevolence, as God treats his human subjects. "It requires no great depth of natural philosophy to discover," Styles writes, "that God has made this lower world, and all the life with which it teems, subservient to the will of man" (164). As evidence for his claims, Styles frequently makes the argument that animals instinctively acknowledge human superiority, and willingly submit to it:

> The relation of dependence and inferiority makes its appeal to every generous feeling in the human heart on behalf of those who, conscious of their relative condition, ask for our protection while they yield to our sovereignty. The dependence of inferiority, which constitutes man the lord of the domestic creatures which gather around him, and offer themselves and their lives for his comfort, convenience, and sustenance, calls upon him to exercise his authority with mildness, humanity, and justice. (168)

Styles's argument for animal welfare is cast in religious and political terms, and rests on a naturalized animal subjection and human sovereignty. Styles's construction of animal subjectivity suggests that humans should be kind to animals based on an animal conduct that reinforces human superiority. Because they willingly submit to human governance, this rationale suggests, animals deserve kindness and justice. If humans rule over animals as kings rule over their subjects, they must exercise good governance. And indeed, animal inferiority cast in such political terms seems an obvious assumption given Victorian liberalism's hierarchical logic of civilization, progress, and natural rights.[1]

Importantly, Styles also compares humans to a shepherd, positioning animal welfare as pastoral power. In his chapter "The Claims of the Inferior Creatures as Recognized and Enforced in the Holy Scriptures, and Especially by the Religion of Christ," Styles notes "how entirely this spirit of humane and tender consideration for the happiness of animals,

---

[1] In *Liberalism and Empire* Mehta demonstrates how these liberal notions contain within them strategies for exclusion that often sanction discrimination against non-Western subjects. The same strategies define animal–human relations in the period. See also Mehta, "Liberal Strategies of Exclusion."

under all its forms, pervades both the Old and New Testaments" (199). He references Psalm 23, "The Lord is my shepherd," and describes the picture it inspires: "the shepherd's care is incessant to defend, to sustain, to lead, and to cherish. His rod and his staff are with his flock; at sultry noon, he conducts them to the shade ... he leads them to a place of safety, or braves for them and with them, inclement seasons and ravenous beasts of prey" (199–200). The shepherd is self-sacrificing for the good of his sheep, yet his material benefits – sheep are property and capital – remain unstated. These two rationales for animal welfare, human sovereignty and pastoral power, locate animal–human relationships in the sphere of governmentality and demonstrate the extent to which hierarchical constructions of animal subjectivity, or what I call the regulation of animal conduct, were essential to arguments for animal welfare.

If legislative discourse posited domestic animals and wild birds as subject to humankind and incorporated them into the strategies of governmentality, the RSPCA confirmed and expanded this subjection in its construction of animal subjects who are content with and desire an animal–human hierarchy. The RSPCA, which Harriet Ritvo labels a "quasi-governmental institution" (*Animal Estate* 145), was formed as a direct response to anti-cruelty legislation and aimed to supplement the law through moral education and policing of animal–human relationships. Grounded in Christian principles, the RSPCA consistently used human dominion and animal interiority as evidence for their claims. The Society's conceptions of animals as thinking, feeling, and desiring creatures – as more than property – spurred numerous constructions of animal subjectivity, yet they were often far from liberating. If legislative discourse subjected animals to humankind through strategies of liberal governmentality, the RSPCA confirmed and expanded this subjection through constructions of animal subjectivity. Such constructions function as a regulation of animal conduct that controls and exploits animals while aiming to protect them. Although most often understood as a revolutionary turning point in cultivating more humane animal–human relationships, the RSPCA brought animals into a political community while keeping them subjected to humankind. As such the RSPCA reflects a major feature of Victorian liberalism: to expand and bring more subjects into its power networks. It also highlights the extent to which liberalism works by creating and maintaining hierarchies, even in rights-based discourses.

At the same time, however, the organization's construction of animals as subjects with thoughts, feelings, character, and individuality cultivated a striking *liberalized* animal subject. While animal subjectivity was often posited in relation to human superiority, it nonetheless created an animal subject directly influenced by liberal thought, most especially discourses of character and liberal cognition. This liberal creature simultaneously challenges and reinforces the carnophallogocentric logic that structures Victorian liberalism, thus demonstrating that humans were not the only subjects regulated by liberalism's exclusionary frameworks. Recognizing a liberalized animal subject invites us to reconsider the boundaries of the liberal subject and understand how multiple kinds of subjects were liberalized, even if they did not have the political participation which in part defined the liberal subject. Animals were not merely anthropomorphized creatures with little connection to the political sphere; rather, attempts to bring them into a political community demonstrate the wide-reaching effects of governmentality and the political agency certain conceptualizations of animals had throughout the period. Animal subjectivity reinforced liberal principles while often, although not always, challenging liberalism's anthropocentric structure.

In this chapter I examine a selection of animal welfare texts from 1838 and 1839 connected to the RSPCA, then move to an analysis of the Society's journal *Animal World*, started in 1869. I demonstrate how the RSPCA functioned as a mode of power over animals, one which, at times, cultivated a liberalized animal subject who challenged assumptions about both animals and humans. Most often, however, animal welfare discourse kept animals within exploitative power structures. I end with a brief examination of the Vegetarian Society (1846), which began as a temperance movement concerned with the health of the nation, and the London Vegetarian Society (1888), which broke from the national organization because of its more radical socialist politics. Both organizations throw into relief the conservatism behind the RSPCA and its reliance on liberal thought, and advocate an alternate political status for animals. Not only did the Vegetarian Society critique the RSPCA for neglecting to advocate for vegetarianism, but the London Vegetarian Society posits animals as part of a universal brotherhood, articulating a radical equality lacking within RSPCA discourse. Taken together, anti-cruelty legislation, the RSPCA, and the vegetarian societies demonstrate how animals were regulated by governmentality, yet at times challenged the primacy of a liberal human subject. Animal welfare discourse, I suggest, cultivated a liberalized animal subjectivity that regulated both animals and humans, and exposes the limitations of incorporating animals into liberal political structures.

The RSPCA's Pastoral Power

The Society for the Prevention of Cruelty to Animals aimed to revolutionize human feelings toward animals. The Society's prospectus states, "The object of the Society is 'the mitigation of animal suffering, and the promotion and expansion of the practice of humanity towards the inferior classes of animated beings'" (*Records* 201). The announcement of the Society in *The Times* stated,

> it was desirable, not only to prevent the exercise of cruelty towards animals, but to spread amongst the lower orders of the people, especially amongst those to whom the care of animals was intrusted [*sic*], a degree of moral feeling which would compel them to think and act like those of a superior class, instead of sinking into a comparison (in which their inferiority was now unfortunately acknowledged) with the poor brute. ("Society" 3)

Such statements emphasize that the Society aimed to regulate mostly lower-class humans while reinforcing animal–human differences and human superiority. The announcement exposes the Society's class-based politics and its desire to regulate working-class subjects; it reflects liberalism's focus on moral rather than economic reform. The prospectus further highlights their shared religious and political aims, by explaining that

> much remains to be done towards the entire accomplishment of the humane views of those who in various ways have recommended the great moral and Christian obligation of kindness and compassion toward the brute creation ... by the discouragement of cruelty and insensibility of heart, in the treatment of inferior creatures, human beings will be rendered more susceptible of kind impressions toward each other, their moral temper will be improved, and consequently, social happiness and genuine philanthropy must, infallibly, be strengthened and enlarged. (*Records* 201)

The indirect duty exposed here reflects the rationale used in anti-cruelty legislation debates, which found its first articulation in Locke's *Some Thoughts Concerning Education*: by treating animals well, social order will prevail.

Although those in the Society saw themselves as a moral organization aiming to publish "Tracts, Sermons, and similar modes of influencing public opinion," they were also a policing force, seeking "to adopt measures for Inspecting the Markets and Streets of the Metropolis, the Slaughter Houses, the conduct of Coachmen, &c-&c ..." (qtd. in Moss 23). As with anti-cruelty legislation, concerns over individual liberties grew with the growth of the RSPCA's force of inspectors. For example, during an

1844 legislative debate about a horse-slaughtering bill, one MP stated "that this Bill was admitted to proceed from the Society for the Prevention of Cruelty to Animals. That alone he would consider a sufficient reason for opposing it, as no encouragement ought to be given to societies for meddling with everybody's business but their own" (*Hansard's* LXXVI: 1334). Later commentators such as Brian Harrison have pointed toward the state's reluctance to infringe on personal liberties and privacies when regulating animal–human relationships. Harrison demonstrates how the aims of the RSPCA conflicted with liberal ideals of a decentralized government, individual freedoms, and privacy; he claims the Society "clashed with longer-established and decentralized rural traditions of self-government" (801). Yet working-class regulation fits well within liberal ideals of teaching appropriate social behavior. Moral regulation of not just humans, but animals as well, was always a goal of the RSPCA; such regulation exemplifies governmentality's goal of indirect government.

The RSPCA further operates through pastoral power in its constructions of animal subjectivity. Explaining the limitations of using Foucault's notions of disciplinary power to analyze Victorian power structures, Lauren Goodlad emphasizes that "Britain's ruling classes strove to govern *indirectly*: to implement parliamentary power in ways that encouraged self-help, philanthropy, voluntarism, and local government" (*Victorian Literature* 14). She claims pastorship more accurately describes Victorian power relations: "Foucault's essays on governmentality reformulate the paradox of disciplinary individualism by introducing human agency, and, in theory, de-emphasizing the state. Foucault now identifies the power to individualize with *pastorship*, the ancient Christian concept of the shepherd's intensive care for his flock" (18). While for both Foucault and Goodlad this power ultimately takes place within human–human relationships, I suggest not only that pastoral power may be more appropriately located within Victorian animal–human relationships, but that understanding these relationships as pastoral power highlights how liberal thought regulated animal subjectivities. Although the RSPCA conflicted with liberal ideals of restricted state power in favor of individual liberties, it strove to make both animals and humans self-regulating individuals through forms of pastorship.

Foucault stresses that pastoral power "is fundamentally a beneficent power," and that "the essential objective of pastoral power is the salvation (*salut*) of the flock" ("Security" 126). The shepherd must watch over the sheep's conduct, which results in an individualizing power whereby the shepherd carefully shields each individual sheep. Foucault writes,

> it is a mode of individualization that is not brought about by the designation or marking of an individual's place in a hierarchy. Nor will it be brought about by the assertion of the self's mastery of self, but by a whole network of servitude that involves the general servitude of everyone with regard to everyone and, at the same time, the exclusion of the self, of the ego, and of egoism as the central, nuclear form of the individual. It is therefore a mode of individualization by subjection (*assujettissement*). (184)

In this formulation, animals are individuals whose conduct is regulated by a caring and concerned human. The sheep and shepherd are equalized through shared disinterest, and subjection exists on both levels. Yet the goal of pastoral power is to guide, conduct, and disseminate proper social and moral behavior. For Foucault, pastoral power's movement from the sheepfold to the church "gave rise to an art of conducting, directing, leading, guiding, taking in hand, and manipulating men, an art of monitoring them and urging them on step by step, an art with the function of taking charge of men collectively and individually throughout their life and at every moment of their existence" (165). Once institutionalized, pastoral power works as a form of "governing men" (165) that regulates subjectivity. I argue that the RSPCA's representations of animal subjectivity regulate animal conduct as part of the larger government of animals. Although most animals cannot self-regulate to the extent humans do, RSPCA discourses suggested that they did so, and this influenced how humans understood and related to them. Such animals are individuals inscribed in the Christian discourse of duty and a liberal discourse of disinterest, as they recognize their role in the hierarchy of beings created by God. This *acknowledgment* of divine hierarchy constructs animals as complicit in their own subjection and highlights "the tension between care and control" (Pandian 90) at the heart of pastoral power.

Animal welfare texts submitted to the RSPCA's 1837 best essay prize demonstrate how pastoral power influenced constructions of animal subjectivity and illustrate the strategies used to bring animals under liberal governance. While John Styles was the winner, William Drummond, a Unitarian minister with close connections to the Society – they had previously approached him requesting a sermon on the moral duties to animals – published *The Rights of Animals and Man's Obligation to Treat Them with Humanity* in 1838. William Youatt, the Society's veterinary surgeon who helped the animals of the poor, published *The Obligation and Extent of Humanity to Brutes, Principally Considered with Reference to the Domesticated Animals* in 1839. All three essays reflect the Christian spirit of the RSPCA, as they base their arguments on the belief that God gave humans animals for their use; humans should thus protect and treat them kindly. In other words, humans should provide good governance. This framework rests on subordination, as all essays construct animals as the willing subjects of humankind. At the same time, however, such constructions figure a liberalized animal subject with character, reason, and moral qualities. As the liberal subject ultimately self-regulates, these animal qualities mark a liberal creature on par with, if not exceeding, the liberal human subject.

Youatt's text figures domestication as a politicized moment: the domestication of animals mirrors the removal of humans from nature into a political community that submits to governance. Animals gain certain protections by giving up natural liberty, as they are imagined as participating in a social contract. In Locke's formulation, "The only way whereby any one devests [*sic*] himself of his Natural Liberty, and *puts on the bonds of Civil Society* is by agreeing with other Men to joyn [*sic*] and unite into a Community, for their comfortable, safe, and peaceable living one amongst another" (*Second Treatise* 330–331). In *A Fragment on Government*, Jeremy Bentham similarly claims, "When a number of persons (whom we may style *subjects*) are supposed to be in the *habit* of paying *obedience* to a person, or an assemblage of persons, of a known and certain description (whom we may call *governor* or *governors*) such persons altogether (*subjects* and *governors*) are said to be in a state of *political* SOCIETY" (40). Although Alasdair Cochrane emphasizes that contract-based political theory has often been a means of excluding animals and denying them justice, RSPCA discourse used it to bring animals into a multi-species political community (23). For example, Youatt imagines animals as members of this political community, as he suggests that domestic animals are often "far happier" (8) than they would be in the wild, and that "Some of the noblest of them are reclaimed from their state of nature, and subjugated to us in order to help our weaknesses, and to supply our wants" (11). In the same way Locke's members of civil society put on certain "bonds," or Bentham's subjects obey a governor, so too are Youatt's domestic animals subjugated to the human. Yet they remain happier by gaining certain protections. Domestication is further figured as a liberal civilizing mission: to be "reclaimed from their state of nature" suggests a progressive movement from nature to culture. Participation in such a society requires, however, appropriate conduct that certain animals are represented as internalizing.

Youatt and Drummond represent domestic animals as willingly entering into positions of subjection, thus reinforcing "consent as a fundamental ground for the legitimacy of political authority" (Mehta, *Liberalism* 59). In this figuration, animals properly conduct themselves within human society, consenting to human authority. Youatt claims horses "become not only our willing slaves, but by intuition they understand all that we require of them. They become a part and portion of ourselves. The finger can scarcely have touched the rein or the heel the side, ere all that we wish is accomplished" (85). Subjection here occurs both willingly and instinctually, suggesting that Kathleen Frederickson's claims that instinct is a way out from liberal subjectivity apply only to humans. Even animal senses and epistemologies are imagined as directed toward the human: "On account of the situations in which they are placed," Youatt explains, "and the services which they are designed to render man, the organs of sense are far more powerful in the inferior creatures than in the human being" (39). Similarly, "The superior acuteness of his senses prepares the animal for his own provision and safety, and for our service" (41). This combination of willpower, instinct, and superior senses, and the desire to direct them toward the human, epitomizes the construction of animal subjectivity under pastoral power. By describing human power as taking place at the physical level, Youatt articulates animal subjection within a biopolitical discourse suggesting that animal bodies hold the rationale for their own subjection. And precisely because of their desire to enter into subjection, animals deserve proper governance. Drummond similarly grants animals agency, but only as a form of submission. "All animals," he writes, "particularly whose services are most required, as if conscious that they were ordained to be subject to man's dominion, yield to it without reluctance, asking in return only to be treated with humanity" (82–83), stating further that "Many animals seem to forego their natural instincts or to employ them only for the service and profit of their benefactors" (83). Animals can thus "yield," "forego," and "employ" themselves, and even suppress their instincts for the benefit of humankind. In a liberal multispecies political community, animals undergo a self-renunciation and internalize their role as disinterested workers in a capitalist system.

However, if Youatt imagines animals as subjects willingly entering a political community with humans, he also succeeds at imagining them as liberalized subjects. Not only does he articulate at length the mental qualities of animals, such as the association of ideas and imagination, he also endows them with qualities specifically attributed to liberal subjects: character, detachment, and disinterestedness. Youatt writes, "There is, in those domesticated slaves which we have selected from the rest, a pureness of detachment, a nobleness of disposition, and a total disregard of self-interest, which cannot fail, one would think, of endearing them to us, and protecting them from ill-usage of every kind" (87); "I pass to another division of our subject – *the moral qualities*. What, of brutes? Ay! and strongly developed, and beautifully displayed, and often putting the biped to shame" (64); and "Friendship! Is there a surer test of nobleness of character than sincerity and permanence of friendship? The brute is capable of it to an intense degree. We do not, perhaps, see many instances of it. We do not see many in the human being" (79). Here animals resemble not only the ideal liberal subject, but a liberal subject exceeding the human. Detachment, as Amanda Anderson argues, had "profound bearing on moral character" (*Powers* 6); here detachment is pure and animal disinterest is "total." Animal moral qualities exceed and "shame" the human. Such qualities, often understood as valued in mid-century, are here seen earlier in the animal world, raising questions about the progression of the liberal subject more broadly. Might the liberal subject be molded on an idealized animal subject? For not only does the liberal animal subject exceed the human, but here it is articulated before the mid-Victorian emphasis on character and liberal cognition.

Thus even as animal protection is a strategy of governmentality that incorporates self-regulating animals into a political community, it destabilizes hierarchies produced by Victorian liberalism: animal versus human, instinct versus reason, uncivilized versus civilized. However, such liberal qualities, even if they undermine the animal–human hierarchy on certain levels, ultimately reinforce animal oppression. For even if these animal subjects exceed the human, their liberal qualities are projected toward the human; it is precisely because of their liberal qualities that they should be subjected to and protected by human governance. In this instance, liberal subjectivity regulates otherness, again highlighting the limitations of projecting liberal categories onto the animal world.

While Youatt and Drummond praise animal epistemology and find moral and physical animal qualities that rival the human, Styles suggests nothing is superior to human reason. In his formulation, even animals acknowledge its superiority, and thus humans should govern them well:

> Though man is the last link in the chain of rational beings, yet, in comparison with those creatures, who are without the verge of undying intellect, he is almost a divinity ... The fowls of heaven, although they make their nests on high, and seek an asylum in the clouds, his reason controls and brings down to his feet ... All the creatures with which man is surrounded, feel instinctively that he is their sovereign. In addition to the majesty of intellect, there is something in his form and carriage that inspires

awe; so that all animals in their natural state, feel his superiority, and either approach him with love, or fly from him in terror. (19–20)

Styles connects sovereignty to good governance as he emphasizes that "as it regards the animal race, man, that should be their protector, because he is their sovereign, is their persecutor and their tyrant" (21). While Styles's text shares many qualities with Drummond and Youatt's, it differs in its more explicit use of political language. Styles's tendency to collapse the religious and the political emphasizes the extent to which animal welfare was a form of pastoral power with roots in Christian discourse, and used to secure the government of animals. Styles's claim that "Man, as the subject of moral government, is bound to regard every creature in its relation to God" (116), emphasizes this interconnection between morality, government, and the regulation of both animal and human subjects. For animals should be governed well precisely because "We can make an animal understand, and obey and recognize authority" (139), and "You can create in a brute the sense of right or wrong. To imagine that animals have not a character induced by education, is to labour under a strange delusion; in reference to the standard of duty under which they are placed, they have their virtues and their vices. What will not many of them do and suffer to please their master"? (139–140). Here animals are imagined with the "inward monitor" of character with which they regulate their own conduct (Smiles 413); they self-regulate in ways similar to how Samuel Smiles famously articulates the willpower behind character in *Self-Help*: a "principle, or conscience, dominating in the character, and exercising a noble protectorate over it; not merely a passive influence, but an active power regulating the life. Such a principle goes on moulding the character hourly and daily, growing with a force that operates every moment" (403).

The constructions of animal subjectivity articulated by Styles, Youatt, and Drummond demonstrate the difficulties of arguing for animal protection based on animal interiority and capacities. They expose the limitations of projecting human notions of the subject onto animals, especially when they function within a regulatory framework. Derrida emphasizes the deficiencies of a human juridical framework for animal rights and highlights the tensions between animal welfare ideology and animal liberation. As he argues throughout his late work on animals, the notion of the subject at the core of Western juridical logic is grounded in hierarchical and regulatory concepts such as reason, consciousness, speech, and citizen, which have oppressed women, non-Western subjects, the lower class, and animals. By constructing liberal notions of subjectivity, RSPCA discourse keeps animals within a regulatory framework that continues to exploit animals today. The Victorian liberal subject, most often understood as only human, can in fact be expanded to certain types of animals; yet this subject is regulated under exploitative power networks. By liberalizing animals, liberal hierarchies are destabilized only to a limiting extent; for the liberal qualities animals are granted reinforce and perpetuate their subjection.

These early Victorian animal welfare texts confer onto animals a subjectivity constituted by subordination, yet such subordination brings them into political community with humans. This construction of animal minds functions as the knowledge of such minds, emphasizing Foucault's articulation of how the regulation of subjectivity works in relation to pastoral power: "this form of power," he claims, "cannot be exercised without knowing the inside of people's minds" ("Subject" 333). Drummond, Styles, and Youatt posit themselves as authorities on animal cognition and present constructions of animal desire as fact. Yet by constructing animals in this way, these writers confirm and reinforce an animal–human hierarchy that keeps animals in positions of subjection, not only philosophically, but also materially, through exploitative labor practices. By suggesting, for example, that animals are willing workers in the production of capital, animal welfare discourses solidify a capitalist system of animal exploitation. Positioned as social reform, animal welfare emphasizes how institutions constructed with liberal principles reinforce those very ideologies that made Victorian liberalism so contradictory and destructive to marginalized subjects. Yet certain constructions of animal subjects can undo the very ideologies that liberalism sought to maintain. By claiming that animals have superior liberal qualities – character, disinterestedness, and detachment – these writers open the sphere of liberal subjectivity. If the white British male was envisioned as the liberal subject par excellence, the incorporation of animals into a political community destabilizes human supremacy even as it seeks to reinforce it. This liberalized animal subject was necessary to sustain the government of animals: by constructing animals as desiring human control, animal welfare secured the social and political domination of them.

The RSPCA's *Animal World*

The RSPCA continued to offer essay prizes throughout the period, but as the century progressed they were mostly offered to children. As one RSPCA member noted, "Who will deny that childhood is the best time for making good impressions upon the mind, and for imbuing it with sound and humane principles?" ("Late" 195). In 1872 *Animal World* published three pages of extracts from an essay contest for children, and although more than thirty years later, the rationale for animal welfare and the construction of animal subjectivity remains largely consistent with that found in earlier texts by Drummond, Styles, and Youatt. These extracts emphasize the Lockean belief that kindness toward animals cultivates social order, and argue that one should be kind to animals because of human dominion and animal submission. At the same time, children note the possibility of animal superiority:

> "Kindness to animals is a very important thing; it is everybody's duty to be kind to animals, because they are dumb and are not gifted with speech as we are; therefore if we hurt them they cannot tell us, and with kindness we may train them to love us, and come at our command." – Mary Carter
>
> "We may learn a great many lessons from animals, such as forgiveness, unselfishness, love, usefulness, and obedience." – Ann Ashdown Evans
>
> "I cannot think how man, the noblest piece of creation, made in the image of God, can so far forget himself as to ill-treat dumb creatures that are sent for his use and amusement, and are entirely at his mercy. They are in many respects far superior to man, for man has the gift of reason: yet sometimes the humble faculties of the brute creation are so well exercised as to put to shame the negligence of those who are gifted with an immortal soul. How often are we told in Holy Writ to go and learn of the animal creation our duty? From the bee we learn industry, from the dog we learn faithfulness, and from every animal there is something to learn." – Howard F. Rowden ("Extracts" 197)

The striking similarities between these extracts and early animal welfare texts emphasizes how pastoral power remained the primary power structure that governed animal welfare discourse throughout the Victorian era. The Society's efforts to educate citizens, particularly children, demonstrate how liberal education worked alongside pastoral power as a strategy of governmentality. Indeed, the goal of the journal was, above all, education. *Animal World* underscores the extent to which animal welfare embraced liberal principles and projected liberal ideals onto the animals and humans it aimed to regulate. While much mid-Victorian animal welfare discourse remains the same as that used earlier in the period, *Animal World* presents an intensified liberal creature who reinforces pastoral power while putting pressure on liberal concepts used to dominate animals and other humans. *Animal World* demonstrates how animals can teach humans to be better liberal subjects; bringing animals into a political community as actors and agents in the public sphere offers a more-than-human liberal politics in which animals influence social and political change.

Animal World was first published in 1869, and by this time the RSPCA had become a large and influential organization. Not only had it succeeded in impacting the development of anti-cruelty legislation, but it also brought humane education into schools. The journal entered the public sphere during the height of periodical publishing, and noted the absence of a journal dedicated to animals. The first issue explains, "Journalism has become a mighty public voice, and thousands of newspapers and magazines are issued daily and weekly dedicated to man's welfare ... But where shall we look for one journal devoted to the interests of the next grade in nature's scale? Animals who cannot talk surely require an advocate" ("Our Object"). The content of the journal was highly variable and its wide variety of articles demonstrates a desire to reach multiple audiences and represent a large portion of the animal population. *Animal World* included features on different species (both domestic and wild), relating to their "natural history" or how to train and handle them; articles about major figures in the animal welfare movement; poetry; fiction; animal autobiographies; news about animals; legislative updates; extracts from the press about animals; letters to the editor; RSPCA annual meeting notes; news from sister branches; sermons, articles on animal rights and ethics; extracts from natural history texts; book reviews; lists of animal-cruelty convictions; and illustrations. The goal of the journal was to educate the public and advocate for animal welfare in the legislative realm and at the individual level. As such, it emphasizes how throughout the century animals were increasingly seen as members of a political community and participants in the public sphere. Yet although animals were envisioned as political actors and liberalized subjects, the journal highlights the extent to which animals needed a regulated conduct in order to enter into a political community with humans.

The journal is specifically liberal in its aims and format: it emphasizes one must tolerate the opinion of others, especially "minor differences" ("Our Object"). By embracing a combination of training citizens and legislators in animal welfare, it works at the level of the individual and the state. *Animal World* promoted education throughout all levels of society, and the places in which the journal circulated emphasize its connection to social reform and state institutions: "hospitals, prisons, reformatories, convict establishments, workhouses, reading-rooms for the working classes, soldiers, and militiamen" ("Annual" 172). Within less than two years of publication, *Animal World* "has become a standard reading book in many hundreds of schools, and circulates in most of the British colonies" (173). As such, the journal was involved in social progress at home and abroad.² It was also immensely popular: it was praised for well-written articles, beautiful illustrations, and its successful aims. An ad for the journal in 1871 notes that "Upwards of 600 journals have spoken well of it, and no unfavorable criticism has yet appeared" ("The Animal World" 207). Although they stress in "Our Object" that they hope to be apolitical, their rationale for the journal is figured within political terms. "As king having dominion," the article states, "should he not protect his subject?" As in earlier animal welfare texts, animal protection is figured in terms of good government, one that all citizens take upon themselves. Animal welfare is decentralized, as all humans are encouraged to act as good governors over animals and regulate other citizens; *Animal World* helps them do so.

Animal World is an important journal in the history of the government of animals, as it uses specifically liberal strategies to encourage better government and posits animals as liberalized subjects with a political voice. It shows how liberal governmentality brought animals under its strategies and into the sphere of democracy. Importantly, the journal itself is envisioned as the journal not of the RSPCA but of animals. The opinions of the press, published in the journal's second issue, note that "The brutes of creation have at last got a journal," and that *Animal World* will be "the living tongue of the poor dumb beast" ("Opinions" 48). Articles consistently represent animals as having a voice within the political sphere. In an article titled "Contagious Diseases (Animals) Act, 1869," the author asks readers to "bear in mind that the responsibility is now fairly on the Government (from which it cannot escape, if it would), and that a population of living, sensitive beings, five times more numerous than that of human beings, are having their plea for justice heard by the Government." Animals are envisioned as political actors: not only are they imagined as directly addressing the government, but the state cannot ignore their claims. As such they participate in a form of representative government wherein their claims will be heard.

One of the more noticeable aspects of how the journal liberalized animals was the extent to which it included individualized animal voices through the signed opinion piece and animal autobiographies. In her reading of the *Fortnightly Review*, Elaine Hadley argues that the journal's decision to require a signature "carried with it a specifically liberal philosophy concerning the meaning and value of individual opinion"

---

² There were many instances of readers writing in to discuss the need for sister societies in the colonies. Animal welfare thus contributed to the civilizing mission of the imperial project.

(*Living* 125). She suggests that "individual opinion" expressed character and made individuals "*liberal* subjects" (129), and acted as mid-century liberalism's "version of social agency" (9). In *Animal World*'s announcement about their "Correspondence" column, the editor consents to public discussion, so long as it is "carried on tolerantly and concisely" ("Correspondence"). He also emphasizes that the opinions are *individual* opinions, and not those of the journal. Thus the "Correspondence" column provided an avenue for public discussion and individual opinions about animals; what is most striking is that animals were often imagined participants in these discussions, and thus given a form of social agency.

For example, the June 1870 issue includes "An Appeal from a Brute to Road-Makers," in which "A Poor Omnibus Horse" appeals to state legislators to fix the roads. The horse writes,

> Is there no legislator in that great house at Westminster upon whom the mantle of [Richard] Martin can fitly descend? No one will befriend those who cannot help themselves? A short Bill making it compulsory on those who have the making of roads to make them what they should be . . . would save thousands of dumb animals from cruel and unnecessary suffering, and add to the comfort of those whom they so patiently serve.

A letter from "An Old Leicestershire Fox" does not specifically call out to legislators, but addresses vivisection during the years it was debated in parliament: "I would rather be hunted fairly (not dug out) with a good chance of escape," he writes, "than be caught in a cruelty trap like a rabbit, or be caught and sent up to London to be dissected alive" ("Reynard"). While the Horse and the Fox attempt to enact change on a legislative level, "A Dog's Appeal," signed "A Collie," speaks about animal character and the corrupting nature of humans. The dog asks, "Is it not wrong of men and women to try to foster the vices they are themselves so often subject to in us?" Finally, "A Raven's Appeal from St. Leonards-on-Sea" begs readers to see raven character differently and stop regarding them as "bad omens," in the hopes of better treatment. Such examples reinforce Hadley's argument that individual opinions reinforce character, and extend it to the animal world, whereby animals critique human character and ask for political change. While the animals are often unnamed, they are presented as individuals with a moral authority over the humans who treat them poorly. The inclusion of these signed pieces in the "Correspondence" section imagines animals as participating in a public, rational discussion to encourage legislators to continue acting on their behalf, and asks humans to be better liberal subjects. Their "opinions" give them a form of agency central to liberal subjectivity.

As well as imagining animals as agents in the public sphere, the presentation of animal character was one of the main aims of *Animal World*. It consistently printed articles regarding the consciousness of animals, their loyalty, their desire to serve humans, and ultimately, their desire to be submissive. The focus on animal character frequently occurs with animals castigated throughout society, suggesting they have the ability to progress to a higher state of civilization.[3] For example the journal worked hard to change the public opinion of cats, who were often viewed as vermin rather than pets, and were thought to be more attached to the house than to its occupants. *Animal World* reported on the yearly cat shows at the crystal palace, which first took place in 1871, and used this as a way to alter conceptions of cat character. In "Another Great Cat Show," the author notes, "The cat is really a despised creature – despised and defamed by men who have not the capacity nor the habit to make correct observations" (40). The author explains how such views affect feline political representation: "Even many of our justices of the peace regard this feline organism as unworthy of the protection of the statute made to prevent cruelty to domestic brutes" (40). Major critiques of the cat revolve around feline character: they are "thieves" and "treacherous" (40), yet the author attributes this to poor human governance. For if one is kind to cats "you see the development of a high moral quality – confidence," which produces "perfectly affectionate cats, as innocent of treachery as most cultivated moralists are" (40). After giving examples of feline character, such as a cat who let a starving kitten eat her breakfast, or another cat who allowed a mouse and her children to "share his bed" (41), the author argues that cat shows will elevate feline character. They will induce humans to treat them better, and "Pussy will advance morally under his tuition" (41). In writing about the 1872 cat show, the author claims,

> We are not only convinced by arguments, but have undoubted evidence that this show is accomplishing a grand reform in the interest of cats, not only in their treatment and education, but in the cultivation of a higher race of animals, and in the consequent elevation of the species. They are fast losing their old classification with noxious animals, as vermin; and the tendency of these exhibitions is to raise their status, and in the future to make them universally cherished and esteemed as pets and property, instead of fair game for cruel sports. ("Cats")

---

[3] The loyal dog was the most venerated animal throughout Victorian society and culture, and *Animal World* reflects this obsession with canine loyalty. Nearly every issue had an example of canine loyalty, from other newspapers or reader testimony.

The explicit liberal political language of this argument – "reform," "cultivation," "elevation," and "raise their status" – connects the journal's presentation of cats with not just political reform but more pointedly with liberal cultivation of character. In such examples human governance influences feline character; good governance, *Animal World* argues, cultivates in animals a disposition that reflects back onto human superiority. Loyalty – a quality venerated within the dog – can also be found in cats, and for this reason humans should form good relationships with them.

The construction of feline character also worked on the level of the individual. While cat shows promoted a eugenics wherein "Best breeds will be propagated, and weakly, unhandsome, and useless individuals will consequently be rare" ("Cat Shows" 145), cat autobiographies present liberalized animals with good moral qualities that speak well of human domination. Coming directly after an article on the 1873 cat show, the autobiography of Toby, who was entered in the show, highlights how education cultivates appropriate animal–human relationships that encourage a self-regulating animal character. Toby "felt how kind my friends were, and resolved to repay them the only way I could, viz., by showing as much affection as lay in my power, and by attention to their wishes ... I can only attribute my superior manners to the care with which I was educated, and for which I shall thank my friends" ("Toby's"). Toby's "superior manners" are a direct result of training, here figured as education, and are directed back onto the human in the form of affection and attention. Such manners – indeed, Toby's domestication and cleanliness – are represented in the accompanying portrait (Figure 2.1). Toby's character further manifests in his claim that "I think I am as peaceably disposed as most cats, and would never fight at all except for the sake of upholding my own opinions." The violence associated with cats is here turned into social agency and figured in liberal terms. Another cat autobiography placed next to Toby's – "The Autobiography of Another Cat. By Mow Wow," ends by destabilizing animal–human difference while reinforcing human authority and the master–servant relationship. "I never could understand the vast difference that was supposed to exist between cats and men," Mow Wow states, "Certainly man is the lord of the creation, and superior to us in some things; but under-estimating us and calling us names ... only induces the cruelty with which we are too often treated" (147).

Throughout the journal, animal autobiographies serve a direct political role. In the case of cats, the goal was better treatment at the hands of citizens and the state. The same goes for birds; during the years of arguments about wild bird legislation, autobiographies of individualized birds appear frequently. By presenting individual animals with character

Figure 2.1 "Toby. – A Portrait by Harrison Weir." *Animal World*, vol. 4, no. 49, Oct. 1873, p. 145.

and a desire for human control – a French Partridge, for example, notes, "I prefer limited liberty with comparative security, to wild freedom and its unpleasant contingencies" ("The Autobiography" 154) – animals in need of better or more political representation are introduced to readers as liberalized animals. Their liberal qualities, however, reinforce their subjection to the human.

The animal character cultivated throughout *Animal World* portrays "character building as the outcome of pastor-like relations" (Goodlad, "Character" 13) between animals and humans, where training is consistently articulated in terms of education.[4] Through associations with laws, governance, and social reform, animal character is explicitly political and reflects Mill's conceptions of character as Goodlad summarizes them: "subjectivity is no static and pre-political artifact of self-ownership or natural rights, but the contingent product of politically charged character-building practices such as domestic care, education, and citizenship" (13). Indeed, the cultivation of animal character and inclusion in the political sphere relies on a construction of subjectivity figured as an education in accepting human norms and hierarchies. Throughout *Animal World*, animals register a moral improvability: with proper governance they too can cultivate moral character. Although not citizens in a literal sense, animals were increasingly recognized as members of a political community. Combined with the political nature of *Animal World*'s representations – the inclusion of animal voices in the public sphere – animals become liberal creatures whose subjectivity is directed toward human authority and the state. RSPCA discourse suggests animals deserve state protection not because of any claims to natural rights, but because of their moral character.

While Samuel Smiles emphasizes that "Character is human nature in its best form" (396), *Animal World* suggests it may also be animal nature in its best form. Qualities such as morality, loyalty, integrity, and self-regulation are believed to exist in the animal world, even if only in certain animals. Liberal norms, I suggest, were thus in part influenced and perpetuated by Victorian conceptions of animal subjects. The political sphere becomes more-than-human, suggesting that animal–human relationships and animals themselves regulated liberal human subjects. Not only did humans cultivate their own character through appropriate relationships with animals, but looking at how animals demonstrated qualities admired by humans encouraged them to craft those same qualities in themselves. If animals can build character, so can humans. In this sense governmentality becomes a mesh of animal and human actors, extending our understanding of the Victorian political sphere. Jane Bennett's attempts to figure a more-than-human democracy are relevant as we uncover the ways animals

---

[4] For example, an 1872 article on dog training is titled "The Education of Animals."

became part of Victorian drives toward democracy. Her suggestion that multi-species communities are cultivated through a heterogeneous "'public' coalescing around a problem" (108) applies well to how the Victorian public "coalesced" around the problem of governing animals. Animals had political agency in crafting moral liberal subjects, who in turn helped encourage more legislation on behalf of animals. Animals and humans work together to accomplish political change and give animals a political voice. Although the representations of animals I discussed are human products, they nonetheless encourage humans to consider animals as part of a larger political community.

Thus while constructions of animal character always reflect back onto the human – indeed, they are ultimately evidence of human power and governance – they also invite us to rethink the limits of the liberal human subject, which was in part envisioned in relationship to animality and influenced by what were seen as animal qualities. As we saw at the beginning of this section, children were inculcated with beliefs that the animal world had much to teach burgeoning liberal subjects: "forgiveness, unselfishness, love, usefulness, and obedience ... from every animal there is something to learn" ("Extracts" 197). This asks us to reconceptualize how we understand not just liberalism's control over animal subjects, but also the limits of the political when its terms become more-than-human. Even though animals were envisioned as educating and in part creating the liberal subject, they were also constructed to desire an animal–human hierarchy within an exploitative social and economic system that kept them subjected to humans. Projecting human political categories onto the animal world, in this case, reaffirms human superiority and domination even as it affords animals a limited amount of political agency.

Vegetarianism, Socialism, and Universal Brotherhood

An early article from the Vegetarian Society's journal *The Truth-Tester* gives a rationale for vegetarianism that may have been surprising to Victorian readers.[5] Formed in Manchester in 1847 by leaders of the Alcott House – a cult-like group inspired by the principles of William Cowherd and the Bible Christians – the Vegetarian Society promoted a diet, lifestyle, and set of ethics that brought one closer to Christian principles

---

[5] The journal of the Vegetarian Society went through many name changes, including *The Truth-Tester* (which incorporated the Alcott House's journal *The Healthian*), *The Vegetarian Advocate*, *Vegetarian Messenger*, and *The Dietetic Reformer and Vegetarian Messenger*.

and salvation.[6] On the surface, the Society seemed relatively uninterested in animal welfare and more concerned with human health and individual salvation. While an 1847 article advertising an upcoming vegetarian conference and announcing a desire to form the Society describes "the slaughter of animals as a violation of the laws of humanity," the author suggests that the Society would work to "secure the practical benefits of improved habits of diet to society generally" (Simpson 20). Yet the Society had radical moments, especially when it came to describing animal–human relationships from a religious perspective. While it was a common belief that God gave animals to humans for their own use, one writer in 1848 believed it was the other way around:

> With much more apparent reason, therefore, might it be said, that man was created for these loathsome creatures, than that sheep, oxen, and other animals, were formed for his use; since they are not indispensable to his health and happiness. Whatever man can press into his service – whether for food, raiment, or pleasure – whatever can be made to minister to his necessities, real or imaginary, – these his pride and selfishness prompt him to believe were given solely for his use; and because the flesh of gregarious and other animals is found to be nutritious, he concludes that the sole design of the Creator in imparting vitality to them, was to supply him with food, clothing, and other conveniences: but few men who think seriously on the subject, will consider the inference a just one. (Horsell 65)

Whereas the RSPCA argued that humans should treat animals well because they were tasked with governance of the animal world, members of the Vegetarian Society claimed that God gave animals life, and humans had no right to take it away. Such arguments undermine human superiority and highlight the limitations of pastoral power in achieving justice for animals. Indeed, the Vegetarian Society stated that one of its objects was to formulate and adopt a principle of "universal brotherhood" ("Adjourned"), thus placing animals and humans on a more level plane than was ever articulated by the RSPCA. Both the Vegetarian Society and the London Vegetarian Society (LVS) throw into relief the conservatism behind the RSPCA and offer not just a revolution in human morals, but a larger systemic change: a destruction of the capitalist system that exploits children, women, the working class, colonized subjects, *and* animals. The vegetarian societies demonstrate how, through its promotion of capitalism,

---

[6] For other discussions of the Vegetarian Society, see Colin Spencer, *The Heretics' Feast: A History of Vegetarianism*. In *The Bloodless Revolution: A Cultural History of Vegetarianism from 1600 to Modern Times*, Tristram Stuart briefly discusses the formation of the Society. See also the website of the Vegetarian Society, which gives a concise overview of the Society's formation ("History").

liberal thought can never be revolutionary, and will continue to keep both animals and humans in positions of subjection and oppression.

Since the Romantic period especially, vegetarianism has been associated with radical politics. To be sure, some vegetarian discourses simply promoted the health benefits of relinquishing meat, such as George Cheyne's medical treatises, while vegetarians like William Cowherd's Bible Christians, who in 1809 pledged to abstain from meat, saw meat-eating as a product of the Fall. As we saw in Chapter 1, arguments for animal rights often claimed that harming animals made humans more brutal, and these arguments extended to vegetarianism. Eating meat, early vegetarians such as Joseph Ritson argued, makes you more vicious and evil, and even contributes to war: "That the use of animal food disposes man to cruel and ferocious actions is a fact to which the experience of ages gives ample testimony" (qtd. in Spencer 233). While the practice itself stretches back thousands of years, the Romantic era's concern with human rights, social justice, and the negative effects of industrial capitalism spurred a much more politicized version of vegetarianism. John Oswald's vegetarianism, for example, was connected to his anti-imperial and revolutionary politics. After traveling to India to fight for the British against Tipu Sultan, Oswald became disillusioned with the violent imperial project, traveled around India, and adopted Hindu principles against eating animals. Scholars of Romantic-era vegetarianism emphasize that not only was killing and eating animals figured as a brutal form of human tyranny, and thus symbolically associated with political tyranny, but that meat-eating was associated with the upper class. As Tristram Stuart argues, "Predation was symbolic of social inequality, and most people could not afford to eat meat, so for Oswald vegetarianism was also an act of solidarity" (301). Timothy Morton similarly reads Percy Shelley's vegetarianism as a "revolt against what he conceived to be the hierarchical powers which controlled consumption, production and culture" (*Shelley* 1). Thus while vegetarianism had roots in health and religious principles, it was also a larger critique of a class-based hierarchical social system that exploited not just the poor, but animals as well.[7]

Throughout its publication during the Victorian period, *Animal World* remained mostly silent on vegetarianism. It published numerous articles about the horrors of the cattle trade and cruelty in private slaughterhouses, yet instead of advocating for vegetarianism, the RSPCA looked for better

---

[7] David Perkins briefly discusses vegetarianism in *Romanticism and Animal Rights*.

methods of transit and advocated humane slaughter.[8] In other words, it wanted to keep animals within an exploitative and deathly capitalist system. Especially during the 1870s when concerns arose about cruelty and public health in the meat industry, articles detailing its atrocities spurred only a few readers to write to the journal advocating vegetarianism.[9] Their arguments follow the lines of the Vegetarian Society, which advocated vegetarianism as "a principle which will tend essentially to true civilization, to universal brotherhood, and to the increase of human happiness generally" ("Adjourned").[10] True humanity and social justice, they argue, could not be accomplished if one ate meat and contributed to an unjust and inhumane system. Similarly, one reader wrote to *Animal World* in 1878 that "it is impossible to teach humanity and kindness and gentleness to men while they eat meat. You may succeed in some few cases, but you will always find that the majority will continue to withstand your efforts and go down to the grave as empty of love and goodness as is the carcase they have been eating" (Hayes 184). Others point out the need for consistency, and suggest that raising animals for slaughter will encourage "debased and cruel notions of animal life" (Ivens).

The RSPCA, however, did not agree with such arguments. During their 1874 jubilee meeting, one member stated,

> It is obvious that the mere fact that the operation is painful to an animal is not in itself a sufficient ground for forbidding it. Animals which are killed for food have to undergo a certain amount of suffering; but the object in view is justly held to override the inconvenience of slaughter to the animals in question, and all that can be done is to require that the slaughter should be conducted without any wanton or unnecessary pain. ("Our Jubilee" 115)

The editor of *Animal World* even responded to one concerned reader critiquing those who "delight in torturing and destroying the defenceless" and "justify slaughter-house cruelties by saying that flesh is sent for us to eat, or else that his body requires it for his sustenance" (Shipman). The editor responds with claims of human dominion and worries over animal extinction:

---

[8] From its inception, the RSPCA was cautious of vegan and vegetarian views, believing that, as they stemmed from Pythagoras, they conflicted with Christian ideals. In fact, in 1832 they fired secretary Lewis Gompertz – who advocated veganism – for his anti-Christian views. See Kean (36–37).

[9] For a discussion of Victorian concerns over slaughterhouses and the meat industry, see Paula Young Lee's collection *Meat, Modernity, and the Rise of the Slaughterhouse*.

[10] When the London Vegetarian Society broke off from the Manchester organization, it included these same words in its own constitution ("Constitution" 51).

as the God who made carnivora made their teeth and their instinct to eat flesh, may we not presume He intended them to eat flesh? And does not the same remark apply in less force to man? Vegetarians have a good object in view; but, desirable as it appears to be, the extinction of flesh-eating animals we fear, is necessary to accomplish it, including mankind. (Shipman)

Vegetarianism, it seems, was too radical for the RSPCA.

At first glance, it may seem as if the vegetarian societies were just as anthropocentric as the RSPCA, concerned more with human than animal welfare. After all, while both vegetarian societies discussed the inhumanity of the meat industry, and claimed it was unjust to eat animals, arguments about political economy, temperance, good health, and Christianity were made much more often than those about animal welfare. And the Vegetarian Society's staunch individualism can be read as a form of pastoral power that makes no substantive efforts to produce wider systemic change. At the first annual meeting of the Vegetarian Society, one member emphasized that "if reform does not commence within the individual, no legislative enactments will ever produce it ... Hence, before we ask for legislative enactments, let individuals, and all of us, use our best endeavors to aid ourselves in social improvement to the best of our abilities" ("First Annual" 16). Indeed, their arguments often follow Kant's notion of indirect duty, wherein a certain relationship to animals is important only in how it benefits human communities and salvation. The LVS especially was deeply concerned with the conditions of the working class, and advocated vegetarianism as a way to save money and battle low wages. Unlike *Animal World*, their journals avoid long articles on animals or how to treat them well, opting instead for recipes, articles on fruit, arguments for and against vegetarianism, the plight of the working class, England's colonies abroad (especially Hinduism in India), restaurant reviews, legislation, women's rights, unions, and, primarily in the LVS's journal *The Vegetarian*, articles about socialism, liberalism, individualism, liberty, and war. Although *Animal World* claimed to be apolitical, its politics emerges through its engagement with legislation and its endorsement of a certain kind of animal–human relationship. The LVS, however, took no pains to hide their politics. And indeed, their larger political engagement and critique of capitalism is what made these two societies so radical. Their *lack* of engagement with animals specifically is what allows them to remove animals from the oppressive discourses of governmentality and pastoral power. Animals are not actors or subjects in the ways they are in RSPCA discourse; they are rarely liberalized subjects. Yet whether or not it was possible to understand animals as subjects, or the kind of subjectivity they had, did not matter; they were part of a "universal brotherhood" that called on humans to treat all life with justice, respect, and liberty: "God hath chartered the animals with the liberty of life," argues one writer. "They who deprive them of life, transgress the will of God" (Barmby).

In *Affective Communities*, Leela Gandhi outlines the London Vegetarian Society's anti-imperial and socialist politics. For Gandhi, the LVS moved away from the "will to governmentality" (92) and utilitarian ideology of earlier animal welfare groups like the RSPCA; governmentality and utilitarianism were also associated with colonialism and nationalist discourses of meat-eating. While I discuss intersections between animality and anti-imperial politics in Chapter 6, here I argue that the vegetarian societies removed political understandings of animals from the regulatory nature of governmentality. Through positioning animals within a "universal brotherhood," the vegetarian societies emphasized intersectional social justice and advocated a more humane anti-capitalist social system. Animal subjects enter into a political community precisely through their shared suffering with other humans at the hands of capitalism, not as liberalized subjects who happily take part in their own exploitation. In "Socialism and Vegetarianism," for example, published in *The Vegetarian*, Henry Salt claims, "We can never be a humane people, so long as the working classes are sacrificed, body and soul, to the greed of their oppressors, or while the 'lower animals' are regarded as mere 'live-stock' and food-producers for man." He further emphasizes that real social justice means acknowledging larger oppressive systems:

> A Vegetarian, who protests against the cruelties inflicted on the victims of the slaughter-house, cannot consistently be an opponent of a system which holds out a prospect of relief to the victims of the sweater's den; a Socialist, who (rightly, as I think) denounces those who live on the labour of others as robbers and "blood-suckers," ought not to be able to regard with complacency the horrible traffic in flesh.

While the RSPCA imaginatively posits animals as political actors, here animals enter the political sphere through their imbrication in a larger oppressive system. They are subjects not just because they feel pain, but because they have a life that was *not* given to humans by God. Capitalist practices exploit such animal life, while also keeping the lower class in miserable and inhumane conditions. The vegetarian societies thus critique animal welfare's insistence on the regulations and hierarchies resulting from the government of animals. From their standpoint, governing well means refraining from claims to knowledge of animals' inner life, and most importantly, to rid oneself of the social hierarchies that reinforce animal and human oppression. The vegetarian societies did not promote regulation of the animal world; they promoted animal and human liberation.

That vegetarians must practice social justice for all, not just animals, is made clear by Henry Salt's larger political views. He was involved in the London Vegetarian Society, formed the Humanitarian League in 1891, which "existed to fight injustice, inequality and cruelty to all creatures including humans," and believed that the RSPCA did not go far enough in its politics (Spencer 287). As Leela Gandhi shows, Salt's 1886 pamphlet "A Plea for Vegetarianism" was highly influential to Mahatma Gandhi's views of animals and social reform. Salt's 1892 *Animals' Rights: Considered in Relation to Social Progress* stated blatantly that any unnecessary suffering inflicted on animals was incompatible with humanitarianism. Indeed, his critiques of pet-keeping – he saw pets as animals who were "turned into a useless puppet" existing for "the mere idle amusement" of his or her owner (34) – highlight the extent to which his views strayed from the mainstream. As a committed socialist, he instructed fellow vegetarians to take up the principles of socialism; his recommendation for vegetarian readers was Frank Fairman's 1888 *Principles of Socialism Made Plain*. Fairman emphasizes that socialism is a critique of individual property and profit: "This, then," he writes, "is the criticism which Socialism passes upon the present state of society ... that the one great evil which afflicts humanity ... is the unlimited right of private property and accumulation; and that unless this power is restricted, if not abrogated, all other reforms will be useless" (10). Private property, according to Fairman, gives wealthy humans unlimited sovereignty, as "the absolute, unlimited right of individual property in land is seen to carry with it the absolute right of life and death" (17). While Fairman's concern is with lower-class women, children, and men, vegetarian readers would make a direct connection to the animal world. One of the founding concepts of liberal government, private property and its protection, here allows unfair human sovereignty over animals. Private property reinforces the notion that animals are property and that humans yield the right to let them live or make them die.

While socialist thought critiques the subjection of animals to liberal governmentality, Fairman offers an animal politics that destabilizes the primacy of liberal capitalism. Instead of conceptualizing political communities as a movement out of nature, Fairman suggests socialism has a model in animal communities: "I remark that nothing approaching the individual accumulation of property is known among the lower animals, not even those which have reached the highest stages of intelligence, so far as to live in communities, to make provisions for future necessities by laying up stores of food, and even to keep domestic animals, as some species of ants do" (15–16). He further explains – without the regulation of animal conduct – that even their division of labor provides a remarkable model:

> No one can reasonably contend that the lower animals are possessed of more powerful benevolent impulses, or less powerful selfish ones than human beings, yet we see highly-organized communities continued generation after generation for thousands of years, in which *personal* accumulation is utterly unknown, but where the whole society flourishes or decays together, these members sharing in the benefits derived from the common labour of all, though that labour is in some cases remarkably sub-divided. (16)

Although Fairman rarely discusses animals throughout his text, and suggests vegetarianism is a superficial remedy for poverty, *Principles of Socialism Made Plain* offers an animal politics that destabilizes human superiority and refrains from regulating animal conduct. As Brian Massumi explains, animal politics "calls on the human to become animal, not on animals to renounce vital powers long wrongly assumed to be the sole province of the human" (52). While Massumi here challenges critiques of anthropomorphism, to embrace animal politics is to relinquish human sovereignty and the liberal subject, and locate alternate relationships within animal communities. Unlike liberalism, which regulates both animals and humans through governmentality, and projects regulatory forms of subjectivity onto animals, socialism renounces – but never fully – human superiority.

This chapter began with a prize essay from the RSPCA that highlights how animal welfare discourse constructed animal subjectivity within pastoral power. Such constructions kept animals within exploitative social systems that reified human power and solidified systems of subjection. As such, the ethics of the RSPCA ultimately reflect back onto human superiority. The vegetarian societies, however, sought to critique intersectional forms of oppression at the hands of capitalism; rather than cultivate an animal subjectivity that admired the human, they developed a radical equality through the notion of universal brotherhood. While the RSPCA's prize essays reflect back onto human superiority, the following prize essay from the LVS critiques the human self-interestedness at the center of Victorian animal welfare. Published June 15, 1889, Leo Michaels's "Best Method for Organised Propaganda of Vegetarian Principles" argues that "There can be no perfect ideal man or woman, nor perfect social condition, without the triumph of the principle of Vegetarianism." Yet this cannot be self-serving: "The man who is a Vegetarian through fear of parasites or sickness, is like one who is religious because he is afraid of going to hell." While the vegetarian societies were regulated by religious principles, as was the RSPCA, there is no belief in absolute human dominion over animals. Indeed, faith in a perfect society must rely on "the abolishment of the slaughterhouse and butcher's shop, and every other form of cruelty to man and beast." Universal brotherhood, a concept frequently appearing throughout all vegetarian societies' journals, destabilizes anthropocentrism. Michaels emphasizes this lack of self-interest through promoting a love that includes both animals and humans. Like his reformulation of Christian-inspired animal–human relationships, this love is not anthropocentric nor liberal: "The love of which I am writing is not the mere gush of a good-natured liberalism, that so often boasts of its charity, and yet loves nothing so much as its own ease in Zion."

Animal welfare and anti-cruelty discourse signaled a profound shift in how animals were incorporated into a liberal political community. This shift affected not just how animals were physically treated, but how they were imagined as sentient and thinking creatures. As the government debated whether or not to bring animals into a political community, and how to do so, a competing set of ideologies structured the construction of animal subjectivity. Indeed, as Alasdair Cochrane suggests, "Asking how political communities ought to govern their relations with animals involves asking more than simply what laws they should enact" (2). It means altering how animals are viewed as subjects, and refiguring their role in society. Although creating an almost revolutionary shift in animal–human relationships, such as imagining animals as thinking, feeling subjects, many of the most well-meaning animal welfare advocates reified the position of animals as subservient to humankind and its economic systems. In the following chapters, I demonstrate how the Victorian novel takes up the issues discussed in these first two chapters, and through its animal characters, pushes the limits of liberal thought, especially in its relationship with alterity. Rather than reifying animals into hierarchical relationships with the human, the animal characters I examine challenge liberal ideologies and offer an animal politics that exposes and revises the many contradictions of Victorian liberalism. While not always finding solutions for how to incorporate animals into a political community, the novels I discuss highlight the radical potential of animal characters, and offer possibilities for pushing liberal thought beyond its normative anthropocentric framework.

PART II

Democracy, Education, and Alternative Subjectivity

CHAPTER 3

'Tame submission to injustice is unworthy of a Raven'
Charles Dickens's Animal Character

> The capitalist flourishes, he amasses immense wealth; we sink, lower and lower; lower than the beasts of burthen; for they are fed better than we are, cared for more. And it is just, for according to the present system they are more precious.
> – Benjamin Disraeli, *Sybil*

> It is worse to be compared to a beast than to be one.
> – "Jeremy Taylor on Animals"

> The conclusion would be that the political, ethical, social, philosophical problem of our days is not to try to liberate the individual from the state, and from the state's institutions, but to liberate us both from the state and from the type of individualization linked to the state. We have to promote new forms of subjectivity through the refusal of this kind of individuality that has been imposed on us for several centuries.
> – Michel Foucault, "The Subject and Power"

The first two chapters marked the nineteenth century as a period inaugurating wider political representation for mostly laboring animals. Significantly, this took place alongside movements for working-class representation. In the year of Queen Victoria's coronation, the 1835 Cruelty to Animals Act was extended to Ireland. The law built on Martin's Act and penalized animal fighting; required the feeding of confined horses, donkeys, and other cattle; and regulated horse slaughtering. One year later, the Chartists presented their National Petition and People's Charter to parliament in their own attempt to gain more political representation. Although the years 1838 and 1839 saw the publication of animal welfare texts, the banning of dog carts in certain parts of England, and debates about cattle slaughter, the 1839 Chartist Convention and Newport protests signaled that the working class was no closer to attaining the political representation they demanded. Indeed, in his 1840 *Chartism*, Thomas Carlyle noted how animals were getting more attention than the Chartists, claiming that instead of trying to "interpret" the desires of the working class, parliament was discussing "Smithfield cattle, and Dog-carts, – all manner of questions and subjects, except simply this the alpha and omega of all!" (8). While the lower class was animalized, described by Carlyle as "wild inarticulate souls ... like dumb creatures in pain, unable to speak what is in them" (9), animals such as dogs were valorized and anthropomorphized. Landseer's famous 1837 painting *The Old Shepherd's Chief Mourner*, for example, exemplifies conceptions of the loyal dog that circulated throughout the period. In 1840, while the working class struggled for representation, the Society for the Prevention of Cruelty to Animals gained its "Royal" designation, giving it both legitimacy and direct connection to the state.

Debates regarding political representation for the working class and laboring animals often focused on liberal ideologies of character: "self-restraint, perseverance, strenuous effort, courage in the face of adversity" (Collini 36).[1] And according to liberal political discourse, working and domestic animals had more character than the working class. As we have seen, the incorporation of animals into the juridico-political sphere relied on conceptions of animal character in which animals were constructed as liberalized moral subjects who accepted domination. Such constructions were often placed next to a brutal and immoral working class that needed to learn how to treat animals kindly in order to cultivate their own character. Significantly, the incorporation of animals and the working class into representative politics put pressure on the role and character of the government. While parliament argued over if it should protect animals, legislators who debated the 1832 Reform Bill worried that expanding the franchise would "entirely annihilate our deliberative character, and will reduce us to the mere function of speaking the will of others from day to day" (*Hansard's* II 1091). Debates about wider representation thus concern the nature of governmentality and the logic controlling its subjects: how should a population of animals and working people be properly conducted and represented?

---

[1] Critical consensus is that character becomes a prominent political category in the mid-Victorian period, seen especially in Mill's valuation of character in connection to individuality. Janice Carlisle explains that for Mill, "Character involves how one human being acts or is acted upon by other human beings and by their shared circumstances. Character inevitably comprises one's thoughts, desires, and impulses, but it is known most accurately through one's choices and actions" (*John* 1), while Goodlad describes Mill's notion of character as "human potential" ("Character" 19). Hadley emphasizes the class-based nature of Victorian liberal character, arguing that "Although touted as that subject of all subjects who transcends hierarchy and classificatory constraints, the liberal character is a class character" ("Past" 18).

Social reform novels supplemented the regulatory effects of a class-based governmentality by giving voice to the poor while reinforcing middle-class character. Elizabeth Gaskell and Charles Dickens especially expanded the scope of political representation and aimed to induce sympathetic legislators, social reformers, and the middle class to help, or at least care about, the working class.[2] They cultivated a positive working-class character while illustrating what a productive relationship between the lower and middle classes within the confines of capitalism could look like. The ending of *Mary Barton*, for example, features Mr. Carson's wish "that a perfect understanding, and complete confidence and love, might exist between masters and men," and that workers will be "bound to their employers by the ties of respect and affection, not by mere money bargains alone" (388). Such politics reinforces class hierarchies perpetuated by liberal ideology and do little to better the working conditions of the poor. The idea that the working class would work for their "masters" out of "respect and affection" is strikingly similar to the constructions of liberal animal subjectivity discussed in previous chapters: both subjects are happy to work in an exploitative capitalist system. Thus even sympathetic constructions of working-class subjectivity function as an animalizing discourse that suggests the working class willingly participates in oppressive master–servant relationships. Even as they stage productive political debates, as Amanda Anderson argues in *Bleak Liberalism*, social reform novels privilege pastoral power by advocating top-down power relationships to guide working-class conduct. They cultivate character as a means to induce social change and better working-class political representation, yet the political community they represent reproduces unequal social systems that mostly work for the good of capitalism.[3]

Although Dickens's social reform novels have been critiqued for their "sentimental radicalism," and for positing middle-class morality, domesticity, and paternalism as solutions to social inequities, Dickens also suggests that the character of liberal governmentality must be revised.[4] He often makes this argument by way of animal characters. For alongside sympathetic representations of the working class, Dickens's early novels represent

---

[2] Carolyn Betensky argues that social-problem novels were invested in cultivating bourgeois subjectivity to feel sympathy for both the poor and the bourgeois readers themselves.
[3] To nuance ideological readings of the social reform novel, Amanda Anderson claims that argument and the representation of a lived political commitment should be read as central to the political novel's liberal form (*Bleak* 79).
[4] Walter Bagehot characterized Dickens's novels as promoting "sentimental radicalism." See Bethan Carney, "Introduction: 'Mr Popular Sentiment': Dickens and Feeling," for a discussion of the term.

animal characters who resist the individualizing logic of liberal bourgeois ideology present in animal welfare discourse. In fact, I suggest his animal characters often contain a radicalness human characters do not, as his discourse on animality revises descriptive notions of character cultivated by liberal governmentality.[5] By animal character, I mean animals as literary characters *and* the morality and interiority with which they were imagined, thus connecting their novelistic representation to a larger political sphere associated with liberal character. This is not far from Alex Woloch's double meaning of character: "character as social being (a person *is* a character) and character as inner quality (a person *has* a character)" (53). I argue that although Dickens often reifies working-class character within pastoral power, his animal characters question the results of cultivating hegemonic forms of character. Indeed, the fact of their being minor characters functions as a way out of liberal forms of individualization: the fact that they are on the novel's periphery highlights their inability to be fully circumscribed by governmentality. Dickens's destabilization of human governance over animals reflects larger hierarchical modes of cultivating character and subjectivity, bringing animals within the novel's critique of liberal governmentality. Dickens suggests liberal character is an animalizing force that regulates the conduct of both animals and the working class, and inscribes them into social hierarchies. The alternate animality he offers exposes how often liberal governing structures fail to adequately represent their populations.

Through examining Dickens's animal politics, I argue that reading animal characters by way of liberal discourse invites a reconsideration of animalized subjects, asks us to reexamine notions of animality, and shows the limits of legislating based on a top-down construction of character regulated by pastoral power. By resisting forms of subjection perpetuated by animal welfare discourse, Dickens's animal characters move beyond the oppressive logic of liberal governmentality, allowing for a larger critique of animality and the hierarchies that create it. For although novels such as *Oliver Twist*, *Barnaby Rudge*, and *Hard Times* represent animals with liberal qualities that coincide with political protection, such as cognition, reason, and emotion, they also represent animals with alternative subjectivities that privilege alterity, resistance to governance, and non-rational

---

[5] Goodlad argues that as opposed to prescriptive forms of character, which place "the onus on individuals or classes to meet … the qualifications for citizenship," in descriptive character "social particularities" of individuals were emphasized, such as class, race, gender, and species ("Character" 18). Descriptive character especially reinforces hierarchies already in place.

epistemologies. Dickens's literary animals challenge descriptive notions of character conducted through pastoral power, in which animal subjectivity is consistently liberalized and positioned in relationship to an animal–human hierarchy. Such representations destabilize human power and authority over animal subjectivity, and thus the animal–human hierarchy maintaining it.

I suggest this incorporation of animal characters into the Victorian novel is an alternate form of political representation for domestic animals, as Dickens's animal characters often deemphasize moral character as a requirement for political participation and representation. Dickens creates animal subjects whose subjectivity exceeds the more restrictive subjectivity cultivated by governmentality, and envisions animal subjects within a political community in ways that challenge representations from anti-cruelty legislation and animal welfare discourse. Following Alex Woloch, I understand the representational space of the novel as reflecting demands for democracy, and include animals in his formulation of minor characters. Dickens's animal characters compete and jostle for space with human ones, which places them on a more horizontal plane of political representation. Dickens cannot always remove his working-class characters from the constraints of pastoral power, yet he often displaces his animals from this regulating force. While Dickens's animal characters reveal the politics that keeps animals confined within an animal–human hierarchy, they also exhibit the tensions within his politics. Although Dickens imagines animals exceeding their social position, and critiques pastoral power's regulation of conduct, he cannot imagine the kind of society that can contain them. However radical it may be, Dickens's animal subjectivity remains a site of imagined political resistance that ignores the very real material conditions affecting the lives of animals and humans. Dickens's animal characters thus demonstrate the difficulty of incorporating animals into existing liberal political structures, and the potential they had for disrupting them.

Charles Dickens's Animal Politics

In a set of essays from 1850 published in *Household Words*, Charles Dickens uses a raven to trouble human constructions of animal character. In "Perfect Felicity in a Bird's-Eye View" and "From the Raven in the Happy Family," Dickens writes from the viewpoint of the raven forced to live in John Austin's "Happy Family," a collection of "animals of opposite natures living in one cage" ("John Austin"). Metaphorically, Austin's animals represent an ideal disinterested populace, wherein subjects place the good of a democratic whole before individual needs. A handbill for the spectacle emphasizes the extent to which it demonstrates disinterestedness, liberal character, and equality: "In this collection, revengeful passions are not known; the weak are without fear, and the strong without the desire to injure" ("John Austin"). The fact that this display and others began circulating in the 1840s during heightened demands for democracy suggests it was representative of attempts to cultivate good relationships between the predators and prey of the human world.[6] If "We may learn a great many lessons from animals, such as forgiveness, unselfishness, love, usefulness, and obedience" ("Extracts" 197), as RSPCA discourse suggested, then a cage full of predators and prey living together should influence cooperation among opposing human interests. Indeed, these essays critique the lack of disinterest among social reformers and government officials. Putting together a disparate list of rulers, clergymen, and governing bodies, Dickens emphasizes the self-interest of those with power. The raven states,

> This is what *I* say: I want to see men do it. I should like to get up a Happy Family of men, and show 'em. I should like to put the Rajah Brooke, the Peace Society, Captain Aaron Smith, several Malay Pirates, Dr. Wiseman, the Reverend Hugh Stowell, Mr. Fox of Oldham, the Board of Health, all the London undertakers, some of the Common (very common *I* think) Council, and all the vested interests in the filth and misery of the poor into a good-sized cage, and see how *they*'d get on. ("Perfect" 200)

Imagining the Board of Health negotiating with the London undertakers, or an Archbishop next to an anti-Catholic Church of England clergyman demonstrates the conflicting interests structuring governmentality and influencing not only the beliefs and daily actions of average citizens, but also the governing institutions that create policy, regulations, and reform. Self-interest is the governing mentality, which highlights how representative government and its institutions fail the population, and remain unable to productively preserve heterogeneous modes of thinking.

Dickens's political critique is intertwined with animal character, suggesting his animal politics is intimately connected to those of the human world. Animal and human character are regulated through a governmentality that perpetuates its own stability rather than the good of the population. In the first essay, the raven laments his position as a spectacle as he claims, "What

---

[6] Keridiana Chez briefly analyzes "Happy Families," and cites an 1844 *Chambers's* article discussing the spectacle (25–26). In the 1840s, Henry Mayhew wrote that Happy Families "are so well known as to need no further description here" (299), and includes a description from a man who claims John Austin exhibited his collection before Princess Victoria in 1833 (301).

right has any man to require me to look complacently at a cat on a shelf all day?" (199). The raven posits his subjection as a result of a larger governing structure, and suggests training is a form of national education that benefits only the governing body:

> I want to know why I am called upon to accommodate myself to a cat, a mouse, a pigeon, a ringdove, an owl (who is the greatest ass I have ever known), a guinea-pig, a sparrow, and a variety of other creatures with whom I have no opinion in common. Is this national education? Because, if it is, I object to it. Is our cage what they call neutral ground, on which all parties may agree? If so, war to the beak I consider preferable. (199)

Given Dickens's suspicion of a state education that reified oppressive social positions, the raven's question – Is this national education? – suggests that training restricts freedom and imposes hegemonic and oppressive forms of character. Not only should the audience know that the Happy Family is a delusion, their attraction to it should cause self-reflection: humans should practice cooperation among disparate interests and viewpoints. He claims that the humans who visit Austin's spectacle should be "ashamed to look me in the eye!" (201); for not only does he avoid making "half the pretences that are common among you men!" (201), but after discussing the Mouse's claims that "you don't take half the care you ought; of your own young, and don't teach 'em half enough" (202), the raven claims, "You are a nice set of fellows, certainly, to come and look at Happy Families, as if you had nothing else to look after!" (202). The misrepresented animal speaks back, not about human superiority and a willingness to be subservient, but about hypocritical human character, the government of animals, and the character of governmentality. Animality, the raven suggests, is a human construction reaffirming positions of power; and the negative qualities some humans project onto others, and define as animality, are most often found within themselves.

In "From the Raven in the Happy Family," the raven further critiques human desires to classify animals according to supposedly innate characteristics that reflect positively upon the human. "I want to know who Buffon was," he says. "I'll take my oath he wasn't a bird. Then what did *he* know about birds – especially about Ravens?" (203). The raven compares his position as a spectacle in a cage, where he is trained to restrain his "animal nature," to scientific delineations of animal character: "Your friend Buffon, and some more of you, are mighty ready, it seems to give *us* characters" (204). Education and scientific discourse manipulate and subjugate, resulting in misrepresentation: "I tell you what. I like the idea of you men, writing histories of *us*, and settling what we are, and what we are not, and calling us any names you like best. What colors do you think you would show in, yourselves, if some of us were to take it into our heads to write histories of *you*?" (203). He asks, "Would you like to hear about your own temper and forebearance? Ask the Dog. About your never overloading or ill-using a willing creature? Ask my brother-in-law's friend, the Camel, up in the Zoological" (204). When taken seriously, animal viewpoints undermine anthropocentric constructions of character regulating animal–human relationships, and the hierarchical logic structuring them. Such constructions, the raven suggests, result in an imagined animal submission of the kind perpetuated by animal welfare discourse. For he exclaims, "Tame submission to injustice is unworthy of a Raven. I croak the croak of revolt, and call upon the Happy Family to rally round me. You men have had it all your own way for a long time. *Now*, you shall hear a sentiment or two about yourselves" (207). The raven demands a democracy in which animals have a participatory voice and their point of view is taken seriously. He rejects human desires to assert a hierarchical position over animals through training and classification, and imagines animals as revolting against the regulation of their conduct and constructions of their character. Like the animals found throughout *Animal World*, the raven participates in public discourse and deliberative democracy. He has liberalized qualities and offers his opinion – a Victorian form of social agency – but rejects them through his critique of human superiority and governmentality.

Revolting against hierarchy and human domination, the raven petitions for a more democratic mode of animal–human relations, and calls on his animal brethren to join his organizing efforts. He destabilizes the authority of human knowledge and language – "You are mighty proud about your language; but it seems to me that you don't deserve to have words, if you can't make a better use of 'em" (206) – and thus the authority and character of a governing body. While we could understand Dickens's critique of Austin's collection as a disinclination for democracy, his problem lies with governing structures and their mentality, rather than the democratic whole. Austin's collection represents a grotesque form of democracy, social cooperation, and disinterestedness, founded on the illusion of equality and functioning through a subjection that erases difference.[7] The animals' disinterest, seen in their ability to "suppress"

---

[7] In his reading of *Barnaby Rudge*, Patrick Brantlinger locates a "grotesque" populism, in which "misrule has so deluded and deformed the common people that they themselves emerge ... as a nightmarish caricature of what the common people might have been if wisely ruled" (59).

their animal natures, results from the human trainer, whose interests lie in financial gain. Dickens's critique of Austin's animals is not with the idealized democracy they represent, but with the capitalist governing structures through which humans construct and classify subjects under their domination. Given J. S. Mill's later claims that "national education" is one of the ways "a form of government or set of political institutions affects the welfare of the community" (*Considerations* 230), Dickens's essay works as an exposé of a failed democracy.

The raven from the Happy Family offers a telling insight into Dickens's animal politics. Although there is no evidence he was a member and supporter of the RSPCA, as Arthur Moss previously claimed, Dickens praised the organization in a letter to its secretary, John Colam: "I have a high opinion of the Society you represent," he writes, "and believe that it does a great deal of good" (*Letters* X: 359). Philip Howell suggests that, in part through Percy Fitzgerald's characterization of Dickens as "the Landseer of fiction," his representations of dogs helped "canine *emancipation*" and the inclusion of dogs within a civic community (26–27). Noting that even though Fitzgerald's essay is somewhat hyperbolic, Howell asks us to take seriously the fact that Dickens is often represented as a formative figure in the animal welfare movement. Dickens's most prominent engagement with animal welfare comes during debates about relocating Smithfield Market from London to the suburbs in the 1850s, during which *Household Words* ran a series of articles encouraging readers to support its removal. Often read as a reflection of Dickens's public health concerns, these essays illuminate how both animals and humans are negatively affected by capitalism's drive for profit. Ron Morrison argues that Dickens's 1850 essay "The Heart of Mid-London," co-written with *Household Words*'s sub-editor W. H. Wills, at first perpetuates stereotypes that drovers were innately cruel members of the lower class and RSPCA critiques of lower-class animal cruelty, but ultimately exposes the need for governmental regulation of slaughterhouses ("Dickens"). Indeed, Dickens and Wills's descriptions give credence to naturalist Edward Jesse's 1825 claim that "England is the Hell of dumb animals" (qtd. in Ritvo, *Animal Estate* 126), as they vividly describe the "positive horror," "punishing and torturing," "mute agony," and "panorama of cruelty and suffering" (104) that Mr. Bovington witnesses in a state of stupefaction.

For Dickens, Smithfield represents the inhumanity of London, a lack of governmental interference where it is actually needed, and exposes capitalism's encouragement of self-interest at the expense of the humane treatment of both animals and humans. Indeed, in both *Oliver Twist* and

Great Expectations, Smithfield signifies a lack of control over the fates of the protagonists, and is a telling sign of London's vices. For journalist and playwright Douglas Jerrold, a close acquaintance of Dickens, Smithfield was comparable to a workhouse; the treatment of animals and the working class are aligned through bad governmentality. In his 1843 article "The Beauties of the Police," for example, Jerrold describes a beggar who compared the workhouse to Smithfield: "He would risk starvation and the cold comfort of a stone-step for his bed; but, then, his child would be with him in his misery: they would not be separated like cattle in the pens of Smithfield" (qtd. in Ledger 116). Like Jerrold, Dickens saw similarities between capitalism's objectification of animals and humans, thus elevating the status of animals in his politics. Yet as Patrick Joyce argues, even the desire to regulate slaughter was another mode of governmentality, further aligning the poor and animals within a discourse of moral character and "self-mastery" (88).

Critics who discuss Dickens and animals often emphasize his well-known fondness for dogs, with the caveat that he shot his beloved dog Sultan, who bit a servant.[8] Howell locates Dickens's dogs outside of sentimentality and a glorification of domesticity, claiming they are "more messily ambiguous than their role as home helpers suggest, and not simply (like Dora Copperfield's Jip) as icons of domestic incompetence" (39). Rather, his dogs "refuse to be deadened and disciplined by domesticity"; Dickens "delights" in the street dogs and the ways they challenge the authorizing effects of a well-ordered and moral domesticity (44–45). Monica Flegel reads Dickens's male dog–human relationships as representative of "a cross-species homosociality," seen in Sikes from *Oliver Twist* and Hugh from *Barnaby Rudge*, who represent "a savagery that cannot be subsumed within the middle-class version of domesticity and the concomitant versions of manhood being constructed within early and mid-Victorian fiction and culture" (*Pets* 119). While Dickens's dogs challenge his valuation of domestic and gendered ideologies, I adopt Howell's suggestion that we take seriously Dickens's figuration as a canine emancipator, and more importantly, uncover the relationship of his animal characters to his negotiation of liberal governmentality and pastoral power.

As seen through his essay on the Happy Family, Dickens's animal politics is actually quite radical, as it critiques capitalism's cultivation of

---

[8] This story is related in Kreilkamp, "Dying" (92–93), and in Beryl Gray, *The Dog in the Dickensian Imagination* (58–59). According to his daughter Mamie, Dickens would relate Sultan's fate with "comical seriousness" (Gray 59).

self-interest, advocates for self-representation, and destabilizes hierarchical structures perpetuated by governmentality. Indeed, Dickens's alignment of animal and working-class suffering situates his animal politics within that of the late-century London Vegetarian Society, rather than the RSPCA, an organization Marx and Engels labeled as perpetuating bourgeois ideology and hierarchical social structures.[9] Not necessarily concerned with animal welfare, Dickens's animal politics challenges human constructions of animal subjectivity to show the limitations of pastorship and the oppressive ways governmentality works with capitalism to organize and represent its subjects. Goodlad suggests Dickens shows Victorian society is "shepherd-less" (*Victorian Literature* xii), but we might also read him as suggesting it is filled with bad shepherds. Foucault's description of a "bad shepherd," one who "only thinks of good pasture for his own profit, for fattening the flock that he will be able to sell and scatter" ("Security" 128), highlights governmentality's close relationship with capitalism. In his representations of working-class animals and humans, Dickens shows how capitalism and governmentality work together: he represents a working class consistently animalized by the forces that are supposed to represent and conduct them well – the government, the aristocracy, and the middle class – and by the social and economic forces that subject animals and humans to a life of grueling work, poverty, and suffering.

Friedrich Engels exposes such animalization in *The Conditions of the Working Class in England*, as he emphasizes there is no inherent animality in the working class, but rather that governmentality's close relationships with capitalism makes them like animals: "They are hunted like game, and not permitted to attain peace of mind and quiet enjoyment of life" (108–109); "they either bow humbly before the fate that overtakes them ... or they are tossed about by fate, lose their moral hold upon themselves as they have already lost their economic hold, live along from day to day, drink and fall into licentiousness; and in both cases they are brutes" (129); and "Once more the worker must choose, must either surrender himself to his fate, become a 'good' workman, heed 'faithfully' the interest of the bourgeoisie, in which case he most certainly becomes a

---

[9] In *The Communist Manifesto*, Marx and Engels write that "members of societies for the prevention of cruelty to animals" are "desirous of redressing social grievances, in order to secure the continued existence of bourgeois society" (242). They claim that in this form of Bourgeois Socialism, "the proletariat should remain within the bounds of existing society, but should cast away all its hateful ideas concerning the bourgeoisie" (243). Representations of animal subjectivity perpetuated by the RSPCA, who are represented without any "hateful ideas" concerning their middle-class caretakers, confirm Marx and Engels's analysis.

brute, or he must rebel" (130). Engels points out the failure of what Gaskell advocates in *Mary Barton*, and exposes it as an animalizing discourse: to become a "good worker" is to become a "faithful" loyal animal. Indeed, in Disraeli's *Sybil*, the hand-loom weaver Warner highlights how animalization results from capitalist drives for profit: "The capitalist flourishes," he explains, "he amasses immense wealth; we sink, lower and lower; lower than the beasts of burthen; for they are fed better than we are, cared for more. And it is just, for according to the present system they are more precious" (115). Warner's comment emphasizes how the working class was both animalized and made lower than animals, as political concern for animals was at times more accepted by the government and the middle class than the plight of the poor; or as James Turner argues, was perhaps to some middle-class Victorians "a more acceptable object of benevolence" (54). Yet while Disraeli advocates for pastoral power's paternalism, Dickens shows the limitations of good government and critiques the dual animalizing discourse – to be like an animal in negative terms, or like a faithful animal in bourgeois terms – that structures liberal governmentality's care for the poor. For indeed, Mr. T. Attwood made a similar construction between loyalty and the working class when he brought in the Chartist Petition on June 14, 1839: "The men who signed the petition were honest and industrious – of sober and unblemished character – men who have uniformly discharged the duties of good members of society and loyal subjects, and who had always obeyed the laws" (*Hansard's* XLVIII: 223).

In his chapter on Dickens, Woloch's arguments about the relationship between the amount of character space, or minorness, and social stratification rely on the above passages from Engels, emphasizing that animality is also part of this relationship.[10] This triangulation of minorness, stratification, and animality structure Dickens's animal politics, in which he critiques constructions of animality under capitalism, and exposes liberalism's speciesist logic that values civility, constraint, and reason. Woloch emphasizes that Dickens's novels "constantly dramatiz[e] the distortion that is a consequence of minorness," and that "the division of labor, so central to nineteenth-century social and economic theory, is also the social process most profoundly

---

[10] The translation from which Woloch quotes Engels emphasizes even more fully the animalizing nature of industrialization: "They are goaded like wild beasts and never have a chance of enjoying a quiet life"; "*Whether they submit passively to their fate or take to drink*, they are equally no more than animals"; and "He may submit to his fate and become a 'good worker,' 'faithfully' serving the interests of the middle classes – and if he does so he is absolutely certain to become a mere animal" (qtd. in Woloch 163–164).

implicated in the character-systems of nineteenth-century fiction" (156). Characterization, then, is a result of and reflects a character's place in capitalist society, and I suggest this relationship between economics and representation also applies to animal characters.

In his reading of *Great Expectations*, Ivan Kreilkamp hesitates to label animals in Victorian literature minor characters, instead describing them as "semi-characters" whose status is reflective of their treatment as "semi-human" ("Dying" 82). "What I mean by this," he argues, "is that animals, or certain privileged domesticated animals, are given names and invested with personality and individual identity, but that this status is unreliable and subject to sudden abrogation" (82). Kreilkamp further links social status and characterization, but does not connect this to an animal politics. He claims,

> Generally denied the status of a protagonist or developed character in such longer narratives, animals, when they are so represented, can embody alternative, non-novelistic temporalities – anecdotal, minor, interrupted. An animal character is, perhaps by definition, an incomplete or fragile character, one whose continuity over a long span of time or pages cannot be guaranteed or anticipated, and whose presence in a long novel may implicitly challenge that very form's presumption that individual identity can be maintained over a long duration. (84)

To extend Kreilkamp's claim, I suggest the liminality of animal characters reflects their imbrication in Victorian capitalism's division of labor: their lack of substantial political representation and protection, the valuation of some animals over others, and the construction of animals as willingly taking part in an exploitative economic system. Animal fragility and liminality is linked to the strategies of governmentality that extend to animals, most especially pastoral power, animal welfare, and human exceptionalism. Yet Dickens's animal characters are often removed from governmentality's character discourse and expose the limitations of speaking for, or the lack of representation of, London's poor *and* animals. As such, I suggest Dickens's animal politics is most clearly articulated on the level of character, rather than within his larger stance toward animal welfare, which is ambiguous at best. Dickens, like Engels, argues that animal and human animality is a result of governmentality and the strategies that maintain it: pastoral power, bad shepherds, and a utilitarian ideology that objectifies Victorian subjects by reducing them to animals or encouraging them to be docile workers, like the loyal animals prized by the RSPCA. His animal politics shows how a multi-species representative democracy fails those whom it should faithfully represent.

Through his engagement with representation and character, Dickens revises hegemonic constructions of animal and human working-class character. As we have seen, character was central to animal welfare and anti-cruelty debates. Liberal animal character – loyalty, recognition of hierarchy, and a willingness to work – was a key strategy for gaining sympathy and political protection for animals. Often this animal character was exemplary of a liberal moral character to which citizens should aspire. Indeed, as animal subjectivity was increasingly constructed in moral, hierarchical, and political language, working-class character was more often at fault for mistreating animals. Yet as I show in the following readings, Dickens critiques the larger governing structures that represent and control his animal characters, thus presenting a more radical animal politics that highlights governmentality's shortcomings for both animals and humans. In *Oliver Twist* and *Barnaby Rudge* Dickens criticizes a hegemonic animal character and thus the larger governing structure of representative democracy. Yet I first move to a brief reading of *Hard Times* to demonstrate the importance of Dickens's animal politics, and the novel's positioning of animal epistemologies as privileged sites of resistance to the strategies of governmentality. Through his radical representations of animal characters, Dickens gives animals an alternative political voice outside the constraints of liberal animal welfare discourse, and deepens our understanding of animals as minor characters. Their liminality, I suggest, may actually be what makes them radical.

The Politics of Animal Epistemology in *Hard Times*

Hard Times begins with animals as facts, reduced to the barest physical qualities, and ends with them as epistemological subjects full of an alterity that remains inaccessible to the human. The novel's transition from Bitzer's graminivorous quadruped to Sleary's wonder over the "wayth of the dogth" (292) charts a move from a utilitarian mode of calculating animal and human individuals, to a place of wonder and fancy beyond self-interest. While critics suggest fancy, as represented by Sleary's circus, is an ineffective political solution to industrialization, others read the novel's circus animals as "vitality, spiritedness, and movement ... a force worthy to oppose the powers of Fact and all that it represents" (Sonstroem 522), which exists in "a world that cannot be comprehended in the language of political economy" (Gold 203). Indeed, *Hard Times* offers alternate ways to understand animals as subjects in a liberal society that reduces them, like the working class, to utility, presenting Derridean moments of "the incalculable and the undecidable" ("Eating" 108). Taking seriously the novel's valuation of animal epistemology as something more than fancy registers an animal politics beyond governmentality's desire to know and regulate its populations. At the novel's end Dickens praises animal epistemology precisely because humans need imagination to conceptualize it; animal interiority relies on alterity, for it resists calculation. However, for all the novel's interest in conceptualizing animals as subjects and positing animal alterity beyond the logics of governmentality, *Hard Times* illuminates tensions between imagining animals outside of pastoral power and conferring on them a moral valuation that inscribes them in a disciplinary framework highlighted by the circus. *Hard Times* thus registers the difficulties of imagining animal subjects and an animal politics in the Victorian period, and locates novels more generally as privileged sites for working through such challenges.

Gradgrind's famous demand to Sissy Jupe – "Give me your definition of a horse" – which causes her to be "thrown into the greatest alarm" (11), raises the question of how to delineate and represent animal subjects in a society privileging them for their utility. For Gradgrind, Sissy's bafflement at a simple question shows that she is "possessed of no facts, in reference to one of the commonest of animals!" (11). Gradgrind assumes animals seen every day in the streets should be easily known because of their pervasive presence. His shock that Sissy knows no "facts" in relation to "the commonest of animals" suggests his utilitarianism defines animals solely by their use value. Bitzer's answer highlights that Gradgrind's desire to know "facts" about horses breaks them into calculable elements that neglect their subjectivity: "Quadruped. Graminivorous. Forty teeth, namely twenty-four grinders, four eye-teeth, and twelve incisive. Sheds coat in the spring; in marshy countries, sheds hoofs, too. Hoofs hard, but requiring to be shod with iron. Age known by marks in mouth" (12). Bitzer's short, declarative sentences reduce horses to physical qualities easily understood by the human, and negate their inner life. Bitzer cuts up the subject in ways Derrida outlines in his critique of utilitarianism's construction of subjects – deciding *who* is a subject or what constitutes it – instead of allowing for alterity and an unstable understanding of subjectivity. Derrida insists on privileging moments of "the incalculable and the undecidable" ("Eating" 108) to avoid the exclusions that come with hegemonic forms of subjecthood. Derrida gestures toward alterity as a space removed from calculation, "so as to remain *other*, a *singular* call to response or responsibility" (110–111). I suggest animals in *Hard Times* function as this unknown space and offer an animal politics that privileges alterity.

Hard Times charts a move from objectifying animals and working-class humans as facts and statistics to acknowledging interiority and alterity. This is exemplified in the meeting between Louisa, Stephen, and Rachel, where Louisa realizes the disconnect between her education and real life:

> For the first time in her life, Louisa had come into one of the dwellings of the Coketown Hands; for the first time in her life, she was face to face with anything like individuality in connexion with them. She knew of their existence by hundreds and by thousands. She knew what results in work a given number of them would produce, in a given space of time. She knew them in crowds passing to and from their nests, like ants or beetles. But she knew from her reading infinitely more of the ways of toiling insects than of these toiling men and women. (*Hard Times* 160)

Standing face to face with Rachel and Stephen, Louisa realizes human beings cannot be reduced to numbers or viewed only in relation to their social utility. Louisa's education, consisting of reason – "the only faculty to which education should be addressed" (25) – disabled her from conceptualizing working-class subjects as anything but a number, fact, or statistic. Indeed, Louisa's lack of education of the sort valued by Dickens is directly connected to animals, as if imagining animals was key to his preferred system of education and mode of conceptualizing marginalized subjects. Dickens informs us that

> No little Gradgrind had ever associated a cow in a field with that famous cow with the crumpled horn who tossed the dog who worried the cat who killed the rat who ate the malt, or with that yet more famous cow who swallowed Tom Thumb: it had never heard of those celebrities, and had only been introduced to a cow as a graminivorous ruminating quadruped with several stomachs. (16)

Dickens's alignment of fictional animals with the kind of education lacking in the Gradgrind household demonstrates that conceptualizing animals requires an imagination that cannot rely on reason and fact. Indeed, Dickens suggests literature is perhaps the most productive space for this to happen. Thus Louisa's revelation about members of the working class as individuals separate from the objectifying logic of governmentality is grounded in an ethic that necessitates stepping away from reason and into an imaginative space whereby animals and humans exist outside a utilitarian philosophy reducing subjects to facts, objects, and utility.

Dickens's valuation of imagination finds its most pronounced moral in Sleary's circus animals. The opposition between Bitzer's opening definition of the horse as a graminivorous quadruped and the dancing horse that prevents him from taking Tom back to Coketown contrasts Gradgrind's language of political economy with the reality of circus life. Yet the moral emerges most fully through Sleary's description of Jupe's dog Merrylegs. After explaining he knew Jupe was dead after Merrylegs returned, only to die soon after, and hearing Gradgrind emphasize Sissy's belief in her father's affection, Sleary explains that Sissy's love is like the "wayth of the dogth":

> "It theemth to prethent two thingth to a perthon, don't it, Thquire?" said Mr Sleary, musing as he looked down into the depths of his brandy and water: "one, that there ith a love in the world, not all Thelf-intereth after all, but thomething very different; t'other, that it hath a way of ith own of calculating or not calculating, whith thomehow or another ith at leatht ath hard to give a name to, ath the wayth of the dogth ith!" (292)

Animal alterity, Sleary suggests, defies calculation and offers an animal politics removed from utilitarian ideology. Aligning Merrylegs's alterity with the necessity of building relationships constructed outside of utilitarian discourses emphasizes Dickens's valuation of animal epistemologies. Although he suggests Merrylegs exemplifies selflessness, not unlike the valorized loyal dog, he most fully posits him as a subject unrestricted by human modes of constituting subjectivity; animals have an inner life outside of discourses constricting the human subject, even if one cannot articulate or define what this inner life looks like. As he does with the raven in the Happy Family, through Merrylegs Dickens critiques capitalism's self-interest, and by extension, the workings of representative government. Dickens privileges Merrylegs's canine epistemology as a space challenging the speciesist logic structuring Victorian society's social and political hierarchies. Merrylegs suggests animal alterity is removed from the strategies of governmentality that construct subjects in terms of facts, reason, and utility, concepts grounding the early Victorian liberal subject.

However, Dickens places his moral onto trained animals and ignores the disciplinary relationship between circus animals and the humans who train them. Although the framing of the novel values animals beyond fact and utility, Dickens sidesteps the problematics of valuing circus animals as radical political figures. Dickens promotes a recognition of animal alterity and rejects human pretensions to delineate animal subjectivity, but neglects to critique alterity's location in a trained animal whose existence is grounded in subjection. Yet he offers us a way to think about animal subjectivity and epistemology in the space of the novel: even if it remains confined to the non-material realm of fiction, Dickens suggests ways to conceptualize the incorporation of otherness into the political sphere that do not rely on capitalist logic. Whereas Merrylegs has political potential to challenge the animalizing, objectifying, and character-driven strategies of liberal governmentality even in his construction as a loyal dog, Bull's-eye from *Oliver Twist* will trouble forms of virtuous character perpetuated by governmentality, offering an even more radical animal politics.

Oliver Twist's Melodramatic Animal Character

Dickens's sentimental and melodramatic critique of the 1834 New Poor Law, *Oliver Twist*, aimed to gain sympathy for the poor who, through institutionalized pastorship, were subject to inhumane and animalizing conditions in the workhouse. For Elaine Hadley, Dickens's use of melodrama – "graphic depictions of gruesome incidents, scenes of physical danger and inflicted torture, plots premised on criminal behavior … an aura of atmospheric menace" (*Melodramatic* 78) – highlights the increasingly class-based social organization of Victorian England's market society and aids Dickens's critique of income inequality. Sally Ledger places *Oliver Twist* in the history of anti–Poor Law literature, which employed melodrama to show the dehumanizing effects of the law. She argues that Dickens

> borrows and builds on many other features of anti–Poor Law literature from the 1830s: he responds to and develops the figure of the beadle in the laughably self-important and venal Mr. Bumble; he emphasizes the effects of the New Poor Law on children in particular; he focuses on the destruction of the working-class family; he explores the role of the surrogate parents spawned by the new legislation; he emphasizes the causal link between poverty and crime; and he exploits to the full the capacity of melodrama and satire for both comic and radical expression. (92)

Dickens's engagement with melodrama and the New Poor Law is not unconnected to pastoral power, as the law epitomized institutionalized pastorship and the inefficacy of dispersed shepherds. As a strategy of governmentality, the law regulated a population of people who were viewed as lacking character and proper conduct. The conditions inside the workhouse encapsulated a biopolitics regulating every aspect of the poor's lives, from their diet to their ability to reproduce, which, as Douglas Jerrold suggested above, animalizes them. Although Dickens critiques many aspects of the New Poor Law, Lauren Goodlad argues the critique fails in its radicalness through "its contrary investment in essentializing virtuous character" (*Victorian Literature* 65). While the novel exposes the middle class's inability to cultivate working-class character, it still holds up the Maylies as exemplary of moral pastorship. Dickens cannot locate a way to cultivate working-class character, Goodlad suggests, nor can he show the middle class as able shepherds. Through its ending valuation of middle-class domesticity, the novel remains firmly embedded in pastoral power.

Yet I suggest *Oliver Twist* offers a radical animal politics that registers rebellious forms of character beyond the regulatory logic of pastoral power. For while Oliver's virtuous character is essentialized as a result of his upper-class genes, Bill Sikes's dog Bull's-eye refuses to remain constricted to essentialized notions of canine loyalty prized throughout the period and circulated as exemplary forms of moral character for liberal citizens to admire and replicate. Bull's-eye's lack of virtuous canine character suggests his conduct is unregulated by pastoral power. As a working-class animal, Bull's-eye refuses the faithful and loyal bourgeois animality Victorians desired in both animals and the working class. Reading *Oliver Twist* by way of its more radical animal politics offers alternate forms of freedom and character outside the pastoral power encouraged by liberal governmentality. For unlike Erskine's robins and the birds discussed around wild bird legislation, Bull's-eye has a freedom independent from human authority. Indeed, he defies authority, having more liberty and equality than most liberalized animals. Further, Bull's-eye's immersion in the melodramatic mode aligns him with a "politics of the people" that sought to disrupt social hierarchy. Following Patrick Joyce, Ledger explains that Dickens's notion of "the people" is defined against a ruling group, one whose "social vision" centered on "key terms such as 'democracy' and 'freedom' rather than class conflict" (4), and I suggest Bull's-eye, even though associated with the novel's criminal class, is an important part of the novel's engagement with freedom, character, and governance.

For although in the end Dickens props up Oliver's innate, virtuous character as a liberal ideal, Bull's-eye offers a non-traditional notion of character that, following Amanda Anderson, seeks to "push beyond traditional conceptions of character, especially of moral exemplarity" and "conceive of political forms appropriate to the current challenges" (*Bleak* 70). As discussed in the Introduction, animal characters in the realist novel are an important political form that revise liberal discourses and demonstrate the importance of engaging with alternative perspectives. Indeed, they illuminate what Pam Morris has identified as the Victorian novel's difficulty of mediating social inclusion and the "problematic of what is perceived as other and alien" (5). Reading Bull's-eye from the vantage of loyal dog discourse and liberal animal subjectivity underscores his political significance and alternative character. Through Bull's-eye, Dickens rejects pastoral power and conduct as an appropriate site for mediating liberal ideals of character, freedom, and governance. Indeed, he suggests one may be better off without a shepherd. Yet although Dickens removes himself from "sentimental radicalism" in his characterization of Bull's-eye, he cannot imagine a place for one who has been shepherdless.

At first glance animals seem fully inscribed in the novel's sentimental discourse. As Carolyn Williams and Nicola Brown note, animals are frequent tropes of Victorian sentimentality and melodrama, used to gain sympathy for women, children, the working class, and pets. Williams explains that like orphans, the poor, and even mutes, animals are "vulnerable and inarticulate figures" who "literalize the suffering of the disenfranchised" ("Melodrama" 202), whereas Brown insists that faithful animals are "the most obvious topoi of literary and visual sentimentality." Indeed, Dickens builds sympathy for Oliver by aligning him with abused animals, suggesting, like Jerrold, that the poor are treated as badly as London's working animals. This alignment reinforces Kreilkamp's claims that animal suffering cultivates middle-class sensibility. This use of animals is highlighted in an early scene taking place outside the workhouse, which introduces how to read animal subjectivity throughout the novel. For animals are not reduced to a symbolic, sentimental function, nor are they completely voiceless. When Mr. Limbkins sees Gamfield beat his donkey before asking to take on Oliver as an apprentice, he assumes that the treatment of poor orphans should be the same as that of working animals. Dickens moves, briefly, to the donkey's perspective:

> The donkey was in a state of profound abstraction, – wondering, probably, whether he was destined to be regaled with a cabbage-stalk or two, when he had disposed of the two sacks of soot with which the little cart was laden; so, without noticing the word of command, he jogged onwards.
> Mr. Gamfield growled a fierce imprecation on the donkey generally, but more particularly on his eyes; and, running after him, bestowed a blow on his head which would inevitably have beaten in any skull but a donkey's; then, catching hold of the bridle, he gave his jaw a sharp wrench, by way of gentle reminder that he was not his own master: and, having by these means turned him round, he gave him another blow on the head, just to stun him till he came back again; and, having done so, walked up to the gate to read the bill . . . .
> Having witnessed the little dispute between Mr. Gamfield and the donkey, he [Mr. Limbkins] smiled joyously when that person came up to read the bill, for he saw at once that Mr. Gamfield was just exactly the sort of master Oliver Twist wanted. (18–19)

This scene suggests that if Oliver goes with Gamfield, he will be treated like the abused donkey, a comparison emphasizing Oliver's "animal-like suffering and abjection" (Miller, "Dark" 29). Limbkins's move from witnessing the beating to viewing Gamfield as "exactly the sort of master Oliver Twist wanted" invites the reader to picture Oliver in the donkey's position, foreclosing the possibility of a sustained sympathetic engagement with the donkey. In this reading the donkey represents Oliver's possible future state resulting from the New Poor Law.

Yet there is another layer to the scene, making it much more radical: the context of anti-cruelty laws and the RSPCA's drive to educate London's working class. In theory the donkey is protected under the 1822 anti-cruelty law, yet it fails to give him adequate protection. Gamfield's melodramatic beating emphasizes both the extent of animal cruelty in London's streets and the failure of the anti-cruelty laws and the RSPCA's drives to reform both working and middle-class conduct. Limbkins's glee at witnessing the abuse shows that the anti-cruelty law – which in part relied on citizens to police and report such cruelty – did not cultivate the desire of all citizens to participate in its enforcement. Yet outside of pastoral power the donkey is removed from discourses that construct him as desiring human subjection. Indeed, the donkey's subjectivity complicates liberal constructions of animal subjectivity, and imagines him with a free subjectivity directed away from human sovereignty. While Dickens contrasts "profound abstraction" with the idea of being "regaled" with a cabbage-stalk to suggest the simplicity of the donkey's mind, it places readers in his subjectivity, making his beating more affecting. While the donkey's thoughts may be humorous and ironic, the melodramatic beating is not. Most importantly, the donkey desires food rather than subjection to humankind; he does not notice Gamfield's commands, suggesting he is not instinctively concerned with acknowledging human authority. Indeed, his mind is centered on food, not his master.[11] Although the donkey's subjectivity is constructed in relation to his master, as his desire for food is linked to Gamfield as a giver of food, the donkey's desire is displaced; instead of desiring to please Gamfield, he desires food. He even wants Gamfield to "regale" him, suggesting that in the donkey's fantasy there is a switch between subject and master. The donkey's

---

[11] Critics posit Oliver's asking for more food at the workhouse as a way to humanize him in an institution dehumanizing the poor. Ledger details this analysis and places the trope of consumption within the radical history of anti-poor law literature and a critique of political economy. Taken in this context, the donkey's fantasies about food can also be seen as a way to remove him from objectification and place him in the novel's critique of pastorship.

displacement of desire moves us into the melodramatic mode associated with radical politics, thus locating the novel's radical politics in animal character and forms of subjectivity unregulated by pastoral power. While the material conditions are unchanged – the donkey will most likely be subject to future beatings – his free subjectivity defies the social hierarchies regulated by governmentality.

Bull's-eye, however, more fully troubles constructions of animals that posit them as accepting human authority. His radical animal politics aligns with the donkey's and offers a subjectivity beyond governmentality's regulatory logic and the moral character it reinforced. Immersed in the melodramatic mode, Bull's-eye exudes qualities of the loyal dog only to move beyond them. For not only is he a mean dog, who "by a certain malicious licking of his lips seemed to be meditating an attack upon the legs of the first gentleman or lady he might encounter in the street when he went out" (100), but he is hardly characterized as a subject of sympathy.[12] Indeed, meditating attacks on gentlemen and ladies, he seems aware of class hierarchies and refuses to honor them. Through Bull's-eye's melodramatic responses to Sikes, Dickens imagines an animal outside of deference hierarchies and challenges constructions of animal subjectivity that privilege human superiority. However, he is unable to imagine a social space for this excessive subject to exist. Dickens thus shows both the possibility of agential and non-deferential subjects and the lack of location for them in Victorian society. If governmentality attempted to cultivate faithfulness and loyalty within working-class animals and humans, Bull's-eye refuses such massifying forms of individuation.

Dickens directly references loyal dog discourse through Bull's-eye's characterization and his death at the end of the novel. The image of the loyal dog was abundant in Victorian culture and used to gain sympathy for animals, a phenomenon epitomized by Edward Landseer's well-known dog paintings.[13] Victorians adored Landseer, especially his paintings representing dogs mourning over their master's graves, such as *Attachment* and *The Old Shepherd's Chief Mourner*, which gained credit for highlighting animal emotion and interiority. As Landseer's paintings emphasize, dogs were often viewed as more loyal than humans. Diana Donald notes that in Landseer's paintings "dogs appeared as saints and heroes, their virtues

---

[12] Chez, however, argues that Bull's-eye helps to elicit sympathy for Sikes and Nancy (51).
[13] Dickens loved Landseer's paintings, and the two were friends. In 1863 Percy Fitzgerald labeled Dickens "the Landseer of Fiction," emphasizing the extent to which Dickens was perceived as invested in representing a sympathetic canine interiority.

equaling or excelling those of the human race" (132), and Kathleen Kete similarly explains that "people owned dogs ... because dogs were faithful and people were not" (*Beast* 24). Kreilkamp describes how "British newspapers and periodicals were in the 1840s and 1850s filled with anecdotes and vignettes about loyal and brave dogs; indeed, to be confined to the sphere of the anecdote would seem to define the Victorian dog's ambiguous position" ("Dying" 83). This tendency continued throughout the period, especially in the RSPCA's journal *Animal World*. The popularity of loyal dogs reinforces my argument that Victorians gave animals liberalized qualities only to the extent that they flattered human superiority. Dickens, however, posits Bull's-eye outside of the loyal-dog anecdote constructed through pastoral power. This gives Bull's-eye more agency and exposes the desire for pastoral power as negative, hierarchical, and even at times grotesque. Dickens exposes it as an abuse of power that reinforces exploitative social practices.

Anecdotes that posit canine loyalty through suicide were highly popular throughout the Victorian era. For example, William Drummond's *The Rights of Animals* describes a dog who commits suicide after his master kicks him. Drummond cites an article that explains:

> "Mr. Burnell Ward, druggist of English-street, in this town, had a favourite little dog, and a few days since, for some infringement of good breeding of which it had been guilty, gave the animal a slight kick. The dog being unaccustomed to receive such treatment from its master, it is to be presumed took the punishment to heart, for it immediately trotted off to the foreshore of the Humber ... to walk into the water with great deliberation, and drown itself. We confess we were at first somewhat incredulous as to the correctness of this story, but on inquiry we have found it to be strictly true." (92)

Such anecdotes hyperbolize liberal qualities while suggesting dogs have no place without a human master. John Styles similarly articulates a story of a dog preferring to die with his master when he writes, "Was no respect due to the Hyrcanian dog, who, when he saw his master's corpse burning on the funeral pile, jumped into the flames and was consumed with it?" (146). This represents a deadly master–servant relationship, while its reference to suttee suggests no social space for a dog without a master.[14] Anecdotes of loyal

---

[14] In her discussion of suttee in "Can the Subaltern Speak?" Gayatri Spivak famously argues that "white men, seeking to save brown women from brown men, impose upon those women a greater ideological constriction by absolutely identifying, *within discursive practice*, good wifehood with self-immolation on the husband's pyre" (101). Loyal dogs were constructed within a similar constrictive ideological discourse, where speciesism follows a similar hierarchical logic of racism and sexism.

dogs thus represent an idealized love and faithfulness connected to their lack of independent inclusion in the social sphere. The dogs are subject to representations of loyalty and thus the conduct of pastoral power; Bull's-eye, however, exposes the constructed nature of such subjectivity.

When placed in this context, Bull's-eye's melodramatic suicide questions human desires for canine loyalty, as Dickens shows that what looks like a suicide was in fact an accident. After Sikes accidentally hangs himself from a rooftop, "A dog, which had lain concealed till now, ran backwards and forwards on the parapet with a dismal howl, and collecting himself for a spring, jumped for the dead man's shoulders. Missing his aim, he fell into the ditch, turning completely over as he went, and striking his head against a stone, dashed out his brains" (428). Instead of illustrating Bull's-eye as a loyal dog who kills himself with his master, Dickens makes Bull's-eye's death a gruesome accident. When Bull's-eye jumps for Sikes's shoulders, he shows the impulse of the loyal dog; his "dismal howl" emphasizes his distress at seeing Sikes in danger. Dickens satisfies expectations for the loyal dog, but takes it one step further; for not only is Bull's-eye's death an accident, but the graphic description of his death – "striking his head against a stone," he "dashed out his brains" – is repulsive rather than sentimental. Indeed, it works in contrast to Landseer's paintings, showing the more disturbing aspects of dogs who stay by or die with their dead humans. Dickens gives Bull's-eye the stereotypical inclination to jump, but extends the action to show a gruesome result of the loyal impulse, challenging Victorian desires for extreme forms of animal loyalty. Indeed, his death is made more significant coming after Sikes's attempt to kill him after he leaves London. Although Bull's-eye dies at the end of the novel, he has the ability to die accidentally, rather than by Sikes's hand, suggesting dogs may not always let their life be determined by humans. Dickens refuses to confine Bull's-eye to the sphere of the sentimental dog, instead destabilizing Victorian impulses to project onto animals narratives of faithfulness. Rather, the Victorian desire for loyal dogs – and thus for pastoral power – is grotesque. While generally Dickens does not offer significant material changes, with Bull's-eye's dramatic and melodramatic death Dickens shows the physical effects of too much pastoral power grounded in speciesist logic. Bull's-eye's accidental death makes him radical, if not a bit clumsy, as it locates him beyond pastoral power. Bull's-eye dies not by virtue of his essentialized loyalty, but by an unfortunate accident caused by his agency.

Thus although Oliver may have an essentialized virtuous character, and little agency throughout the novel, Bull's-eye has a freedom unavailable to the novel's exemplary human protagonist. As Jennifer McDonnell argues, Bull's-eye is "invested with a form of social agency – albeit in uneven and unstable alliance with humans – which, significantly, is denied to the putative hero of the novel, Oliver, to whom things simply seem to happen without his ever having to make them happen" (113). In the same way that dogs had to commit suicide to emphasize their loyalty, Oliver must relinquish his agency to social forces beyond his control to highlight his good character. By refusing pastoral power, Bull's-eye has a freedom of choice denied to Oliver. To be sure, on one level Bull's-eye's often violent agency exposes him as a "criminal animal" onto whom "Dickens offloads undesirable traits" from Bill and Nancy (G. Moore 201). Pointing toward moments where Bull's-eye is characterized as just as mean as Sikes, Grace Moore suggests that Bull's-eye shows how criminality can corrupt even animals (207). Yet when analyzed through the lens of pastoral power, Bull's-eye presents a radical agency departing from deferential constructions. At one moment Sikes curses and kicks Bull's-eye after yelling at him to "keep quiet":

> Dogs are not generally apt to revenge injuries inflicted upon them by their masters; but Mr Sikes's dog, having faults of temper in common with his owner, and labouring perhaps, at this moment, under a powerful sense of injury, made no more ado but at once fixed his teeth in one of the half-boots, and, having given it a good hearty shake, retired, growling, under a form: thereby just escaping the pewter measure which Mr Sikes levelled at his head.
> "You would, would you?" said Sikes, seizing the poker in one hand, and deliberately opening with the other a large clasp-knife, which he drew from his pocket. "Come here, you born devil! Come here! D'ye hear?"
> The dog no doubt heard ... but, appearing to entertain some unaccountable objection to having his throat cut, he remained where he was, and growled more fiercely than before, at the same time grasping the end of the poker between his teeth, and biting at it like a wild beast. (117)

This scene posits Bull's-eye with agency far beyond virtue and loyalty. For not only does Bull's-eye refuse to come when Sikes calls him, but he acts as Sikes's equal. Indeed, the dog's resistance only further infuriates Sikes, and the two begin a violent fighting match: "The dog jumped from right to left, and from left to right, snapping, growling, and barking; the man thrust and swore, and struck and blasphemed ... the struggle was reaching a most critical point for one or other" (117). Bull's-eye fights back instead of sulking, and exhibits power by returning the violent behavior Sikes bestows on him. The similarity of their tempers does not make Bull's-eye a mirror image of Sikes, but posits him outside of a hierarchy where agency is directed toward obeying authority.

Given the animalizing nature of governmentality's relationship with the working class, whether through attempts to cultivate a loyalty to hierarchical structures or through the dehumanizing nature of capitalism, one cannot help but read Bull's-eye as a working-class figure. However, this should not be exclusive of his status as an animal subject with thoughts, feelings, and desires. As we have seen, the changing nature of Victorian society's relationship with animals alongside the intensification of governmentality increasingly focused on character and interiority. Through the donkey and Bull's-eye, Dickens offers alternate forms of subjectivity that suggest new ways of imagining freedom and liberty in an era obsessed simultaneously with social inclusion and exclusion. Dickens locates within animal subjectivity a rejection of state-influenced moral character, which conducted animals and humans toward accepting subjection; outside of pastoral power subjects have the ability to conduct themselves with more freedom. If, as Carolyn Williams explains, "the hyper-expressionistic valence of melodrama actually serves to highlight the *difficulties* of expression in the modern world" ("Melodrama" 203), the melodramatic animals in *Oliver Twist* demonstrate Dickens's difficulty in expressing animal subjectivity in a society where the political status of animals was rapidly changing. For although Bull's-eye operates beyond deference hierarchies and rejects the position of subjection to humankind, he has no place outside of criminal culture. He is an excessive subject excluded from a society structured by pastoral power. Bull's-eye demonstrates an attempt to move toward a more horizontal organization of society that includes animal subjects, and shows how alternate forms of character can challenge hierarchical structures. Yet, like the donkey who receives a beating for fantasizing instead of focusing on his master's commands, Bull's-eye is disciplined for his excessive subjectivity.

Bull's-eye thus demonstrates Dickens's conflicting views of pastorship as they extend to animal subjects. Goodlad reads Dickens's contradictory stance toward pastorship through his "inability to stabilize a prescriptive notion of character – to uphold the moral improvability of each and every individual and to instate reliable pastorship of some kind as the means to achieving that end" (*Victorian Literature* 64), and claims that "Dickens clouds the question of agency so crucial to his contemporaries. The individual of *Oliver Twist* is alternately a morally autonomous and self-directing force, and the powerless pawn of larger forces" (68). Bull's-eye shows that freedom and agency come from beyond the conducting hand of pastoral power that seeks hegemonic forms of moral character. Indeed, given his removal from middle-class domesticity, Bull's-eye's freedom emerges from a lack of shepherds, and ultimately suggests that character, when cultivated by a higher class, results in alternate forms of subjection. Even when one is imagined as "autonomous and self-directing" within structures of pastoral power, this freedom is based on social hierarchy; for a speciesist logic shapes liberal governmentality. Dickens posits a radical animal subjectivity and alternate forms of relating outside the caring hand of pastoral power. Through Bull's-eye, Dickens satirizes pastoral power's loyal dog, yet on a material level, institutionalized pastorship and attempts to get outside of it fail. Because he cannot imagine an alternative social space for the fantasizing donkey and Bull's-eye, he disciplines them, with one receiving a beating, and the other dashing out his brains. *Barnaby Rudge*'s raven Grip, however, represents an animal more connected to alternative character within representative democracy, and suggests the need for heterogeneous subject positions within a democratic field.

Animal Democracy and Alterity in *Barnaby Rudge*

Although written much later, Dickens's critique of Austin's "Happy Family" helps us read the significance of another political raven, Grip from *Barnaby Rudge*. Although George Gissing praised Dickens's "eye for points of character in bird and beast as in human beings" (182), and laments that "The raven deserved a better companion" than Barnaby (182), Grip is often read as a symbol of the novel's violence.[15] Yet Grip was a well-planned addition to the novel: inspired by his two pet ravens of the same name, Dickens told friend and biographer John Forster that "Grip will be strong" (*Letters* 2:219), and quizzed illustrator George Cattermole on "whether you *feel* Ravens in general, and would fancy Barnaby's raven in particular. Barnaby being an idiot my notion is to have him always in company with a pet raven who is immeasurably more knowing than himself. To this end, I have been studying my bird, and think I could make a very queer character of him" (*Letters* 2:197–198).[16]

---

[15] Jerome Buckley gives the most critical attention to Grip, acknowledging his speech "seems more ironic than nefarious" (27).

[16] Dickens's letters detail his relationship with his pet ravens, his most famous being the melodramatic rendering of Grip's death. See his March 12, 1841, letter to artist Daniel Maclise (*Letters* 2: 230–231). Grip was also recognized as a member of the family, as suggested by an 1842 sketch of his four children that includes Grip. See J. Cohen, *Charles Dickens and His Original Illustrators*, chapter 10, "Daniel Maclise."

Eight years after the publication of *Barnaby* in novel form, Dickens revised his original preface by adding a discussion of Grip, informing readers, "The raven in this story is a compound of two great originals, of whom I have been, at different times, the proud possessor" (5). Inspired by naturalist Charles Waterton's "opinion that ravens are gradually becoming extinct in England" (5), Dickens, like Waterton, challenges dominant notions of raven character. In *Essays on Natural History, Chiefly Ornithology* (1838), Waterton explains that he aimed "to do away with the many accusations which ignorance and prejudice have brought forward to injure the character of our feathered tribes" (viii). He argues some birds are "considered by the lower orders as agents, somehow or other, connected with witches, or with wisemen ... who know of things lost, and of deeds done in the dark" (vi). In his essay on ravens, he writes,

> Necromancers of old were noted for their attention to the movements of the raven ... His sable robe and hollow croaking seem to have rendered him of vast importance in those days; when old women were known to travel through the air on broom-staffs, and when the destiny of man was frequently foretold by the flight of birds. Nay, in our own times, the raven has not quite lost all claim to the knowledge of things to come. (271)

Admitting that in the nineteenth century ravens are still associated with necromancy and prophecy, Waterton aims to give a more positive version of raven character. Although Dickens aligns himself with Waterton's goals, Grip has more in common with the raven from the Happy Family.[17] For Waterton's raven embodies liberal moral character: he is "so docile, so clever, and so amusing," with a "noble aspect," and "can scarcely be styled a bird of rapine ... for, in the few inland parts of this country where he is still protected, we hear of no very alarming acts of depredation on his part" (269, 274). Yet through destabilizing the cultural and literary classifications of raven identity, Grip demonstrates the limitations of a structure whereby humans construct knowledge about animal character.[18] Grip illuminates Dickens's animal politics, which are intimately connected to

---

[17] Ackroyd notes that in Dickens's copy of Waterton's book the chapter on ravens had pencil marks (325).
[18] One can also read Dickens's revised preface as a response to Edgar Allan Poe's criticisms of Grip in his 1842 review of *Barnaby* in *Graham's Magazine*. While Grip was the inspiration for Poe's poem "The Raven" (1845), Poe lamented that Grip was not used more "prophetically" in the novel. "The Raven, too," he writes, "intensely amusing as it is, might have been made, more than we now see it, a portion of the conception of the fantastic Barnaby. Its croakings might have been *prophetically* heard in the course of the drama" (129). Poe marks the first in a long line of critics who view Grip in relation to his cultural identity as related to prophecy and evil omens.

his larger critique of regulatory character, negative forms of animality created by liberal governmentality, and a destabilization of the link between property and character at the core of liberal democratic thought.

Barnaby Rudge is set in London before and during the Gordon Riots of 1780, a week-long series of deadly riots incited by the Protestant Association, which protested political and civil liberties for Catholics. The novel is not without relevance to its own political context of the Chartist movement, during which a large portion of the working class demanded universal male suffrage, proof of ballot, abolition of property qualifications for MPs, payment of MPs, and equal electoral districts. Much has been written on tensions within the novel and Dickens's politics regarding Chartism and democracy. Given his fear of mob violence, Dickens could never fully support the Chartist movement beyond the role of a "concerned spectator" (Ackroyd 326). As Ackroyd and Ledger emphasize, Dickens saw certain factions of the Chartist movement as heading for violent civil disobedience. He was also upset by the Chartist's alignment with the Tories and their win in the 1841 election.[19] Even though the novel critiques the corrupt aristocratic authority Dickens associated with the Tories, critics often read the novel as conservative, as it shows the terrifying results of widespread violence perpetrated by the working class.[20] Dickens, critics suggest, was wary of the Chartists' ability to govern themselves and play a role in the political process. Yet even though critics cannot locate much sympathy for the working class and their desire for political participation within the novel, *Barnaby Rudge* explores major themes of nineteenth-century liberal thought – tolerance, liberty, and democracy – and shows how far society must come to achieve them. In this sense *Barnaby Rudge* encapsulates what Amanda Anderson calls bleak liberalism, one with "an acute awareness of the challenges and often bleak prospects confronting it" (1).

A lack of sympathy for the working class is often located in the animality of characters such as Hugh, and the rioters. Certainly, critics have suggested that Hugh's animality is a result of social injustice (B. Stuart 29), and "living

---

[19] See Thomas Rice, "The Politics of *Barnaby Rudge*."
[20] Stephen Marcus emphasizes that Dickens's vivid illustrations of the mob in the second half of the novel "accentuated the similarities between the disturbances of 1780 and what he conceived to be the dangerous circumstances of his own time" (175), while John Butt and Kathleen Tillotson argue that "the events of 1836–41 made the novel almost journalistically apt" (82). See also Peter Scheckner, "Chartism, Class, and Social Struggle: A Study of Charles Dickens," and Scott Dransfield, "Reading the Gordon Riots in 1841: Social Violence and Moral Management in *Barnaby Rudge*."

evidence of a sociopathic condition arising directly out of fractured domesticity and harsh authoritarianism" (Dransfield 79). The novel highlights how human animality results from larger social forces; the novel's rioters, incited by Lord George Gordon, are devoid of any commitment to anti-Catholicism, manipulated instead by Gordon's religious intolerance. Dickens's depiction of animality emphasizes that institutions and social structures perpetuating governmentality – such as the legal system, the church, and class hierarchies – have or perpetuate bad character and create negative character in the population. Indeed, Dickens calls "things of state ... cold and comfortless" (*Barnaby* 284), suggesting little confidence in the state to ameliorate working-class conditions. Through the novel's representation of Dennis the Hangman, for example, Dickens critiques a constitution that legalizes state murder, and admits the mob was "composed for the most part of the very scum and refuse of London, whose growth was fostered by bad criminal laws, bad prison regulations, and the worst conceivable police" (393). Here, the state functions as a bad shepherd who cannot properly conduct its citizens. As such, the novel claims that governmentality cultivates animality within the population it regulates: not only is animality found in the rioters' violence, but the loyalty they show to corrupt aristocrats such as Chester and Gordon typifies a bourgeois animality cultivated by liberalism – one readers are not supposed to support. In this sense animality functions as a negative form of character limiting the ability for political participation. This is not removed from Chartism, as Chartists were animalized by members of parliament, social commentators like Thomas Carlyle, and liberals such as Elizabeth Gaskell and Charles Kingsley (Thompson, *Chartists* 248–250).

Yet through Grip's animal politics, Dickens posits alterity as a way to reject such homogenizing forms of character, as Grip's alterity is a site of resistance to the regulatory effects of state institutions *and* animal welfare. This animal politics demonstrates how understanding animals as subjects with alterity rather than as objects of property destabilizes hierarchical orderings of Victorian society, and reveals how widespread fears over Chartist riots were a result of misrepresentations of the working class *and* the creation of animal-like conditions by forces of governmentality. Grip's characterization further suggests that rejecting the constraints of property opens up subjectivity, destabilizes the link between property and political representation, and registers forms of subjectivity removed from the state. As a minor character, Grip is included in demands for democracy, and makes possible animal subjects existing outside of property, subjection, and pastoral power. Grip encapsulates what Nancy Armstrong describes as "an interiority in excess of the social position that individual is supposed to occupy" (*Novels* 8), and exposes a lack of liberal tolerance for alterity in the public sphere. Grip suggests that Victorian liberal democracy demands conformity through cultivating an individualism based on social and species hierarchies. As a solution, Grip suggests an end to the conducting of the working class by the upper class, and privileges alterity over a homogenized notion of character.

Grip's role as a minor character is thus dual: to refigure animal and working-class character and to expose the political forces that create negative forms of animality prohibiting political participation. For Carolyn Williams, Grip and Barnaby show the working class's lack of historical agency ("Stupidity"), yet Grip also works politically on his own to highlight the constructed nature of animality in relationship to liberal democracy. Grip enters into the political horizons of the novel to show the limitations of representative democracy: not only should the people should speak for themselves without influence from a self-interested political system, but democracy itself requires multiple subject positions beyond liberal bourgeois character.

Throughout the novel, middle- and upper-class characters see Grip as symbolic of the novel's murder mystery and violence, as they associate ravens with necromancy and bad character. Discovering that Mrs. Rudge has contact with a suspicious character, who later turns out to be Mr. Rudge (long believed to be dead), the novel's upstanding middle-class character Gabriel Varden exclaims, "What dark history is this!" as we meet Grip for the first time. Grip exclaims, "Halloa, Halloa, Halloa! Bow wow wow. What's the matter here! Hal-loa!" causing Varden to cry, "'Look at him!" as he is "divided between admiration of the bird and a kind of fear of him. 'Was there ever such a knowing imp as that! Oh he's a dreadful fellow!'" Grip responds, "'Halloa, halloa, halloa! What's the matter here! Keep up your spirits. Never say die. Bow wow wow. I'm a devil, I'm a devil, I'm a devil. Hurrah!' – And then, as if exulting in his infernal character, he began to whistle" (61). Numerous tensions confuse Grip's characterization and his role in the novel. His entrance into the plot, the way characters read him, and his own exclamations of "I'm a devil!" associate him with the novel's gothic elements. Varden's claim a few pages later that "If there's any wickedness going on, that raven's in it, I'll be sworn" (64) reinforces the symbolic classification of Grip as a literary device more so than a minor character.

Yet another layer to Grip undercuts these characterizations, destabilizing human abilities to read raven character. Grip is characterized as neutral when he listens to Edward and Varden "with a polite attention and a most extraordinary appearance of comprehending every word ... as if his office were to judge between them" (61). Indeed, Grip's word choice plays with desires to read him as a "dreadful fellow." While critics generally focus on his exclamation of "I'm a devil!" he also barks, encourages others to "keep up your spirits," and suggests, "Polly put the ket-tle on, we'll all have tea" (148). Grip's repertoire of disparate phrases and whistling demonstrates he does not have a stable character; he troubles human desires to read him according to historical and cultural classifications. For while the novel's middle- and upper-class characters read him as ominous, Grip voices the opposite in word and action, challenging their authority and ability to read animal subjectivity. Grip functions within a "tension between the authenticity of a character in-and-of-himself and the reduction of the character into the thematic or symbolic field" (Woloch 15), as he becomes a character in his own right through undercutting desires to render him symbolic. Middle- and upper-class authority fails at reading animal subjectivity, thus positioning Grip within a field of alterity. Grip is viewed as having poor character, but this is a misreading. We do not know what his true character looks like, but he never contributes to the novel's violence. In fact, his most meaningful action in the plot is uncovering goods stolen during the riots (460). And while his speech may be a result of Barnaby's training, Grip decides what to say and when.

Grip's revisions of popular discourses of Victorian pet-keeping and property remove his animal politics from liberal animal character. Although Harriet Ritvo characterizes the literature of pet-keeping as one "of love rather than one of domination," she notes it represented "the conquest of external nature" ("Emergence" 22). Yet as Monica Flegel argues, even though Victorian pets reaffirmed hegemonic notions of "proper affection, stewardship, conspicuous consumption, and domesticity," they also "stretch our narratives of family and domesticity in ways that acknowledge alternate sexualities, power structures, and ways of understanding time" (*Pets* 6). Grip and Barnaby, I suggest, revise narratives of pet-keeping inscribed within pastoral power, where love and domination work together in ways that are not mutually exclusive. As we have seen, domestic animals were most often constructed as desiring submission to the human, and thus with moral character; yet when Varden asks Barnaby to call Grip, Barnaby replies, "Call him ... But who can make him come! He calls me, and makes me go where he will. He goes on before, and I follow. He's the master, and I'm the man. Is that the truth, Grip?" (62). Grip is only once referred to as Barnaby's pet, in prison nonetheless (465), and is more often described as his companion (378) or friend and brother (456). As Donna Haraway explains, the term "companion" invokes comradeship and implies interdependence between species, emphasizing equality and co-constitution. For "There cannot be just one companion species; there have to be at least two to make one" (*Companion* 12). Further, Barnaby characterizes their relationship as one of co-cultivation, for although Barnaby gives Grip an education, Grip functions as a father figure: "'He takes such care of me besides!' said Barnaby. 'Such care, mother! He watches all the time I sleep, and when I shut my eyes, and make-believe to slumber, he practices new learning softly; but he keeps his eye on me the while, and if he sees me laugh, though never so little, stops directly. He won't surprise me till he's perfect'" (*Barnaby* 143). Such characterizations remove Grip from pastoral power, especially in terms of care, protection, and education, and offer new forms of social organization involving animals that veer from the hierarchy established by liberal discourse. Not only does Grip care for Barnaby instead of the other way around, but the kind of education Barnaby gives Grip is one that destabilizes hierarchy, as it not only gives Grip the ability to speak – long thought to be a human-only quality – but challenges attempts to inscribe him into homogenous forms of liberal character.

Importantly, Grip's removal from constraints of property severs ties between property, character, and political representation. If proprietorship over oneself was a sign of individualism and good character, and having property gave you political representation, being a human's property – and submitting to that role – was a sign of animal character that deserved political representation. Yet, although Grip helps the Rudges earn a living, he is not reduced to a circus animal like Merrylegs, nor is he a commodity:

> Grip was by no means an idle or unprofitable member of the humble household. Partly by dint of Barnaby's tuition, and partly by pursuing a species of self-instruction common to his tribe, and exerting his powers of observation to the utmost, he had acquired a degree of sagacity which rendered him famous for miles round. His conversational powers and surprising performances were the universal theme: and as many persons came to see the wonderful raven, and none left his exertions unrewarded – when he condescended to exhibit, which was not always, for genius is capricious – his earnings formed an important item in the common stock ... though he was perfectly free and unrestrained in the presence of Barnaby and his mother, he maintained in public an amazing gravity. (359–360)

This passage posits Grip as an agent rather than a trained animal; indeed, his performance is not a result of Barnaby's "tuition," but rather his "sagacity" and "self-instruction." Grip is in command of his performances, as they are "surprising," and he does "not always" choose to exhibit them.

In a similar moment when Barnaby and his mother leave the country for London, they stop at the house of an obnoxious and self-indulgent Justice of the Peace to show Grip for money. Grip draws "fifty corks at least, and then began to dance; at the same time eyeing the gentleman with surprising insolence of manner," yet decides for himself when the performance is over (374). The gentleman "desired to have that [cork-drawing] done again, but despite his being very peremptory, and notwithstanding that Barnaby coaxed to the utmost, Grip turned a deaf ear to the request, and preserved a dead silence" (375). Grip's autonomy is especially significant in his characterization as a member of the family. The justice asks how much Grip costs, and "Barnaby looked as though he didn't understand his meaning," and Mrs. Rudge exclaims, "He is my son's constant companion ... He is not to be sold, sir, indeed" (378). This corrupt justice is shocked that a poor family would refuse to sell Grip – "These people who go tramping about the country, a pilfering and vagabondizing on all hands, prefer to keep a bird, when a landed proprietor and a justice asks his price!" (378) – yet he is a companion and member of the family, not property. Indeed, the fact that Dickens points out that this gentleman is a representative of the state underscores the ruling class's inability to conceptualize animals outside of property, aligning him with the other middle- and upper-class characters who misread Grip. Most importantly, Grip's "surprising insolence of manner" (374) and refusal to obey the justice, combined with his figuration as more-than-property, suggests an alternate link between animal character and property: Grip becomes a possessive individual and is thus liberalized, but refuses to obey the social hierarchy associated with moral animal character.[21]

The novel's positioning of Grip between symbol and unreadable subject, pet and companion, property and family member destabilizes the pastoral power that constructs animals as subject to humankind. Grip even confuses Barnaby at times, who tells Lord Gordon, "you had good reason to ask me what he is, for sometimes it puzzles me – and I am used to him – to think he's only a bird" (456). The representation of Grip with alterity posits him as an epistemological subject while destabilizing human power to know and delineate animal subjectivity. As such he refuses the double

---

[21] C. B. Macpherson defines possessive individualism as "essentially the proprietor of his own person or capacities, owing nothing to society for them ... The individual, it was thought, is free inasmuch as he is proprietor of his person and capacities" (3).

forms of subjection Foucault posits as the definition of the subject; Grip rejects subjection to cultural assumptions about ravens and pets, and refuses the subjectivity imposed on domestic animals by governmentality. Grip's alterity presents alternate forms of individuation and highlights the constructed nature of animality more generally. He offers an alternate way to conceptualize relations between animality and violence; for like Grip, the riots and the rioters are consistently referred to as evil. Yet again like Grip, this is a result of poor governmentality rather than an innate animality wired for violent impulses.

Thus, as the novel's figure of animality and alterity, Grip is politicized through his subjection to the state. Placed alongside Barnaby in jail, and read by the jail keeper as a political actor (465), Grip is silenced. He loses his voice, demonstrating a subjection vastly different from his profuse utterings in the novel's first half. Grip's "drooping" head and "rough and rumpled" plumage represent his subjection to state power, and his silence suggests it takes away the voice of animals (468). Barnaby says to his mother, "Who cares for Grip, excepting you and me? ... He never speaks in this place; he never says a word in jail; he sits and mopes all day in this dark corner, dozing sometimes, and sometimes looking at the light that creeps in through the bars ... But who cares for Grip?" (583). Here the state prevents Grip's earlier excessive subjectivity from emerging, as his enclosure in a prison cell results in silence. The bad governmentality Dickens referred to earlier here serves as a poor shepherd for animals as well. Literally entrapped by the walls of the state, Grip's subjectivity is morphed from one that resists classification and a reduced subjectivity, to a subjected state where his agency is prohibited. Indeed, after his release from prison, Grip is "profoundly silent" (660), highlighting the trauma inflicted by the state.

We see a revival of Grip's voice only at the end of the novel, where he is safe inside the domestic sphere. Thus although *Barnaby Rudge* offers multiple subject positions and figures of alterity available for toleration – the working class, the mentally disabled, animals, and Catholics – it still contains alterity and animality in the domestic sphere. Grip and Barnaby have both undergone trauma in the public sphere: Grip loses his voice for a full year, while Barnaby "never could be tempted into London" (660). Through this Dickens suggests there is little space for alterity in the public sphere of political participation and representation; Grip and Barnaby entered into it only to show liberalism's limits when it comes to tolerance and equality. Poor governance results in misrepresentations and misreadings. Liberal claims toward equality, tolerance, and freedom fail alterity and otherness. Barnaby's "love of freedom" (660) has no place in the public sphere.

The alignment of Grip with the rioters highlights the animal politics behind Dickens's representation of the working class and the riots with which the working class is connected, and thus of the Chartists more broadly. As discussed earlier, Chartists and their crowds were often associated with animality and a lack of articulate speech. Thomas Carlyle, for example, calls the five points of the People's Charter "Bellowings, *in*articulate cries as of a dumb creature in rage and pain; to the ear of wisdom they are inarticulate prayers: 'Guide me, govern me! I am mad and miserable, and cannot guide myself'" (42), and describes the working class as "Wild inarticulate souls, struggling there, with inarticulate uproar, like dumb creatures in pain, unable to speak what is in them!" (9). On the other hand, the Chartists saw their crowds as a form of political representation (Plotz 128). The anti-liberal propensities of those with political power, such as Lord George Gordon, cultivate the intolerance that leads to violence, not those with genuine political grievances. By dictating to citizens what they should want or need, instead of reforming government so the marginalized can voice their own desires, democracy will indeed be a nightmare. By acknowledging and cultivating multiple subject positions a democratic society can, ideally, contain its own differences. Until subjects can represent themselves, democracy is impossible. Indeed, the novel's crowd is violent because it is anti-liberal: it results not just from Gordon's bad shepherding, but more appropriately from his intolerance and the inequality perpetuated by bad government.

Given liberalism's reliance on character in debates regarding the working class and democracy, the novel's alternative subjectivities, especially Grip's and Barnaby's, offer the multiple subject positions Chantal Mouffe posits as necessary to democracy. Elaine Hadley's description of someone with liberal character as "a self-possessed individual, literally a subject who possesses its self . . . presumed self-coherent, rational, reasonable, honest, full of integrity, incapable of saying one thing and doing another" ("Past" 12), delineates a regulatory character that rejects alterity and alternative subjectivities. Critiquing individualism's prominence in liberal political theory today, Mouffe asks, "How can we grasp the multiplicity of relations of subordination that can affect an individual if we envisage social agents as homogeneous and unified entities?" (12). She continues to argue that "Some of the key concepts of liberalism, such as rights, liberty and citizenship, are claimed today by the discourse of possessive individualism, which stands in the way of the establishment of a chain of democratic equivalences" (19). Alternative subjectivities such as Barnaby's and Grip's are valued in the novel precisely for their distance from liberal individualism's animalizing discourse. Yet by the end of the novel both are devoid of any significant political power outside of their function as characters in a novel. Alterity, whether in the form of animality, class, or religion, needs incorporation into the democratic sphere, for hegemonic notions of character disrupt liberalism's drive for equality and social inclusion. Dickens suggests the government cannot represent the people by virtue of cultivating character; alternate subjectivities are needed.

Grip's inclusion as a minor character thus synthesizes the novel's engagement with class, animality, and democracy. *Barnaby Rudge* demonstrates that governmentality cultivates forms of character that prohibit political participation. While the reduction of animals to a symbol erases their subjectivity and homogenizes their character, the animalization of working-class unrest and drives for political power expose the speciesism of governmentality. Hugh, the Maypole stable-boy, highlights this animalizing work of the state. Because his mother was hung for stealing food when he was young, he was forced to work and congregate with animals. Hugh's boss and owner of the Maypole Inn, John Willet, reduces Hugh to an animal, explaining that he "'has never had much to do with anything but animals, and has never lived in any way but like the animals he has lived among, *is* an animal. And ... is to be treated accordingly'" (*Barnaby* 99). The relationship between violence and animality is, however, figured as a result of poor governance. Indeed, Hugh's father John Chester, the most corrupt aristocratic figure in the novel, cultivates Hugh's violent behavior and creates in him a surprising submission. This grotesque populism can be linked back to Grip, who demonstrates how poor governance by the middle and upper class results in misreadings and misrepresentations.

When placed in the context of the Chartist movement and the novel's engagement with governmentality, rather than the ominous symbol critics and the novel's characters understand him as, Grip reveals how Dickens envisioned animals in the political sphere and highlights the social and political hierarchies that prohibit democratic equality and fair representation. For Dickens, animals will always be constrained by the speciesism of governmentality. Grip exemplifies the limitations of political forces regulating conduct, and shows that negative characteristics of animalized subjects are a result of poor governance, rather than an innate part of character. Dickens demonstrates how desires to project onto animals certain qualities or characteristics homogenizes their subjectivity and reproduces a social stratification that includes animals and animalized working-class humans. As Woloch explains, nineteenth-century demands for democracy included a visibility that became part of the realist novel's aesthetic. In *Barnaby Rudge*, a "distorted visibility," where "human beings themselves emerge only partially, substantializing the way that subordinate characters, in their intrinsically submerged narrative position, are half-visible," reproduces the subjection of the novel's working-class characters by state power (Woloch 149, 151). In characters such as Hugh, we can only see the animality resulting from his subordination to the state. Grip also registers a tension between being seen and being "half-visible," particularity in the alterity he asserts throughout the novel. The "distortion" resulting from this tension is, according to Woloch, "a consequence of minorness. In the same way, social stratification – along with the division of labor that underlies and is produced by social inequality – is already deeply entrenched" (156). Thus Grip's role as a minor character illuminates how animals and excessive forms of subjectivity were tamed within the political sphere.

Although critics read Dickens as reinforcing bourgeois liberal ideology, and view *Barnaby Rudge* as expressing fears of mob violence, the novel's politics aligns with the Chartist movement's critique of middle-class shepherding.[22] Geoff Eley's summation of nineteenth-century drives for democracy shows how the novel's discourse surrounding Grip challenges liberal ideals critics attribute to Dickens's politics. Using Gladstone's 1864 speech about the Second Reform Bill, Eley argues,

> Liberals bitterly resisted democratic citizenship. In liberal theory, access to political rights required a possession of property, education, and a less definable quality of moral standing – what William Ewart Gladstone called "self-command, self-control, respect for order, patience under suffering, confidence in the law, and regard for superiors" ... In liberal discourse, "the democracy" was synonymous with rule of the mob. (30–31)

Indeed, Thompson's reminder that "Within Parliament, then, 'the people' were clearly seen as the lower orders, the laboring population, whose demand for the vote was associated with at best disrespect for authority and at worst with the intention to overthrow the whole edifice of parliamentary government" (*Dignity* 28), emphasizes negative misreadings of Chartist character. Yet Grip undercuts such liberal beliefs as his character demonstrates that negative attributions, or the lack of the qualities Gladstone praises mid-century, come as a result of bad government. He

---

[22] Thompson gives an example of this in her discussion of how the Chartists wanted the right to control their children's education, and not have the middle class do it for them (*Chartists* 115).

emphasizes the limitations of human sovereignty and the institutions of governmentality in delineating character and subjecthood. The working class, and animals, gain access to the political by exposing the flawed character of governmentality, not their own.

The animal politics of *Hard Times*, *Oliver Twist*, and *Barnaby Rudge* asks for the inclusion of alterity within the public sphere's liberal politics. Yet this can work, these novels argue, only if governmentality – the logic of governance and its extended power networks – allows for the inclusion of difference, rather than its reformation. Institutions governed by liberal thought must cease conducting the marginalized to forms of moral character that accept hierarchical positions and submission to a corrupt and unequal social order. These novels accept the liberalization of animal subjects, yet use it to critique the limitations of liberal thought. By doing so they offer alternative versions of animal subjects and locate liberalism's blind spots in relationship to alterity. As I will demonstrate in Chapter 4, during debates about democracy in the 1860s Victorian liberal thought tried to limit its exclusions and incorporate others through liberal education. Yet this too resulted in a lack of acceptance of alternative subjectivities. I move to children's literature to show how Lewis Carroll's *Alice's Adventures in Wonderland* registers an animal politics that critiques the regulatory nature of liberal education. The novel again becomes a privileged space to present an animal politics that challenges liberal ideologies and shows the need for radical difference in democratic institutions.

CHAPTER 4

Alice in Wonderland's *Animal Pedagogy*
Democracy and Alternative Subjectivity in Mid-Victorian Liberal Education

> "How the creatures order one about, and make one repeat lessons!" thought Alice. "I might just as well be at school at once."
> – Lewis Carroll, *Alice's Adventures in Wonderland*

> I will try to make a meal out of the stuff left out of the feast of political theory done in the anthropocentric style.
> – Jane Bennett, *Vibrant Matter*

> One never eats entirely on one's own: this constitutes the rule underlying the statement, "One must eat well."
> – Jacques Derrida, "Eating Well"

While Chapter 3 briefly discussed Dickens's critique of utilitarian education in *Hard Times*, this was not the whole story of his engagement with political animals. I argued that Dickens employs animals as an integral part of his political message, and offered an animal subject who was, at times, removed from the regulatory discourses of pastoral power. Yet children's literature was also central to the animal politics of *Hard Times*. When Louisa visits the dwellings of the "the Coketown Hands," she realizes that "For the first time in her life, she was face to face with anything like individuality in connexion with them" (106). Louisa's lack of education of the kind Dickens values is directly connected to animals, as if they were key to his preferred educational strategies. For central to Louisa's inability to imagine the other is the fact that she was deprived of children's literature:

> No little Gradgrind had ever associated a cow in a field with that famous cow with the crumpled horn who tossed the dog who worried the cat who killed the rat who ate the malt, or with that yet more famous cow who swallowed Tom Thumb: it had never heard of those celebrities, and had only been introduced to a cow as a graminivorous ruminating quadruped with several stomachs. (16)

Louisa's revelation that working-class individuals should be viewed outside of utilitarian calculation and self-interest is grounded in an ethic that devalues reason and privileges an imaginative space like children's literature. For Dickens, its value lay in its ability to envision an epistemology beyond a cold, calculating reason that views others as subjects, no matter their use value in Victorian society, and locates alterity as a site of rebellion to governmentality. In Dickens's understanding, education influenced by the utilitarian state rejected alternative subjectivities, disallowing social and political reform for non-bourgeois subjects. With more children's literature and alternate understandings of animals, Dickens suggests, social reform is possible.

Dickens's understanding of the political uses of children's literature should not be surprising, for the genre has always been a political tool central to liberal education. The production of children's pedagogy and literature was influenced by John Locke's *Some Thoughts Concerning Education*, which posits stories about and pictures of animals as the best way to help children become proper members of the liberal political sphere.[1] For Locke, Aesop's *Fables* and *Reynard the Fox* are exemplary children's texts featuring animals, as they both "delight and entertain . . . yet afford useful reflections to a grown man" (116–117). The political purpose of such texts is to teach children important social morals, including the internalization of hierarchy and social order; this makes children's literature a productive space for examining how liberal ideology creates power relationships for children to internalize. Locke stressed the importance of kindness toward animals for creating a proper liberal subject, a belief carried into the Victorian era and at the root of social reform movements perpetuated by the RSPCA. Thus, children's literature is inherently grounded in animal welfare discourse. Animals served the political role of translating proper conduct into the space of childhood, drawing children's attention to political and social spheres structured by a liberal framework, while forming their early subjectivity through reading and discussion. The purpose of these animal characters was twofold: entertain while teaching basic reading skills, and produce citizenship

---

[1] Historians and scholars of children's literature have demonstrated the strong influence of Locke's educational theories on the genre; in their readings, Locke's emphasis on entertaining while teaching influenced the children's book trade, particularly beginning with Newberry in the mid-eighteenth century. Seth Lerer explains that "Newberry himself grounded his booklist in the educational theories of John Locke, and the British and American trade in children's books kept up his emphases for decades" (8). Christine Kenyon-Jones, Tess Cosslett, and Colleen Glenney Boggs also discuss connections between Locke, children's education, and children's literature.

through modeling the proper behavior of respecting property, internalizing social hierarchies, and rejecting animality. Beginning with Locke, then, the pedagogical use of animals was politically charged with the goal of turning children into functioning liberal citizens.

Taking seriously the animal politics of children's literature, this chapter examines how the animal subjectivity it constructs reflects, informs, and challenges the goals of liberal education, particularly as children's literature morphs alongside mid-Victorian liberalism. As the genre shifts from didacticism to the fantastic, do animals still maintain hierarchy and teach children social order, or do they embrace J. S. Mill's pedagogy of learning alternative viewpoints?[2] What kind of liberal education were animals giving children, and how was it related to attempts to conceptualize certain animals as legal subjects and give them political representation? I connect these questions regarding the political uses of animals to mid-century debates about liberal education, particularly in relation to the widening franchise and liberalism's incorporation of, or resistance to, alternative subjectivities. Many scholars have emphasized the importance of education to liberalism's political rationality, from David Lloyd and Paul Thomas's claims that liberal education forms citizens for the modern state, to Uday Singh Mehta's argument that education was central to liberalism's ability "to foster successfully a particular self-understanding in which individuals come to view themselves as individuals" (*Anxiety* 6), and Elaine Hadley's understanding of liberal education as vital to "cognitive reform *in* society" (*Living* 58). And in the mid-Victorian period when the widening franchise and expansion of the political community to include animals and colonized subjects was of major concern, ideas of education were more central than ever, and deeply engaged with liberalism's exclusions.

To understand connections between liberal education, animals, and alternative subjectivity, I examine a text that veers from its predecessors most prominently through its use of animals. While earlier texts such as Sarah Trimmer's *History of the Robins* cultivates a paternalistic relationship to animals and the poor, and Charles Kingsley's *The Water-Babies* promotes paternalism and social movement, the animal world of *Alice's Adventures in Wonderland* reorganizes animal–human relationships and challenges the education forming liberal cognition.[3] While Trimmer and

---

[2] See Mill's "Inaugural Address at St. Andrews," which I discuss later.
[3] Carroll's *Through the Looking-Glass and What Alice Found There* also contains many fruitful representations of animals that destabilize hegemonic conceptions of animal subjects. However, I focus on *Alice's Adventures in Wonderland* due to its engagement with education.

Kingsley follow a moralistic and hierarchical liberal pedagogy based on the reinforcement of class, gender, and species, with the goal of social reform, Carroll's unconventional animals unsettle the subject modeled throughout liberal discourse. Through refusing the goals of liberal pedagogy, Carroll's animals teach Alice to disrupt gendered, anthropocentric, and political power relationships based in liberal norms. This education is predicated on Carroll's destabilization of the animal–human hierarchy reinforced by animal welfare discourse. For throughout the text, Wonderland's animals refuse to see Alice in a position of power and authority over them. They destabilize her reason, rather than admire it, as animals were imagined to do throughout animal welfare discourse. *Alice's Adventures in Wonderland* thus critiques the pastoral power associated with self-government and social reform, and undermines the restrictive subjectivity it creates. For instead of teaching Alice kindness and benevolence, Wonderland's animals pester her into an ontological crisis that disrupts her liberal subjectivity. While *Alice* contains a radical animal politics throughout, however, its ending registers Carroll's fears of democracy, as Alice realizes how alternative subjectivity can disrupt political power and result in chaos.

Locke's Liberal Animal Pedagogy

Locke's discussion of animals in *Some Thoughts Concerning Education* lays the groundwork for a liberal conception of animals, and demonstrates their ties to liberal thought. Not only was Locke the first liberal philosopher to write a detailed treatise on education, but he was the first to posit animals as essential to the project of creating good citizens and nation building within a liberal framework. Colleen Glenny Boggs claims Locke posits animals as "the supplement to liberal subjectivity" through their incorporation into language (147), and argues that his pedagogy suggests that affective relationships with animals teach children kindness toward others. For Boggs, Locke's claims about the importance of animals in children's literature "blur the distinction between human beings and animals; animals themselves increasingly become subjects. Instead of seeing animals as a vehicle for human relationships, the animals themselves begin to matter in their own right" (142). In this understanding, Locke is the first liberal thinker to articulate animal–human relationships and animal subjectivity as essential to the political sphere. While Locke most often describes animals in terms of their use value and legal designation as property, he also posits them as the foundation of liberal subjectivity and politics, and of the nation as a whole. Representations of Lockean animal subjectivity possess political power, cultivating core tenets of liberalism such as paternalism, reason, and social hierarchy based on race, class, gender, and species. If early promoters of animal welfare constructed their arguments on claims to the good of the nation, Locke posited this belief in the realm of education and cultural representations geared toward children. Locke's animal welfare is grounded in an understanding of animals as educational and economic capital, which objectifies them through reinforcing their position as property.

Locke's opening dedication in *Some Thoughts Concerning Education* ensures his text is written for the good of the British nation. He explains his treatise should be "suited to our English gentry" and stresses that "the welfare and prosperity of the nation" depends on childhood education, in part through educating children according to their social class and reinforcing class lines (8). While these claims are not explicitly connected to animals, they structure the larger framework for understanding their role in his pedagogy, a project Uday Singh Mehta characterizes as attuning children toward authority and social norms (*Anxiety* 24). Locke registers animals as foundational to the regulation of the political sphere through connecting anti-cruelty ideology and social order. After discussing how kindness to animals helps children learn to "preserve" humankind, Locke explains this is "the true principle to regulate our religion, politicks, and morality" (91). Although the end goal here is to cultivate better human–human relationships, it is founded on animal subjectivity, as Locke stresses that "from their cradles" people should learn to "be tender to all *sensible* creatures" (91; emphasis added). Through representations of animals in literature, and by treating real animals kindly, children become good citizens and help the nation prosper.

Early children's texts such as Trimmer's *History of the Robins* adopt Locke's pedagogy by reinforcing the belief that children should imagine animal subjectivity only in relationship to human goals. In her introduction Trimmer explains that children should not understand her story "as containing the real conversations of birds (for that it is impossible we should ever understand) but as a series of fables, intended to convey a moral instruction applicable to themselves" (1–2). Such statements present animal subjectivity only to reject it, reinforcing beliefs that animals are pedagogical tools rather than subjects in their own right. This convention was common in British children's literature, as Tess Cosslett explains there was anxiety about talking animal protagonists expressed in explanatory prefaces or through the use of a "human mediator" (1). While Trimmer posits the possibility of animal alterity – "it is impossible we should ever understand" the conversations of animals – she rejects it in favor of human goals. Similarly, although it may seem that Locke promotes an early animal welfare philosophy, he suggests animals should be treated well as a pedagogical and political tactic, rather than out of respect for the lives of animals.

Indeed, in his *Second Treatise* Locke reinforces the position of animals as property and capital, emphasizing that treating them well leads to higher profits. Locke's gesture privileges *homo economicus*, the primary subject liberalism produces. He explains,

> For this is no more, than what every Man who loves his own Power, Profit, or Greatness, may, and must naturally do, keep those Animals from hurting or destroying one another who labour and drudge only for his Pleasure and Advantage, and so are taken care of, not out of any Love the Master has for them, but Love of himself, and the Profit they bring him. (328)

Locke's pastoral power reflects the constructions of animal subjectivity found in early animal welfare discourse. Animals work for the "pleasure" and "advantage" of humankind; because of this, one should treat them well. Further, Locke actually negates animal welfare for the sake of animals through his promotion of profit: treat animals well not out of love for them, but for self-love, "and the Profit they bring." This conception of animals is carried over into Locke's pedagogy, where animals become a form of educational capital helping the nation profit. Locke thus opens a space for animal subjectivity in children's literature only to assume that children reject understandings of animals as feeling subjects once they reach adulthood, viewing them instead as capital.

Similarly, in *Some Thoughts*, Locke's example of a proper animal–human relationship in childhood is pet-keeping, which inscribes animals into a position of property. Locke explains that he "cannot but commend both the kindness and prudence of a mother I knew, who was wont always to indulge her daughters when any of them desired dogs, squirrels, or any such things ... but then when they had them, they must be sure to keep them well and look diligently after them, that they wanted nothing, or were not ill used" (91). Locke's praise of the mother willing to give her children any animal they desired, along with his comment that if the animals were not well taken care of, the mother "forfeited their *possession*" (91; emphasis added) demonstrates animal commodification and reinforces their status as property. Here kindness toward animals reflects and aids Locke's founding tenet of the purpose of liberal government: the protection of property. This is reflected in Kingsley's *The Water-Babies*, when Grimes is punished for poaching salmon. The narrator tells his child reader, "when you grow to be a big man, do you behave as all honest fellows should; and never touch a fish or a head of game which belongs to another man without his express leave; and then people will call you a gentleman, and treat you like one" (122–123). Animals are thus included in the political sphere to help structure liberal society, without the possibility of conceptualizing them outside of an anthropocentric framework.

Locke's conception of animals thus presents animal subjectivity but relegates it to a hierarchical position below the human. Children should transfer the morals animals teach them to the human sphere, which simultaneously raises and lowers one's estimation of animals. With animals as teachers at early stages, childhood and animal subjectivity is intertwined, yet children are taught to reject qualities of animality that do not adhere to liberal subjectivity and cognition. Mehta's claims that Locke's pedagogy centered on controlling the passions and encouraging self-restraint links his ultimate rejection of animal subjectivity to a larger discourse of animality (*Anxiety* 131, 137). Although Mehta reads Locke as more concerned with regulating cognition rather than animality, I suggest such regulation is another form of distancing oneself from animals, especially through the cultivation of reason. For although children were supposed to imagine animal subjectivity, they were also to distance themselves from what defined animality well into the nineteenth century: non-reason, instinct, lack of self-government, and appetite. Thus considering Locke's influence on the formation of liberalism and governmentality, to properly imagine animal subjectivity within the liberal political sphere is to reject animality. The animal protected by British citizens and their government is one adhering to liberal thought.

Yet significantly, Locke's pedagogy posits children's literature as a politicized space for imagining animal subjectivity and claiming its necessity; animals are liberalized subjects who recognize and internalize the political world. The salmon in *The Water-Babies*, for example, "are all true gentlemen, and, like true gentlemen, they look noble and proud enough, and yet, like true gentlemen, they never harm or quarrel with any one, but go about their own business, and leave rude fellows to themselves" (112). Locke's promotion of an early animal welfare is most prominent in his valuation of children's literature for advancing animal subjectivity, even if there was anxiety about producing it. Throughout liberal children's pedagogy animals earn a form of representation and have the potential to challenge the dominant political order; children's literature welcomed animal subjectivity while attempting to contain it within the regulatory strategies of governmentality.

The Others of Victorian Liberal Education

After Locke, animals proliferated in children's literature and, alongside animal welfare, remained essential to liberal pedagogy for both children and adults. The welfare of animals was a major part of Victorian social reform, as advocates educated children and the lower class on kind treatment toward them. As Arthur Moss notes, in 1845 animal welfare became entwined with state education, as the National Schools Society "agreed that their teachers should deal with kindness to animals in lessons, and that books on the matter should be placed in school libraries" (197). In the 1850s the RSPCA became even more focused on education, preparing a textbook by 1855, and forming a sub-committee on education in 1857 (Harrison 810, 793). Alongside *Animal World*, the RSPCA published the children's periodical *Band of Mercy*, started in 1879. Both were formed with the purpose of educating citizens in treating animals more kindly, and included numerous articles about the need for humane education at the state level. In *Animal World*'s inaugural issue, for example, a reprinted letter from Angela Burdett Coutts, a major financial supporter of the RSPCA, poses the suggestion "to all persons engaged in teaching, in whatever rank of life, to the President of the Committee of Council for Education, and to the National Society's Board of Education, that some plan should be adopted for inculcating, in a definite manner, principles of humanity towards animals, and a knowledge of their structure, treatment, and value to man." Such education emphasizes pastoral power, indirect duty, and, as in Locke, profit and the protection of property. An article titled "A French Schoolmaster on Humane Education," for example, notes that by teaching kindness to domestic animals, that is, "by not overworking them, and by keeping them in clean and roomy stables, feeding them well, and treating them kindly and gently, a greater profit and larger crops may be obtained than by abusing them." He continues by connecting this to better social behavior: "Ever since I introduced the subject into my school, I have found the children less disorderly, but, instead, more gentle and affectionate towards each other." Animal welfare is no longer confined to children's literature, and becomes directly tied to state education.[4] Yet as we saw in Chapters 1 and 2, animal welfare discourse perpetuated a liberalized animal who desired subjection to the human. This containment

---

[4] See also Monica Flegel's article "'How does your collar suit me?': The Human Animal in the RSPCA's *Animal World* and *Band of Mercy*," which argues that these journals, and the RSPCA in general, aimed to cultivate proper social behavior.

of alternative subjectivity and alterity in liberal norms extended to human others through state-influenced education.

Locke's formulation of the political goals of education carries into the Victorian period, especially through Matthew Arnold and John Stuart Mill's beliefs that education is essential to a civil society, particularly in an era with a slowly expanding franchise.[5] Democracy was frequently discussed alongside the need for national education. J. S. Mill's *Considerations on Representative Government*, for example, emphasizes the belief that good government requires educated citizens, and discusses how essential state-funded national education was to questions of democracy. Mill saw education as one of the most pressing issues of the nineteenth century, while for Arnold it could displace the aristocracy from cultural and political power. Neither Mill nor Arnold posit animals as essential to their pedagogy and the political goals of education. However, in the same way that Locke incorporates animal subjectivity into the political sphere only to reject it, Mill embraces non-hegemonic perspectives only to exclude them. Arnold too expresses the need for an "ideal of greatness, high feeling, and fine culture" (14) for the working class to follow, and advocates for an upper-class culture influenced by the state. Animals are perhaps an extreme of the kinds of subjects British liberalism simultaneously embraced and expelled in attempts to construct subjects who submitted to the state and sociopolitical hierarchies. Like my earlier discussion of the role of animal subjectivity within the political sphere, debates regarding the inclusion of non-normative others into the franchise reflect the exclusionary goals of liberal education, and its attempts to mold a hegemonic liberal subject, even as it embraces the political value of alternative subjectivities.

Major events within the second half of the 1860s influenced discussions of political inclusion and education while, as Herbert Tucker explains, inspiring the movement from "laissez-faire elitism" to "welfare-state participation." In 1865 the Morant Bay Rebellion led to concerns about the

---

[5] There are certainly distinctions between Locke's classical liberalism and mid-Victorian liberalism, and Hadley's distinction proves useful to my focus on animal subjectivity and liberal cognition. In regard to the liberal individual, Hadley argues, "While the Victorian formulation shares its classical predecessor's emphasis on self-proprietorship, Victorian liberal individuality is ... constituted ... in the cognitive realm of devil's advocacy," and thus within the strategies of liberal cognition (*Living* 103). On the other hand, Sartori argues that Lockean precepts of "natural right based on the property-constituting powers of labor" allowed for custom to operate as "the vehicle of liberal norms" in colonial Bengal (70–71). Goodlad argues that mid-Victorian liberalism differs from Lockean liberalism because of its emphasis on character as part of Victorian liberalism's "self-consciously anti-materialist and anti-deterministic cast" ("Character" 12). What remains is a pedagogy that reinforces social and species hierarchies.

morality of the imperial project, while inspiring fears of a working-class rebellion at home. Governor John Eyre's critics made the case against authoritarian rule, thus pushing for reform in England and abroad (Winter, "Morant"). Anxiety over rebellion led, in part, to the passage of the 1867 Second Reform Bill, which expanded the franchise to about 90 percent (Carlisle, "Second"). Education now became a pressing matter of concern. Debates leading up to the Education Act of 1870, which allowed taxes to support religious schools and established a system of primary education through county school boards, often stressed the need for an educated populace. Realizing that the electorate was no longer in the hands of the elite, state actors debated moving toward a welfare system that helped equalize the inequalities highlighted by the Reform Act (Boos). These events emphasize how the goals of liberalism, whether through legislation or education, were to keep social rebellion at bay.

Indeed, education was one of governmentality's individualizing powers regulating liberal subjectivity and cognition. Lauren Goodlad claims that mid-Victorian beliefs about popular education highlight the ambivalence of the middle class's paternalistic relationship to the lower class. In contrasting conservative and liberal viewpoints on education, Goodlad explains that resistance came from the conservatives, "many of whom believed that education could make the working class discontent with their lot. Liberals, on the other hand, saw education as integral to building character" (*Victorian Literature* 167). Goodlad's distinction posits the possibility of education giving rise to a resentful alternative subjectivity, rather than the normative one liberals hoped to cultivate. Lloyd and Thomas similarly argue that liberal education taught citizens to accept their subjection. Beliefs in the regulatory role of education spanned the empire, as Gauri Viswanathan claims that British education in India attempted to control non-Western subjectivity. State-influenced education thus demonstrates mid-Victorian liberalism's reluctance to welcome non-bourgeois subjects into a democratic community; representative government was not for everyone, and one's inclusion relied on their liberal cognition.

Mill demonstrates that, like animals, non-bourgeois subjects must be educated with a regulative liberal subjectivity if given more political power. In his "Inaugural Address at St. Andrews," given during his time as a member of parliament (1865–1867), Mill suggested that there was "no reading more profitable to students" (175) than Locke. Mill himself never read much children's literature, nor does he praise its benefits in the way Locke does. While animals remain excluded from his pedagogy, in *Principles of Political Economy* he critiques a kindness toward animals exercised in service to the human. Although Mill described the benefits of his extraordinary childhood education in his *Autobiography*, the closest he comes to laying out an actual pedagogy is in his "Inaugural Address," geared toward higher education. Here he stresses the necessity of an intellectual and moral education open to alternative viewpoints; understanding others can aid intellectual development and social progress. Mill's awareness of the importance of learning about non-British subjects through their language – "Without knowing the language of a people," he claims, "we never really know their thoughts, their feelings, and their type of character: and unless we do possess this knowledge, of some other people than ourselves, we remain, to the hour of our death, with our intellects only half expanded" (146) – emphasizes the benefits of alterity to liberal education. Mill's focus on the language of others stresses his desire to understand alternative subjectivities rather than impose Western thinking onto them, even though he so often does this in his other writings.

Yet Mill's statements on alterity are hardly radical. In her reading of Mill, for example, Sarah Winter argues that liberal pedagogy promoted an "ethnographic knowledge" of generalization rather than cultural particularity, used to "support normative ethical and political applications" ("Mental" 431–432). And as Mehta has demonstrated in *Liberalism and Empire*, the subjection of imperial subjects was at the core of liberal philosophy's obsession with education and progress; education was a means of progression toward what was understood as a more civilized European rationality. In a reading of Locke and Mill, Mehta explains that "The universalistic reach of liberalism derives from the capacities that it identifies with human nature" – everyone is born free and equal – yet "behind the capacities ascribed to all . . . there exist a thicker set of social credentials that constitute the real bases of political inclusion" ("Liberal" 429). Categories such as race, gender, and class limit the extent to which humans can achieve desired qualities for political inclusion. Within liberal education, then, alternative subjectivities should be examined and taken seriously, yet reined in by an education in liberal norms and subjectivity. Hadley's observation that mid-Victorian liberalism prizes individuality and eccentricity at the same time it "seeks a normative order" (*Living* 53) emphasizes liberalism's contentious and contradictory relationship to otherness and alterity, which, outside of imperial and anthropological discourses, is seen most fully in liberalism's relation to pedagogy and demands for democracy. Like animals, these alternative subjects are included only to be shaped by liberalism's exclusionary politics.

Mill's writings on democracy emphasize this resistance to alterity and an expanded franchise. Although Mill privileges alternative viewpoints, worries

Alice in Wonderland's *Animal Pedagogy* 145

that a monopolized state-sponsored education hinders individualism and diversity, and eventually refused to support demands for democracy until women were included, he has a very normative subject in mind when discussing the franchise. Throughout *Considerations on Representative Government*, Mill constantly seeks to exclude the working class and imperial subjects from any kind of political power. He hopes that "Means might be found of giving a further extension to the privilege [of plural voting], which would connect it in a more direct manner with superior education" (338), and claims that obtaining parish relief should exclude one from the franchise (332). He believes some non-Westerners are "unfit for liberty" (209), and that people in a state of "savage independence" require a despotic ruler (232). Mill's beliefs about the relationship between education and democracy suggest that education reinforced a normative Western liberal subjectivity and a hierarchical social order. Without it, democracy was to be feared rather than embraced. T. H. Huxley's description of the educated liberal subject highlights this regulatory nature of education:

> That man, I think, has had a liberal education who has been so *trained* in youth that his body is the ready *servant* of his will, and does with ease and pleasure all the work that, as *a mechanism*, it is capable of; *whose intellect is a clear, cold, logic engine*, with all its parts of equal strength, and in smooth working order; *ready, like a steam engine, to be turned to any kind of work* ... one who, no stunted ascetic, is full of life and fire, but whose passions are *trained* to come to heel by *a vigorous will*, the *servant* of a tender conscience. (86; emphasis added)

Such qualities are not far from those Mill requires in citizens capable of representative government: "industry, integrity, justice, and prudence ... the qualities of mental activity, enterprise, and courage" (220).

Ultimately, mid-Victorian discourses on education lack room for alternatives to an education connected to social reform and political exclusion. The liberal pedagogy of Locke, Mill, and Arnold sought to expel subjects rather than bring them into the political fold. Lloyd and Thomas explain how the function of mid-Victorian education was

> to be devoted, even to the most advanced liberals and radicals, to processes of normalization. Its function is to train the young for participation in forms and institutions which are already established and outside whose terms it is virtually impossible to imagine social relations and cultural forms that are not simply aberrant or primitive. To imagine or exist otherwise flies in the face of a common sense which designates the alternative either to be violent, as in Arnold's working-class "mobs," or to be less than fully civilized, as in Mill's savages, colonial subjects and working classes. (126)

Without creating a simple alignment between the working class, colonized subjects, and animals, although the subjection of these groups often rested on their supposed animality, I include animals as another sight of contention within liberal education. During the Victorian era animals proliferated within cultural representations, which, following Lloyd and Thomas, were linked to the state and subject-formation. Animals flooded literature for children and adults, and the RSPCA aimed to cultivate morality by teaching kindness toward animals. Representations of animals, however, also had to adhere to a normative subjectivity for appropriately educating citizens, and if animals were to receive more political protection. Indeed, throughout *Animal World*, animal training is most often referred to as education; such language emphasizes the liberalization of animal subjects and exposes how liberal education was geared toward obedience of social rules.

Alice's Adventures in Wonderland has been read from a wide array of perspectives, from psychoanalysis and feminist theory, to evolution and thing theory. However, it has yet to be placed in its political context and engagement with Victorian liberalism. As a conservative, Carroll demonstrates how much alterity can disrupt the political sphere. Indeed, based on the novel's ending chaos, Carroll seems to register the disorder resulting from alternative subjects with political agency. My reading, however, suggests that *Alice*'s combination of mid-Victorian discourses on liberal education and animal pedagogy destabilizes a subjectivity founded on reason, social hierarchy, and middle-class morality. For when the novel's talking animals are read from the vantage of animal politics, they promote a radical and subversive pedagogy that disrupts hierarchy and normative subjectivity. Through upending the goals of liberal pedagogy, Carroll's animals offer Alice an education in the political power of alternative perspectives. Through her interactions with them, Alice learns the political potentialities arising from taking seriously alternative subjectivity. *Alice*'s unconventional animal characters, who embrace non-reason and disrupt the moral discipline meant to result from sports and games, subvert the liberal subject modeled within Victorian political discourse. That is, Carroll's human politics shows the need for liberal pedagogy to avoid political disorder; the novel's animal politics, however, suggests that non-normative subjectivities hold the power to disrupt an unfair political system. Through Carroll's unconventional animals, children's literature becomes a subversive space for an animal politics that resists governmentality and the normative subjectivity it cultivates. Such political agency, however, remains relegated to the spheres of fantasy and dream worlds.

Liberal Education, *Alice*-Style: Eating Well in Wonderland

Lewis Carroll believed education was essential to Victorian society, but did not support state influence in its manifestations. He opposed examinations, then heavily in vogue and one of the exemplars of mid-Victorian education, but was furious when, in 1864, Oxford University proposed legislation to lower standards and allow more students into it (M. Cohen 82). According to Morton Cohen, Carroll "considered the lowering of standards degrading and believed the new dispensation harmed both mathematics and classics" (83). Although Carroll did not approve of examinations, he believed that if used they should be demanding, highlighting his belief that lowering the standards of University entrance would "cheapen" education (M. Cohen 82). Shuman's work on the "repressive social functions" (8) of mid-Victorian examinations helps us read Carroll's reluctance to support them as a dislike of state power, while his frustration over an expanding student body suggests an anti-democratic stance. Carroll's unwillingness to embrace state-influenced education is not as surprising when we learn of his dislike for the liberal party; he was a conservative and admired Disraeli. References suggest his disdain for political and social agitation, which he believed Gladstone and his party encouraged. A series of anagrams of William Gladstone suggest as much: "I, wise Mr. G. want to lead all," and "Wild agitator! Means well" (*Diaries* II 277). These emphasize Carroll's belief that liberal electors are "brutal" (*Diaries* II 275), and show his fears of an expanded franchise. He was, however, interested in creating voting systems that represented the majority, and followed debates regarding electoral reform. Carroll attended readings of the Second Reform Bill, wrote pamphlets on voting in the 1870s and 1880s, and sent amendments of the Franchise Bill to Lord Salisbury in 1884. Carroll desired fairness, but without the possibility of an uneducated majority. Like other conservatives, he dreaded the possibility of rebellion against the dominant social order.

The above debates about education and democracy were circulating in the 1860s while Carroll was revising *Alice* for publication. The novel's engagement with education is so pervasive that Alice exclaims, "'How the creatures order one about, and make one repeat lessons! ... I might just as well be at school at once'" (136). However, the text's constant declarations of anti-morality suggest *Alice*'s pedagogy is different from the middle-class emphasis on moral reform. Jack Zipes's claim that *Alice*'s most "radical statement" is its lack of "moral purpose" suggests the novel challenges the educational status quo (xxii). Carroll's text is representative of a new moment in children's literature that reaches beyond a didactic purpose and into the realm of social critique, and grapples with a politics striving to incorporate new subjects while maintaining social and political hierarchies. While Jessica Straley has shown that mid-Victorian children's pedagogy was influenced by evolutionary theories of recapitulation, which assumed a liberal progressive movement of civilization from animal to Western human, *Alice*'s animal pedagogy encourages Alice to become more animal-like, rather than transcend an uncivilized animal irrationality. For moving from animal to civilized human required that children learn liberal norms. Indeed, Herbert Spencer's scientific pedagogy, which Straley describes as "exercises in observation, experimentation, and deduction," emphasizes reason and empirical thinking (590), elements of liberal cognition. Yet Wonderland's animals teach Alice to move beyond the confines of Victorian society, use liberal cognition only to reject it, and stand up to excessive political power. They cultivate an animal politics, which "calls on the human to become animal, not on animals to renounce vital powers long wrongly assumed to be the sole province of the human" (Massumi 52). Through representations of animals who reject human superiority and embrace nonsense, *Alice*'s animal pedagogy demonstrates how radical representations of animals upend the effects of governmentality.

Alice's lessons in alternative pedagogy most often happen by way of her appetite, something she would have been taught to control as a young Victorian girl.[6] The size changes resulting from Alice's alimentary desires propel her into animal perspectives and ontological crises, giving her an education in alternative subjectivity. The animals challenge Alice to eat well, what Derrida refers to as a political, rather than "theoretical imperative," to "protect the other's otherness" and accept their alterity

---

[6] Scholars have discussed in detail the heavy focus on Alice's appetite. Like Nancy Armstrong, who suggests that regulating one's appetite is tantamount to controlling sexuality ("Alice"), Carina Garland argues that through controlling her appetite, Carroll controls Alice's sexuality and agency. Similarly, Nina Auerbach finds in the novel's discourse about appetite a connection between Alice and the Cheshire Cat: "The core of Alice's nature, too, seems to lie in her mouth: the eating and drinking that direct her size changes and motivate much of her behavior, the songs and verses that pop out of her inadvertently, are all involved with things entering and leaving her mouth" (39). As Garland suggests, Carroll was "disgusted" by a "ravenous" appetite in female girls (26), yet in my analysis Alice's appetite has much political potential. More recently, Michael Parrish Lee argues that the *Alice* books "deploy eating more radically to remap the novelistic social, merging literary character, and indeed 'the human,'" with things (490). His analysis focuses on connections between evolutionary theory and commodity capitalism, connecting "economic appetites" with the struggle for life (487). Other scholars such as Rose Lovell-Smith read *Alice* in light of natural history and Darwin's theory of natural selection, suggesting that "Carroll's reversal of the usual direction of the natural history gaze insinuates that humans may not be superior to 'nature' but may merely be animals themselves" ("Eggs" 28). See also Lovell-Smith, "The Animals of Wonderland: Tenniel as Carroll's Reader"; Gillian Beer, *Alice in Space*; and Akira Lippit, *Electric Animal* (126–143).

("Eating" 111). Derrida understands eating metonymically, as experience with, seeing, speaking of, identification with, and understanding the other ("Eating" 115). With this sense of eating and her ravenous appetite, Alice challenges the "conceptual machinery" of liberal subjectivity ("Eating" 109). Through her meals, Alice anticipates Jane Bennett in "mak[ing] a meal out of the stuff left out of the feast of political theory done in the anthropocentric style" (ix). *Alice's Adventures in Wonderland* dramatizes Bennett's desire to highlight "the material agency or effectivity of nonhuman or not-quite-human things" (ix), and show their political potential. For the food Alice eats during her time in Wonderland instigates an affective response that often challenges her worldview and forces her to see beyond a liberal, anthropocentric perspective. Akira Lippit's claim that "The inability of Alice to maintain a size relative to her surroundings dramatizes the dynamic that allows animals to overshadow human beings in a radically free economy of language" (140) further emphasizes the extent to which Alice's eating disrupts liberal education. For the animals also weaken Alice's hold on language, the very foundation of liberal subjectivity. As I demonstrated above, Victorian political discourse desired the reform of alterity, not its acceptance. Through eating well and debating with Wonderland's animals, however, Alice throws Wonderland's political system and her own liberal subjectivity into disorder, thus achieving a level of political agency refused to her above ground.

Alice's Adventures in Wonderland opens with a reference to Lockean pedagogy, for reading with her sister, Alice has no books with pictures. "What is the use of a book," she thinks, "without pictures or conversations?" (51). Alice's boredom is dissipated through the entrance of an animal, and her travels down the rabbit hole suggest she will enter a space where animals and conversations become educational. Alice's grown-up desire for conversations foreshadows the educational forms of debate in which she will engage with the animals of Wonderland, and demonstrates her eagerness to expand her thinking. Alice's entrance into Wonderland through a rabbit hole signals her simultaneous entry into three spaces: the colonial, the political, and the animal. The reference to New Zealand and Australia, or the "antipathies" (53), emphasizes the alterity and otherness of Wonderland, particularly in the Victorian imagination.[7] Nancy Armstrong and Daniel Bivona have read *Alice* in relation to imperialism and

---

[7] Ronald Reichertz explains that the trope of the upside-down world was a familiar one in nineteenth-century children's literature, yet this was not often conceptualized as a specifically animal world. Gillian Beer more recently labels Wonderland an "egalitarian" and "*sideways*" world (*Alice* 4).

colonial discourse, suggesting Alice enters Wonderland with a Eurocentric view she cannot shake off. Such readings emphasize that Alice enters a world in which she will encounter alternative subjectivities, and Alice's Eurocentric worldview can further be confirmed as a liberal one.

In an animal world of unreason, Alice tries to comprehend a new environment by relying on her education. Yet on entering Wonderland, the tools she has received from her above-ground education fail her, and "this was not a *very* good opportunity for showing off her knowledge, as there was no one to listen to her" (53). Alice's lack of self-understanding and her changing size work together to offer non-reason-based perspectives, allowing her to question above-ground power relationships. After drinking from the bottle labeled "Drink Me," Alice shrinks to an animal perspective, able to fit through a passage "not much larger than a rat-hole" (55). Eating from the box "Eat Me," Alice zooms up to nine feet tall and no longer knows who she is: "'I wonder if I've been changed in the night? Let me think: *was* I the same when I got up this morning? I almost think I can remember feeling a little different. But if I'm not the same, the next question is, 'Who in the world am I?' Ah, *that's* the great puzzle!'" (60). Alice's existential question suggests she is already moving beyond liberal discourses focused on self-improvement rather than self-understanding. Although she attempts to see if she "know[s] all the things I used to know" (61), multiplication, geography, and memorization fail her. So does her liberal ideology, when Isaac Watts's "Against Idleness and Mischief" becomes a poem about laziness, otherness, and appetite. Alice's transformation of Watts's industrial bee to the symbolically charged crocodile, "the quintessential sign of alterity" (Leighton and Surridge 255), represents an incorporation of otherness into liberal pedagogy.

While Alice's failed education disrupts her subjectivity, Wonderland's animal pedagogy allows her to examine both her subject position and that of animals. The tears she cries due to her education's failure help her understand human domination over animals, and challenge her own entrapment in the domestic sphere. For Alice, these are similar forms of domination. Using phrases from her French book, she offends the nearby mouse by asking, "Où est ma chatte?" (64). The mouse's response – "Would *you* like cats, if you were me?" (64) – inspires Alice to question her relationship with her pet cat Dinah and Wonderland's rejection of Dinah. His question gives Alice the possibility of imagining animal perspectives. For when Alice finds herself subjected to Wonderland's animals and ordered around by the White Rabbit, she sees animals in positions of power over her. "How queer it seems," Alice says, "to be going messages for a rabbit! I suppose Dinah'll be sending me on messages next!" (75). Alice imagines herself in Dinah's position after learning from the White Rabbit that animal and human roles can reverse, and from seeing how different the world looks from an animal perspective. Indeed, the animals' fear of domestic animals – above-ground dogs and cats – suggests a rejection of liberalized animals and a call to imagine alternate animal perspectives. Alice learns a crucial distinction between domestic animals above ground and those in Wonderland: animals in the real world must be subject to humans, not the other way around. Alice says, "I don't think ... that they'd let Dinah stop in the house if it began ordering people about like that!" (75), showing a recognition of how animals must remain submissive to humans.

The text's alignment of Alice and Dinah demonstrates Alice's refusal to submit to Victorian patriarchy, as cats were frequently paired with feminists or other deviant women in Victorian culture (Ritvo, *Animal* 22–23). Beginning to see through animal perspectives and understand the logic of eating in Wonderland, Alice challenges the patriarchal structure in which she is enmeshed. As she understands the impossibility of human subjection to animals above ground – Dinah is property, not proprietor – Alice fantasizes about a reversal of power relations: "And she began fancying the sort of thing that would happen: 'Miss Alice! Come here directly, and get ready for your walk!' 'Coming in a minute, nurse! But I've got to watch this mouse-hole until Dinah comes back, and see that the mouse doesn't get out!'" (75). As Nina Auerbauch explains, "Alice fantasizes her own identity actually blending into Dinah's" (36), and imagining herself in an animal perspective allows Alice to challenge her own subject position. For she next claims that she is "quite tired of being such a tiny little thing!" (75) and takes another drink from the bottle she knows will change her size. In this moment of fantasy, inspired by the White Rabbit and learning to see from animal perspectives, Alice protests patriarchal social structures. Her attempt to break out of the rabbit's house metaphorically highlights a desire to leave the domestic sphere. Here, Wonderland's education exposes hierarchical positions rather than reinforces them; Alice learns that if animals can switch their subject positions, so can she.

Wonderland's animals make Alice's ontological crisis worse by questioning the normalcy of a liberal perspective. Gillian Beer has emphasized that "Alice herself seeks mutuality through dialogue" (109), and that through the text's many dialogues between Alice and Wonderland's animals Carroll "satiriz[es] the tradition of pedagogic dialogues, then domineering over the Victorian educational system" (121). I read such dialogues as a form of devil's advocacy, in which the creatures challenge Alice to defend her own opinions and take theirs seriously. Through playing devil's advocate, what Hadley describes as a technique of mid-Victorian liberalism that "fosters a cognitive expression of social alterity, and . . . organizes the otherwise incommensurable contents of social difference" (*Living* 81), the animals use a strategy of liberalism to disrupt it. Alice participates in forms of liberal cognition usually taken on by the white male liberal subject, but the results are much different. Indeed, these scenes are representative of the kind of discussion advocated by Mill in *On Liberty* – "There must be discussion, to show how experience is to be interpreted" (25) – yet the results do not solidify Alice's own opinions and individuality. Through devil's advocacy animals educate Alice in stepping outside a liberal perspective and understanding the politics of alterity. Rather than educate her in Victorian morality, the animals pester Alice until her liberal subjectivity collapses. Such discussion incorporates a rebellious animal subjectivity into liberal forms; for while overall Wonderland's animals do not exemplify liberal cognition – most lack objectivity, reticence, reason, and sincerity – they use devil's advocacy to disrupt what Alice understands as objective, empirical, and normative. Although Mill explains that "The steady habit of correcting and completing his own opinion by collating it with those of others, so far from causing doubt and hesitation in carrying it into practice, is the only stable foundation for a just reliance on it" (*Liberty* 25), Wonderland's animals elicit a sense of doubt and hesitation in Alice, as they use discussion to question liberal normativity.

Chapter 5's title, "Advice from a Caterpillar," reinforces the educational aspect of the conversation between Alice and the Caterpillar. Instead of an encouraging conversation, however, he badgers Alice into conceptualizing alternative perspectives. Alice finds herself unable to answer the Caterpillar's forceful question, "Who are *you*?" (83), and tries by relating her experience of changing sizes to his future experience of becoming a butterfly. The Caterpillar's rejection of this alignment suggests that animal and human experiences are not equitable, and that Alice's subjectivity is not normative. Whereas children often saw similarities between themselves and animals in children's literature, here they are rejected in favor of an animal–human difference that disrupts liberal subjectivity, confusing Alice to the extent that she loses her self-knowledge. The Caterpillar's constant challenging – "It isn't," "Not a bit," "Why?" (84) – throws Alice outside of her knowledge base and asks her to imagine alternative perspectives and ontologies. Here devil's advocacy, taking place in a nonsensical space, counteracts what it was supposed to reinforce: reason, disinterestedness, and the organization of social difference. Alice, however, is speechless, as she has learned she cannot organize difference according to liberal standards.

Thus the one moral the Caterpillar gives Alice – "keep your temper" (84) – is not to reinforce good behavior but to accept contradiction and debate. However, this lesson does little to reassure Alice of her individuality. Her difficulty in imagining epistemological differences, and her claim that "three inches is such a wretched height to be" (88), suggests her education above ground trained her to assume her perspective is normative. *Alice*, however, extends experience to the non-normative, non-reason-based animal world, as the Caterpillar teaches Alice that she *cannot* organize social difference according to an individualized way of perceiving the world. Indeed, when told that an animal perspective of three inches is just as good as a human perspective, Alice can only answer that she is "not used to it!" (88). The Caterpillar destabilizes an animal–human hierarchy by questioning normative experience and, in contrast to animal welfare discourse, through his own refusal to prize human subjectivity over that of the animal. In effect, he exists outside of a subjectivity regulated by pastoral power – a technique of governmentality – further contributing to Alice's disrupted self.

If the Caterpillar rejects Alice's attempt at equating animal and human experience, the Pigeon schools Alice in rethinking species delineation, taking seriously animal perspectives, and understanding eating well as an ethical imperative. While Alice is at first "delighted" to enter into such a drastic alternative perspective, with her neck reaching out of the trees, minutes later she is unsure of her identity (90). Convinced she is a serpent, the Pigeon demands, "'Well, *What* are you? ... I can see you're trying to invent something!" (90). Alice's response signals hesitation, or perhaps an awareness that the species hierarchies structuring Victorian society do not exist in Wonderland: "'I – I'm a little girl,' said Alice, rather doubtfully" (90). In a conversation spurred from devil's advocacy and focused on eating, Alice sees fine gradations between the differences and similarities that structure the animal–human divide, and thus liberal rationality. As Zoe Jaques suggests, Alice learns that "one's status as human or animal can be merely a matter of perspective" (47). Not only are species and social hierarchies destabilized in Wonderland, but, like the Caterpillar's, the Pigeon's severe questioning renders Alice's perspective non-normative. Through playing devil's advocacy, the animals challenge Alice to decide what constitutes difference: if girls eat eggs, according to the Pigeon, then they are indeed a kind of serpent. Such nonsensical thinking, even with logic behind it, contributes to the collapse of Alice's understanding of difference and destabilizes the authority of language, a marker of human superiority.[8]

Alice has further learned that animals have a response and point of view. From the Pigeon's point of view, Alice is a kind of serpent; this causes her to grapple with alterity and alternative perspectives, disrupting her identity as a young girl. For Derrida, recognizing that animals have a "point of view regarding me" and that they have a response is one of the major ethical imperatives of animal–human relationships (*Animal* 11). Understanding eating metonymically, Derrida explains that "nothing will have ever given me more food for thinking through this absolute alterity of the neighbor or of the next (-door) than these moments when I see myself seen naked under the gaze of a cat" (*Animal* 11). Such food for thought is another way of eating well, which as we saw above, puts pressure on hegemonic forms of subjectivity. As Alice attempts to return to her normal size, she too has learned the ethical imperative of eating well, for she now respects otherness and imagines alternative perspectives: coming upon a small house, she realizes that at her height she "should frighten them out of their wits!" (91). But perhaps most importantly, Alice now questions the arbitrary nature of the categories organizing social difference. This allows her to behave in a way that accepts difference and alternate epistemologies, rather than reforms them.

While the above-ground world trained and constructed animal and child subjectivity to internalize social difference, Wonderland's animals undo this training through educating Alice in non-hegemonic perspectives, and breaking out of constructions that keep animals within pastoral power. Instead of internalizing human authority, they reject it and show how non-reason questions the liberal norms structuring governmentality. The animals participate in forms of mid-Victorian liberalism, such as discussion and devil's advocacy, yet use it to move away from the kinds of thinking liberalism normally produces. In other words, by imagining animal subjectivity outside of liberal discourses of reason, education, animal welfare, and pastoral power, the novel's animal politics cultivates a space where techniques of liberalism are used to undo its hegemonic and exclusionary thinking. Alice's education in eating well and devil's advocacy helps her

---

[8] Beatrice Turner suggests logic exists within Wonderland's madness and nonsense. Such logic, however, "can be an alienating exercise, and in fact an appeal to logic usually signifies a point at which Alice's understanding of the world is about to confront a disconcertingly different one" (248). The Mock Turtle's conversations about education further contribute to the text's destabilization of language.

challenge the carnophallogocentric categories forming the liberal subject. Alice's own notions of animals change as she experiences the familiar in an epistemologically unfamiliar fashion. The animals and animal–human relationships with which Alice is familiar – domestic animals, representations of animals in children's literature, and meat-eating – are defamiliarized as Wonderland challenges the liberal logic structuring them. Carroll thus places Alice into epistemological and ontological crises, which will help her disrupt the political. *Alice's* animal politics – embracing non-reason, rejecting human authority, and perverting liberal cognition – suggests that only when liberal subjectivity loses its hegemony can political change occur. Governmentality thus attempts to contain and reform alternative subjectivities due to their ability to disrupt its regulatory techniques.

Alice's Political Power

While Alice's fall down the rabbit hole signals her entrance into an animal world, it also marks her arrival into the political sphere. In Wonderland Alice participates in political processes, from engagement with the sovereign to courtroom trials. In this way, *Alice*'s animals participate in the Lockean tradition of teaching children how to enter the public sphere. Yet instead of teaching Alice to submit to social order, they teach her to question political power. Although *Alice's Adventures in Wonderland* demonstrates the chaos that could ensue from bringing alternative subjectivity into the political sphere, its animal politics suggests that space can be made for someone like Alice, who has learned to challenge the excesses of political power through embracing alternative subjectivity. For in three specific scenes the political is a nonsensical space over which Alice exerts control: the caucus race, the Queen's croquet grounds, and the trial. In the first scene, when Dodo suggests that "the best thing to get us dry would be a Caucus-race" (68), logic and order collapse. The animals "began running when they liked, and left off when they liked, so that it was not easy to know when the race was over" (68). The animals' use of the term "caucus" suggests their desire to take part in the political, and their inability to do so; they have not the reason needed to participate. As Bivona informs us, in Victorian England "caucus" was often a pejorative term used to refer to a committee that aimed to convince electors to vote a certain way (147). Yet here it highlights the lack of order resulting from a radical equality. For although Alice finds the whole thing "absurd" (70), the Dodo's wishful thinking – "*Everybody* has won, and *all* must have prizes" (69) – suggests a democracy in which all participate. Given the exclusionary space of caucuses in general, the animals attempt to construct a more equal political sphere. Alice, however, senses the impossibility of democracy, as the animals ultimately show her how absurd and unreasonable the political process can be.

Through turning a political event into a literal race, Carroll also disrupts the order and discipline sports were meant to maintain. Within liberal pedagogy, sports played the role of "maintaining order and building character," while training young citizens in the skills necessary for a strong military and imperial rule (N. Anderson 49). As Kathleen Blake emphasizes, even Samuel Smiles approved of sports "for their cultivation of mind and body" (201). The caucus race thus further contributes to a non-liberal pedagogy, wherein the animals show Alice that political order can be destabilized. If "Amusements, exercise, games, and sport were defended for improving health and morals" (199), in *Alice* they disrupt liberal pedagogy and the political order it was meant to maintain. For like the caucus race, the croquet match exposes how games can upend power relationships, rather than reinforce them.

While the caucus race demonstrates a lack of order and illogicality within electoral politics, the croquet match establishes the unfair political advantage and excessive power of the aristocracy. Alice finds the game nearly impossible to play, unfair, and "confusing," particularly on account of "all the things being alive" (119). Indeed, the use of live animals demonstrates the objectification of animals within the political – they become croquet balls and mallets – and reflects early debates over anti-cruelty laws and their relationship to class. Carroll demonstrates the hypocritical implications of the upper class using animals for sport and highlights the absurdity of aristocratic pastimes involving animals.[9] Although Alice tries to keep these animals objectified, they make the game impossible to play:

> just as she had got its [the flamingo's] neck nicely straightened out, and was going to give the hedgehog a blow with its head, it *would* twist itself round and look up in her face ... and, when she had got its head down, and was going to begin again, it was very provoking to find that the hedgehog had unrolled itself and was in the act of crawling away. (117)

The flamingo's and hedgehog's resistance reflects animal agency and causes a game of civility to become absurd and uncivilized. Although these

---

[9] Kathleen Blake emphasizes that Carroll was a critic of animal sports, fearing it led to a lack of morality (172–179).

animals are subjected to state power, their resistance and disruption demonstrates how excessive power results in futility: the game cannot be played. With the use of live animals and the queen ordering executions throughout, the croquet match becomes a grotesque and nonsensical version of an aristocratic pastime, ultimately critiquing the objectification of animals within the political and social spheres that early liberal thinkers such as Locke reinforced.

The Queen also marks Carroll's alignment of the aristocracy with excess sovereignty, a power Alice finds unreasonable and thus rejects. While the aristocracy was understood as the pinnacle of civilization, Carroll represents it as uncivilized. Alice's inner thought when meeting the Queen and her subjects – "Why, they're only a pack of cards, after all. I needn't be afraid of them!" (114) – demonstrates a refusal to take seriously Wonderland's monarchy, denouncing power that arises from luck, or one's birth. Able to conceptualize alternate power relations after her education from Wonderland's animals, Alice recognizes the nonsensical and excessive in too much state power. She responds to the Queen's power by calling her command to chop off her head "Nonsense!" (114). If liberal education forced one to internalize state power, Alice's alternative education has taught her to reject it. After experiencing altered power relations, Alice can now disrupt them on her own.

The appearance of the Cheshire Cat's head marks the illogicality within state grounds while providing the avenue for Alice's power. Understood as a non-liberalized version of a domestic animal, the Cheshire Cat represents resistance to domesticity and political power, and the irrationality of excessive state power. The King, Queen, and executioner all seek Alice's advice on cutting off the cat's head, even though the endeavor makes no sense, registering a form of deliberative democracy. After hearing their arguments Alice reinscribes animals into the domestic sphere as property by claiming, "It belongs to the Duchess: you'd better ask *her* about it" (121). Alice becomes the sovereign, if only for a brief moment, yet her endeavor to place the Cheshire Cat within the confines of pet-keeping is fruitless; the cat's ability to appear and disappear, and his current state of existing without a body suggests he remains outside of domestic and state power. Alice has come to understand how alternative subjectivity disrupts power relationships, and thus now tries to reorder Wonderland according to her own logic. After experiencing the world of animal politics, Alice embraces the safer realm of liberal human politics.

As such, Alice's entrance into the courtroom marks her desire to insert reason and order into the political sphere, and emphasizes Carroll's conservatism. Realizing that Wonderland's politics functions outside of above-ground logic, Alice repeatedly upsets the courtroom in an attempt to quell chaos. Indeed, her growing size represents her political power, while the courtroom's chaos and motley array of jurors represents Carroll's fears of democracy. It also marks the failure of bringing animals into the political; Alice's comparison of spilling over the jury box to upsetting a bowl of goldfish shows the fatality of animals within the political sphere. Alice has gained power through taking seriously alternative subjectivities, yet she ends up reinscribing them into familiar positions. Indeed, Jaques argues that although "Carroll plac[es] so many ontological challenges in her path," Alice's "personal quest remains to try to keep that same humanness intact" (53). Through the challenges to liberal subjectivity an animal politics endorses, Alice has gained the power to upset the political and social order, an important feat for a young girl. Her schooling in the nonsensical allows her to locate it in the political, and attempt to remove it. Yet the result is hardly radical; although she learns to step outside of a liberal worldview, she finds herself back within it. Having gained power, Alice sees the need for order, something impossible without the guiding rule of reason and normative liberal subjects.

Conclusion: *Alice*'s Animal Welfare and the Limits of Liberalism

While Carroll shows the impossibility of including animals in the political sphere as active citizens, and ultimately paints a negative picture of democracy, he makes a pointed critique of animal–human relationships in general. Whereas animal welfare inscribes animals into pastoral power, in both of Carroll's Alice texts animal subjectivity resists hierarchy. Indeed, if *Alice* can be read as promoting animal welfare, my analysis shows it is quite radical. Animals direct their desires away from the human, they reject human superiority, and resist their objectification within the social and political spheres. Yet just as the novel's animal politics exists only within a dream world, so does Carroll's reworking of animal welfare discourse take place only in the space of fiction. Carroll was a critic of vivisection, yet his arguments for its immorality rest not on its treatment of animals, but in how vivisection affects human character. In "Popular Fallacies about Vivisection" he writes that the biggest evil of vivisection is "in the effect produced on the operator ... The hapless animal suffers, dies, 'and there an end': but the man whose sympathies have been deadened, and whose selfishness has been fostered ... may be the parent of others equally brutalised, and so bequeath a curse to future ages" (1194). Carroll's logic reflects Locke's argument for the kind treatment of animals, reinserting animals into an anthropocentric framework that negates the valuation of animal lives in and of themselves.[10]

Yet within *Alice's Adventures in Wonderland* and *Through the Looking Glass*, Carroll calls for eating well: respect for the other beyond the objectifying logic of anthropocentrism. Through forcing Alice to meet her meat, Carroll posits animal subjectivity within the ultimate objectification and eradication of animal subjects, and "refuse[s] to allow the animality of meat to be obscured" (Jaques 48). In *Alice's Adventures in Wonderland*, Alice learns to refrain from talking about animals as food, putting her outside a liberal view that objectifies animals. When the Mock Turtle tells Alice, "and perhaps you were never even introduced to a lobster," she "began to say 'I once Tasted –' but checked herself hastily, and said, 'No, never'" (132), showing an awareness of her meat's animal life. Similarly, in *Through the Looking Glass*, after Tweedledee recites "The Walrus and the Carpenter," Alice says, "'I like the Walrus best ... because he was a *little* sorry for the poor oysters'" (*Annotated* 187). Alice's later introduction to a leg of mutton literally requires her to conceptualize the subject status of her meat, where "eating becomes a question of responsibility" (Guyer 160). Carroll's construction of animal subjectivity and the understanding Alice gains toward animals thus reworks the animal welfare discourse created by the hegemony of pastoral power in liberal education. Carroll envisions animals outside the exclusionary nature of liberal subjectivity, yet demonstrates how central the containment of animals and alterity was to the workings of governmentality.

The Victorian novel, in its manifestation as mid-century children's literature, has the potential to critique the function of animals within liberal discourse and their constructions through governmentality. Alternate animal subjectivities destabilize core concepts of liberal politics and expose contradictions within its philosophies: claims of inclusion while excluding many, the promotion of agency and the desire to control subjects, advocacy of individuality and eccentricity, and attempts to conform both animal and human British subjects across the globe. Alternative animal subjectivities also challenge restrictive classificatory categories and the hierarchies they create. *Alice's Adventures in Wonderland* thus offers a new animal pedagogy – indeed, an animal politics – while highlighting

---

[10] In contrast to my argument, Jed Mayer suggests that "human and nonhuman roles are dramatically reversed" in Carroll's antivivisection writing (442). While the human does become the one without morals, the human is still privileged over the animal.

liberalism's limitations in accepting difference. Using animals as educators outside of an anthropocentric and carnophallogocentric framework shows how much potential the consideration of animals as political subjects has for reworking the oppressive and exclusionary logic of mid-Victorian liberalism. Carroll's animal pedagogy also offers reasons for why, throughout the period, liberal discourse strove to keep animals confined to a subjectivity constructed by pastoral power.

PART III

The Biopolitics of Animal Capital

CHAPTER 5

Animal Capital and the Lives of Sheep
Thomas Hardy's Biopolitical Realism

> He recalled how, crossing the ewe-leaze when a child, he went on hands and knees and pretended to eat grass in order to see what the sheep would do. Presently he looked up and found them gathered around in a close ring, gazing at him with astonished faces.
> – *The Life and Work of Thomas Hardy*

> Everything human in the book strikes us as factious and insubstantial; the only things we believe in are the sheep and the dogs.
> – Henry James, review of *Far from the Madding Crowd*

> But if the sheep tried to have a voice in their own affairs, he was afraid that a good many shepherds would be willing to call in the wolves.
> – J. S. Mill, 1865 Speech at Westminster

For many Victorians, sheep were the antithesis of liberal creatures. Although they saw sheep–human relationships as constituting the oldest relationship humans had with other animals, sheep were consistently characterized not as individuals but as a flock that blindly follows a leader. Unlike dogs, for example, sheep were viewed as lacking individuality, courage, and intelligence, foreclosing their ability to participate in a political community composed of individuals. Claims for sheep welfare were thus made not on behalf of their liberal qualities, but "Because they are harmless creatures, and most useful to us, and depend upon us for protection" (Bray 20). The illiberal qualities of sheep made them ripe metaphors for working-class Victorians seen as unable to participate in democracy. In George Eliot's novel of the 1832 Reform Bill *Felix Holt, the Radical*, for example, the Tory family the Transomes "drive their tenants to the poll as if they were sheep" (70), while during the riots that broke out on election day, "rioters ran confusedly, like terrified sheep" (320). Although noting in *On Liberty* that "even sheep are not undistinguishably alike" (75), John Stuart Mill often used sheep as a metaphor for the humans who fall under bad government. In *Considerations on Representative Government*, Mill wrote that without any public duties, to be led by rather than take part in the political process, the human population will be made "a flock of sheep innocently nibbling the grass side by side" (255). Without a proper state education, he argues in *Principles of Political Economy*, where "intelligence and talent are maintained at a high standard within a governing corporation, but starved and discouraged outside the pale," the population will be like sheep guided by a shepherd, yet "without anything like so strong an interest as the shepherd has in the thriving condition of the flock" (333). Sheep are imagined as part of a political community only to the extent that they blindly follow a leader; they are characterized by an inability to exercise political autonomy. While admittedly at times the fault of the governing body – a bad shepherd – the failure of political sheep is ultimately a result of their helplessness, lack of individuality, and tendency to follow the fold.

Although Victorians conceptualized sheep as the antithesis of a liberal political community, Foucault argues that the birth of modern Western politics was inaugurated in the sheep-fold, placing sheep–human relationships at the core of liberal governmentality and its relationship to *homo economicus*. Pastoral power, the relationship of care and concern a shepherd has for the flock, guides the conduct of a population, making power both more dispersed and more benign. As seen in Chapters 1 and 2, animal welfare and the inclusion of animals within a liberal political community operated through pastoral power; the care and concern citizens showed for exploited and abused animals reified their position as subservient to humankind and the interests of capital. The Victorian government of animals resulted in the regulation of both animal minds and bodies, the working together of pastoral power and biopower, to ensure the wide dispersal of power over animal populations. While sheep were cared for through pastoral power, they were also objectified by biopolitical tactics that regulated their lives and bodies, making them physically fit for human consumption and control. Unlike work animals such as donkeys and horses, and dogs who were characterized as companions, sheep were pure capital; their wool clothed England's citizens while their flesh fed them. Sheep thus posed a conundrum to animal welfare advocates and the expansion of liberal governmentality to animal populations: how does one care for an animal who is seen only as capital? How does one include within a political community subjects that are not only property, but property meant for consumption? Can objects of capital be liberal creatures, capable of political inclusion? How does a multi-species political community care for animal subjects ostensibly lacking liberal cognition?

For Mill, sheep-like outsiders can disrupt the status quo, much like the subjects with alternative subjectivity in the two previous chapters. During an 1865 speech he gave when running for parliament, Mill imagines the sheep's perspective, and highlights their ability to revolt. Decrying the influence of money in politics, Mill emphasizes the need for non-hegemonic voices in parliament. He asked the crowd,

> Did they think it was the right and best thing that the House of Commons should be composed exclusively of rich men, or men with rich connections? (*No.*) There were a good many reasons why this was not desirable, and one was that the rich naturally sympathised with the rich. (*Hear, hear.*) The rich had sympathies enough for the poor when the poor came before them as objects of pity. Their feelings of charity were often highly creditable to their dispositions; and, besides, they had almost universally a kind of patronising and protective sympathy for the poor, such as shepherds had for their flocks – (*laughter and cheers*) – only that was conditional upon the flock always behaving like sheep. (*Renewed laughter, and Hear, hear.*) But if the sheep tried to have a voice in their own affairs, he was afraid that a good many shepherds would be willing to call in the wolves (*Cheers.*). ("Westminster" 32)

Although Mill's sheep function metaphorically, as he compares them to a potentially revolutionary working class, he raises the issue of animal perspectives within pastoral power and liberal governmentality. As in the text just quoted, sheep are on the border of a political community even as there is a drive to bring them in. Their inclusion, however, requires a radical revision of the political; taking seriously animal perspectives disrupts the status quo and structure of mid-Victorian representative politics. Animal politics requires an inclusion constituted by difference rather than universalism, one taking the logic of individualism so far that it can disrupt the very politics from which it emerged. Thus if governmentality governed a population rather than a territory, Mill's sheep show the difficulty of including alternative subjectivities within a hegemonic form of political control, and the reality of a representative government that excludes certain populations. Mill exposes how the shepherd guides his sheep only to the extent that they submit to them; his care is self-interested.

Thomas Hardy, a well-known advocate for animal welfare, imagined sheep in more democratic and non-hierarchical ways. In his *Life and Work*, Hardy describes how in discussing his earliest memories, "He recalled how, crossing the ewe-leaze when a child, he went on hands and knees and pretended to eat grass in order to see what the sheep would do. Presently he looked up and found them gathered around in a close ring, gazing at him with astonished faces" (479). These sheep, and Hardy's perception of them, are radically different from the above characterizations. Hardy breaks the animal–human hierarchy by putting himself below the sheep, head to the grass, crawling on his hands and knees. He willingly puts himself into what would be considered a demeaning and diminishing animal-like position to satisfy his curiosity about animal perspectives. By desiring to "see what the sheep would do" Hardy shows an interest in their thoughts and actions, while his reading of their faces as "astonished" projects onto them thought, reason, and emotion. Finally, his special emphasis on the face of the sheep registers a Levinasian ethic grounded in alterity and the gaze of the other.[1] This sheep–human scene destabilizes the animal–human hierarchy and disrupts the representational politics presented above: Hardy is the shepherd, bending down to the level of sheep, to hear what they have to say, and see from their perspective.

By taking political sheep seriously, and reading them *as sheep*, this chapter examines intersections between animals produced for human consumption, biopolitics, and liberal inclusion. I read Thomas Hardy's 1874 novel *Far from the Madding Crowd*, which features a shepherd and his flock of sheep, as a form of liberal inclusion that represents interdependence within animal–human communities. This does not happen by way of representing anthropomorphic sheep who function as individualized minor characters, or through providing detailed descriptions of sheep subjectivity. Rather, through what I call biopolitical realism, Hardy highlights the physical and emotional lives of sheep, and the ways their lives are intertwined with human communities beyond their role as capital. Hardy's lyrical, expansive, and almost microscopic realism includes animal populations while enhancing animal lives through description. This inclusive representation accepts difference and shows animal–human interdependence, especially as it results in social uplift. For although Hardy emphasizes how animals provide capital for the human, he also demonstrates how dependent humans are on the actions of sheep and other animals. Hardy's biopolitical realism thus destabilizes the human individualism at the core of exclusionary liberal capitalism, while giving animals wider political

---

[1] In *Totality and Infinity*, Emmanuel Levinas posits an ethics premised on welcoming and respecting the Other. Key to this ethic is the Other's face, especially the gaze, which "supplicates and demands, that can supplicate only because it demands, deprived of everything because entitled to everything" (75). When later asked if an animal has a face, he said, "One cannot entirely refuse the face of an animal," yet "The human face is completely different and only afterwards do we discover the face of an animal. I don't know if a snake has a face. I can't answer that question. A more specific analysis is needed" ("Name" 49). See Peter Atterton, "Ethical Cynicism," for a discussion of how Levinas's ethics extend to animals.

representation and inclusion. Inspired by Darwinian notions of ecology, Hardy shows a more inclusive liberalism with less desire to maintain hierarchy and reduce animals to their use value, by placing emphasis on animal–human interconnections, community, and freedom. Hardy's biopolitical realism dramatizes a pastoral power that engages with animals as more than capital while simultaneously exposing biopolitics' more regulatory forms.

This chapter analyzes mid-Victorian sheep and their relationships with humans to show an animal politics that resists the objectifying logic of liberal capitalism. Hardy's liberal inclusion accepts animal difference and views sheep as more than capital without inscribing them into regulatory frameworks guided by biopolitical tactics. I place my reading of Thomas Hardy in the context of mid-century cattle industry reform and concerns over the treatment of animals raised for human consumption. I emphasize the biopolitical regulation of these animals' lives, and the fears that arose when humans realized that their negative treatment of animal lives has physical repercussions for their own. By embracing animal capital and profit to better regulate animal lives, animal welfare discourse relied on how animal lives can negatively or positively affect human economies.[2] Thomas Hardy too was concerned with the treatment of animals raised for human consumption, yet he emphasized equality and justice for animals over capitalist drives for profit. *Far from the Madding Crowd*, Hardy's novel about shepherding and pastoral power, demonstrates how his affirmative biopolitical realism offers a form of liberal inclusion and an alternative ethic for relating to animal capital, while exposing the pernicious forms of biopower humans have over animal lives.

Victorian Sheep and the Biopolitics of Cattle Industry Reform

During the 1860s and 1870s, sheep and cattle were at the forefront of animal welfare discourse, this time over how to treat animal bodies destined for capital and consumption. While the Vegetarian Society had been decrying the consumption of animals for years, the RSPCA hoped to regulate the treatment of animals on their way to slaughter and as they met their deaths. As shown in Chapter 3, debates about the removal of

---

[2] The phrase "animal capital" comes from Nicole Shukin's *Animal Capital: Rendering Life in Biopolitical Times*, in which she historicizes the processes that render animals forms of capital. Animal capital "simultaneously notates the semiotic currency of animal signs *and* the carnal traffic in animal substances ... it signals a tangle of biopolitical relations within which the economic and symbolic capital of animal life can no longer be sorted into binary distinction" (7).

Smithfield Market focused not so much on animal cruelty, but on the filth and nuisance created by the market. A similar logic guided slaughterhouse debates twenty years later. Although Copenhagen Fields in Islington became the new animal market in 1855, and Smithfield became a dead-meat market in 1861, there were still more than a thousand private slaughterhouses in London alone, and calls for public abattoirs – in the belief they could be better regulated – continued throughout the rest of the century. Indeed, in 1874 reformers estimated the number of private slaughterhouses as more than 1,429 (Otter 90).[3] In 1875 parliament passed the Public Health Act, which gave local governments the authority to provide and regulate public slaughterhouses, and required owners to affix a notice that they were "licensed" or "regulated."[4] The import of foreign animals also spurred state regulation. The numbers of imported cattle rose in the 1860s, and the 1865 cattle plague, or rinderpest – in which 3 million animals died – led to the 1866 Cattle Diseases Prevention Act, which stipulated that foreign animals had to be slaughtered on arrival, and could not be moved off the coast alive (Perren, "Filth" 141–142).[5] The plague also led to the creation of the first state veterinary service, to deal specifically with animal diseases, and an intensification in the development of veterinary science (Swabe 99, 107–108). While the RSPCA and other humane organizations formed later such as the Humanitarian League in 1891 were concerned with the humane slaughter of animals and the conditions in which animals were transported, animal welfare and legal discourse emphasized connections between animal and human health, and between animal capital and the economy. As Richard Perren emphasizes, slaughterhouse reform came after legislation for the inspection of meat ("Filth" 135), showing the extent to which the government of animals emphasized their status as capital and the ways animal bodies can physically harm human ones. While animal bodies had been under human control for centuries, especially through breeding practices, cattle industry reform marks a heightened concern with how animal populations affect

---

[3] Private slaughterhouses were any building wherein animals were slaughtered. Many were small, or even sheds, and not specifically designed for the purpose of killing (Otter 90).

[4] The governmental regulation of slaughterhouses goes back to 1786, when parliament passed the Knackers Act in response to the stealing of horses, cows, and other cattle. This law required those keeping a slaughterhouse to get a license, which allowed inspectors to enter at any time. For an in-depth discussion of the regulation of animal waste and slaughter, see Atkins, *Animal Cities*.

[5] See also Perren, *The Meat Trade in Britain 1840–1914*.

human ones, how the care of their bodies affects the economy, and how the state should take charge of their bodies.[6]

Debates about animal slaughter and the regulation of animal bodies raised for capital and consumption were influenced less by pastoral power and more by Victorian biopolitics, although the two worked together to maximize control over animals. Foucault locates biopower's intensification in the nineteenth century, and the regulation of animal bodies, both in their cultivation and in their deaths, was a key feature of liberal governmentality's relationship with security and conduct. For Foucault "power's hold over life" equates to "State control of the biological" ("Society" 239–240). This control was a means of security, or "state intervention with the essential function of ensuring the security of the natural phenomena of economic processes or processes intrinsic to population" ("Security" 353). Biopolitics' intensification in the mid-nineteenth century aligned with late-century new liberal ideals; inspired by Darwinian evolution and its implications for collectivism, "biology was replacing political economy as the scientific basis of politics and ethics" (Freeden 93), and state regulation was looked on less as government interference and more as cultivation.[7] Whereas pastoral power regulates conduct, biopower manages the biological aspects of animals and humans. In "Society Must Be Defended," Foucault emphasizes that biopolitics "is, in a word, a matter of taking control of life and the biological processes of man-as-species and of ensuring that they are not disciplined, but regularized" (246–247). Biopolitics gains power from growth in population management, especially through connections to scientific and medical advancement: "biopolitics will derive its knowledge from, and define its power's field of intervention in terms of, the birth rate, the mortality rate, various biological disabilities, and the effects of the environment" (245). As such, biopolitical strategies involve the fostering and enhancement of life, of doing what one can to "'make' live," at the same time they may disavow life and "'let' die" (241). Forms of population management secure and enhance life, and include "every form of indirect murder" (256). Such killing is directly, and ironically, connected to the enhancement of life: "In the biopower system ... killing or the imperative to kill is acceptable only if it results not in a victory over political adversaries, but in the elimination of the

---

[6] For a discussion of cattle breeding in the nineteenth-century, see Ritvo, *The Animal Estate*.
[7] Michael Freeden identifies new liberalism as a shift in emphasis from laissez-faire philosophy, political economy, and restricted government interference to the necessity of government to help citizens attain liberal ideas of freedom and individual development. Inspired by Darwinian evolution, new liberalism emphasized community and the need for state-sponsored social reform.

biological threat to and the improvement of the species or race" (256). The enhancement of human populations was the rationale for killing animals in the cattle industry, as Victorians believed humans need meat to survive. This logic emphasizes how biopolitics easily folds into the politics of death, wherein death is excused and even encouraged. Thus while Foucault registers racism as the focal point for such power, it also works by way of speciesism, of locating "man-as-species" (247) by way of the animal–human divide, as Agamben describes in *The Open*.

Biopolitics secures the market, making it a driver of capitalist practices designed to meet the goal of life enhancement. The regulation of animal life especially works in the interests of capital; animal bodies are controlled, manipulated, and killed to the extent that they secure human populations financially. For even well-fed bodies mean more labor power. Brett Levinson explains that "The overarching model for biopolitics or governmentality, in fact, is not the live body. It is the free market. Biopolitics is an economism before it is a biologism ... for Foucault, the fear of terror, spurring biopolitics, actually results from the appearance of a certain truth: the unpredictability of the market" (247). In this reading, life is enhanced only to the extent it is good for the economy. This relationship between biology and the economy structures an 1873 parliamentary debate about slaughterhouses and the dead-meat industry. The bill under consideration was an amendment to the 1844 Metropolis Buildings Act, which stipulated that in 1874 slaughterhouses closer than 40 feet to a public way and 50 feet to a dwelling house would have to be removed. Unless parliament passed an amendment, many slaughterhouses would close, right at the height of meat consumption.[8] William Brewer, a member for Colchester, worried about what these closures would do to the meat market. He argued that the abolishment of private slaughterhouses would force citizens to rely on the dead-meat market, possibly raising the price of meat overall. He explained that "it was clear beyond dispute that London could not be adequately supplied with meat from this source [the dead-meat market] alone, for although in cool and fresh seasons of the year, London, at enhanced prices, could be supplied to a great extent with dead meat, yet in hot and sultry weather ... London could not depend on the dead meat market" (*Hansard's* CCXV: 489). Not only would regulation create a shortage of meat for London's citizens, but it would also reduce profits

---

[8] In the 1860s, citizens ate an estimated 90 pounds of meat per year, up from 87.3 pounds in the 1850s. The amount jumped almost twenty pounds per person in 1870–1874, when citizens ate an estimated 108.3 lbs. of meat per person (Perren, *Meat* 3).

for butchers. Further anticipating arguments that slaughterhouses need regulations to stop animal cruelty, Brewer

> must notice a most gratuitous charge against a whole class of London tradesmen – namely, that of cruelty to the animals they had purchased for their private slaughterhouses. That would be sheer suicidal folly. No man pursued evil as evil, and for its own sake, in direct opposition to his interest and the strongest motives which could influence human actions. If a short-horn in fine condition were overdriven only half-an-hour the flesh set badly and the market was lost. If the beast had a bruise – and it bruised very easily – the joint in which it occurred was unsaleable. Surely, they would take the best security for good treatment in the interest the man had in the comfort and case of his beast no less than in the pride he felt in the condition of the meat which he displayed in his shop front. (*Hansard's* CCXV: 490)

Brewer suggests that the market will regulate animal cruelty, not legislation, showing his belief in economics as a guiding factor for animal–human relationships. Opponents of the bill, however, argued that the dead-meat trade should be cultivated for the good of the population. Clare Read, a member for Norfolk, "believed it was desirable, both for the health of the community, humanity to the cattle, and the supply of good meat, that the trade in dead meat should be developed as much as possible, and as these private slaughter-houses tended to restrict it, he should offer his opposition" (502). These examples highlight how the regulation of animal populations, and debates about animal cruelty in the meat industry, were discussed in economic and biopolitical terms: animal bodies were regulated in relation to the market and the good of human populations. Debates about animal slaughter give credence to Levinson's claim that "Biopolitical man is *homo oeconomicus*" (249): one regulates life for the good of the economy, their own social uplift, and what we might call *animalis oeconomicus*.[9]

Thomas Osborne resolves the seeming contradiction between liberal decentralization and the wide government control of public health that intensified in the 1830s and 1840s, and extended into and beyond the mid-century, by emphasizing that public health and sanitary science were "intrinsically concerned with *economy*. They were conceived as measures of security, forms of government that saved on interventions and costs in other sectors of the social order" (104). As such public health discourses

---

[9] Further showing connections between sheep and capitalism is Armstrong's discussion of how the wool trade and the enclosure of sheep pastures led to "the eventual emergence of industrial capitalism" (*Sheep* 89), a phenomenon Marx noted when he claimed, "The labourers are first driven from the land, and then come the sheep" (qtd. in Armstrong 89).

and regulations, which spread to the animal population by the 1850s, were strategies of security encouraged by liberal governmentality. By cultivating the population's health, the government ensured a strong economy and citizens healthy enough to contribute to the nation's wealth. Indeed, it ensured a healthy *homo economicus*. These public health movements were a form of pastoral power that conducted the lower class to middle-class morality. As Pamela Gilbert argues, good hygiene and a healthy body resulted in "political fitness" (3). Cleanliness was associated with good morals, and thus state control over the biological was dispersed through social reform movements aimed toward improving the health not only of the poor but of the larger social body. Likewise, the regulation of animals raised for meat and wool ensured a strong economy and a healthy population. As Cara Bray emphasizes in *Our Duty to Animals*, an animal welfare text written for use in schools and printed in early issues of *Animal World*, "not only must we thank the sheep for what it gives us every day of our lives, but for giving England the woollen trade which has employed thousands of poor people for ages past, and which used to make the chief wealth of the country" (15–16). Here sheep are imagined as "giving" their lives and wool, reifying their submission – both mental and physical – to the human. At the same time, conducting citizens to believe in the necessity of the meat and wool industry, and suggesting sheep willingly participate in these industries, secures the wealth of the human population.

Legislators and organizations like the RSPCA thus worked together for the good of animal and human populations. Auberon Herbert suggested as much in the 1873 slaughterhouse debate:

> he trusted that whatever arrangement was ultimately arrived at, the slaughtering of cattle would be so carried on as to inflict the least possible pain on the animals to be killed. For this purpose, efficient inspection of slaughterhouses, public or private, should be provided. He thought that a strong argument in favour of abattoirs was that they afforded ample means of inspection on the part of the officers of the Society for the Prevention of Cruelty to Animals, which were not given by any other system. (*Hansard's* CCXV: 504)

Ultimately, then, within animal welfare discourse around cattle industry reform, there is most often concern for animals only to the extent that their treatment has consequences for human lives and economies. As public health drove regulations of the meat industry – indeed, as we saw only weak slaughterhouse reform came as part of the 1875 Public Health Act – economy and conduct drove the biopolitical regulation of animals within animal welfare discourse. That is, pastoral power and biopower worked together in the interests of animal capital. And indeed, in his discussion of pastoral power, Foucault neglects to emphasize its connection to the interests of capital. For a shepherd ultimately conducts his sheep for the sake of his own profit, cultivating their bodies as capital. When thus taking care of the animal population, pastoral power and biopolitics ensures the well-being of animal capital and the human population.

In the 1870s, animal welfare advocates were concerned not only with animal slaughter but also with the shearing of sheep for their wool. Although considered a relatively benign process and good for the sheep, they suffered from the cold if sheared during winter. With the system of private slaughterhouses, farmers in the country who sold their sheep during the winter would sometimes shear them before bringing them into London, in order to sell the wool as well. If there was a better system for the transportation of dead meat, animal welfare advocates argued, farmers could profit from more animal products and the meat would be better quality. For "what is good for the sheep is good for its owner also" (Bray 19). An 1874 *Animal World* article, "Abolition of Private Slaughter-Houses," describes it thus:

> In the cold month of January the same men consign absolutely naked sheep to the horrible sufferings arising out of journeys made in open trucks, which expose them to the keenest blasts of wind, rain, and snow. This is done with a hope, generally not realized, of securing additional net profit by the separate sale of the fleecy covering which a merciful Creator has given to His creatures to enable them to endure our severe climate ... No doubt if graziers were supplied with the means of sending up their dead meat to London in cool ventilated chambers, they would avail themselves of it: for by slaughtering at their own farms they would profit by the hides, hoofs, offal, and blood, the latter being invaluable as a manure, all of which is now lost to them. The public would benefit, inasmuch as the meat thus slaughtered and conveyed would be found to be in better condition than that of the poor ox or sheep that has just experienced all the miseries of a twelve hours' journey in a cattle truck, succeeded by an agreeable trudge from the railway station to the slaughter-house. (180–181)

Arguments for the better care of animal bodies focus not just on animal conduct, as we saw in Chapters 1 and 2, but more so on the good of the population and the possibility of higher profit for the shepherds. While farmers may try to profit from the wool when sheep are sheared early, animal welfare advocates suggested that even more profit can be made from killing them on their own farms. Arguments further suggested that the meat from sheep sheared early was poor quality, as Cara Bray explains that the punishment for shearing sheep in winter is poor meat (15,16). Similarly, meat from terrified animals was less healthy: "There can be little doubt that the meat of an animal killed after a protracted period of agitation, and after the inhalation of foul vapours, is less wholesome than that of one killed in an undisturbed and unsuspicious state" (Chater and Lester 100). This biopolitical emphasis on animal bodies rather than conduct underscores the capital made from bodies treated well. For animals whose bodies rather than labor function as capital, profit becomes the major rationale for animal welfare.

RSPCA discourse further connects good treatment and profit by suggesting that farmers should be better shepherds through realizing their duty as cultivators of capital. The article "Sheltering Sheep in Bad Weather" emphasizes the shepherd's conduct:

> In a state of nature, sheep and goats, in obedience to a wonderful instinct, search for, and generally find, shelter on the approach of a storm. Is it asking too much of mankind, when such animals are domesticated, and are consequently unable to follow their instinct, that shepherds shall stand in the place of such instinct, and protect their cattle, for the obvious reason that the poor things, surrounded by hedges and kept within enclosures to serve domestic purposes, are unable to protect themselves?

Whereas the animal welfare discourse examined in Chapter 2 argued that animal instinct was constructed for submission, this article suggests that animal instinct is hampered by human intervention. A good shepherd supplements these instincts, protecting animals in the interests of capital. Yet sheep subjectivity was not excluded from arguments for bringing them into the political community. Like writers such as Eliot and Mill, who emphasized the non-liberal qualities of sheep, animal welfare advocates illustrated their helplessness and dependence on humans. Cara Bray emphasized that "Like most grass-eating animals, the sheep is gentle and timid, and seems to ask for the protection of man to shield it from harm; and as long as we hear of man having lived upon the earth, the sheep seems to have lived under his care" (18). Believing that sheep were thoroughly dependent on humans and "incapable of returning to a state of nature" ("Sheep and Lambs" 89), animal welfare advocates asked for shepherds who realized the extent of a sheep's helplessness and regulated their bodies for the good of the human population. Even the London Vegetarian Society saw sheep as capital, explaining that "Man cannot put sheep to a worse use than to eat them. They should be in a measure treated like the land. As it is cultivated to produce corn, fruit, and flax; so sheep should be reared and tended to produce wool ... A sheep that is fed in order to produce mutton and fat, will not produce wool of any merit, and if we persist in having mutton, we must do without wool" ("The Use of Sheep").

The liberal capitalism encouraged by the RSPCA emphasizes profit and reifies animals in a position of capital. Animal welfare discourse perpetuates an animal–human hierarchy in which sheep are in a position of helplessness in relationship to the human, reflecting a sentimental liberalism that remains at the core of many contemporary animal rights arguments. Cynthia Willet describes this as a paternalism wherein arguments emphasize the vulnerability and suffering of dependent creatures rather than their status as autonomous beings (37). Although the focus on bodily suffering challenges oppressive forms of individualism granted to other domestic animals, it ignores the potential agencies, epistemologies, and less hierarchical forms of communities we share with animals. In Victorian animal welfare discourse, sheep are represented as a population needing biopolitical regulation, rather than as individuals who willingly submit to the human; yet they are still affected by the speciesism identified as part of liberal governmentality. This speciesism emphasizes not only mental and moral differences between animals and humans, but also the differences in their bodies and how they are used. Sheep can be subjects of political concern and incorporated into the political community only insofar as their bodies are cultivated for consumption: they should be healthy and free of disease, their flesh should be fresh and free of bruising. Animal biopolitics ensures a healthy liberal human subject, one who treats animals well for the good of capital. Such care cultivates the short life of the sheep and enhances the human population through profit, health, and vigor. Healthy sheep secure the market and the population, contribute to the rise of *homo economicus*, and cultivate a political community in which animals are properly conducted to their deaths.

Thomas Hardy's Animal Welfare: Liberty, Justice, and Ecology

Thomas Hardy's animal welfare was explicitly political and influenced by foundational liberal principles such as liberty, rights, justice, and equality. For example, he praised the Humanitarian League's "readjustment of altruistic morals, by enlarging, as a necessity of rightness, the application of what has been called 'The Golden Rule' from the area of mere mankind to that of the whole animal kingdom" (*Public* 311), and noted "the difficulty of carrying out to its logical extreme the principle of equal justice to all the animal kingdom" (312). He believed in giving animals liberty by keeping them out of cages, off chains, and allowing them an autonomy rare in human societies. For example, one of Hardy's gardeners from Max Gate explained,

> The garden was often visited by a hare which somehow managed to get over the wall which surrounded it. It would eat the carrot tops and do a great deal of damage to other growing plants. Wessex [Hardy's dog] used to try and catch it but without any success, and Mr Hardy, when I told him of its visits and the destruction it caused, said: "I do not mind it in the garden. They are animals, let them carry on." He was very fond of animals and birds, and would never allow me to trap or shoot them however destructive they were to the fruit or vegetables. He insisted that I allow all birds to do as they liked in the garden. (Gibson 226–227)

Hardy lets animals come to his garden even at a loss to himself; to "let them carry on," and "do as they liked in the garden" allows them a freedom not reliant on subjection. By letting animals destroy or take from his garden, he rejects the nature/society divide Locke posits as foundational to political community. As Hardy's garden becomes a communal space for animals and humans, he suggests the possibility of a collectivist animal–human politics, which includes positive liberties for animals. His animal politics arises, in part, from imagining the animal point of view in ways that do not always reflect positively back on the human. He says of the "'lower' animals" that he "hear[s] them complaining in the railway trucks sometimes" (*Letters* III: 74), while after seeing horses in the street in 1888 he wrote, "What was it on the faces of those horses? – Resignation. Their eyes looked at me, haunted me. The absoluteness of their resignation was terrible. When afterwards I heard their tramp as I lay in bed, the ghosts of their eyes came in to me, saying, 'Where is your justice, O man and ruler?'" (*Life* 220). Novelist and playwright Eden Phillpotts explained that Hardy "felt an uncommon regard for animals and revealed strange understanding of his pets, for his imagination enabled him to see life from their point of view and, more or less, to understand what was passing in their little minds. He was never sentimental about them, but always sympathetic and concerned to read their emotions" (Gibson 120). Hardy understood the brutal and confined lives of domestic animals, as he told American novelist Ellen Glasgow in June 1914: "I have often wondered . . . whether I'd choose the lot of a wild or of a domestic animal; and I think, all things considered, I'd choose the lot of the wild" (Gibson 112–113). Domestic animals, he suggests, have little freedom. Indeed, the cruel treatment of animals perhaps inclined him to remark in 1909 that "Freedom, under her incubus of armaments, territorial ambitions smugly disguised as patriotism, superstitions, conventions of every sort, is of such stunted proportions in this her so-called time, that the human race is likely to be extinct before Freedom arrives at maturity" (*Public* 304).

Anna West's *Thomas Hardy and Animals* demonstrates the wide-ranging extent to which Hardy was a humanitarian writer, even though his animal welfare was at times contradictory and not always straightforward.[10] By focusing on his use of the word "creature," which he applied to both animals and humans, West shows how Hardy cultivated an animal ethics that destabilized the animal–human divide, privileged animal alterity, and sought alternative understandings of language, reason, and moral agency. Indeed, Elisa Cohn goes so far as to call kindness to animals Hardy's "paradigm of moral behavior" (168). Hardy saw his writing as central to his involvement with the ethics of the humane movement, and through it he attempted to level the animal–human relationship. The protagonists with which we are to sympathize – Tess, Jude, Sue, and Gabriel Oak – are often associated with animals and have humane relationships with them. In a well-known interview, he characterized his novels as "one plea against 'man's inhumanity to man' – to woman – and to the lower animals" (Gibson 70), showing how his animal ethics were part of a larger desire to bring the excluded into the sphere of moral concern. Throughout his novels and poetry Hardy recognized within animal life knowledges that rival humankind's, imagined animal perspectives, and acknowledged that humans are intimately connected with animals in a series of relationships that move beyond hierarchies perpetuated by sentimental liberalism and the speciesism resulting from governmentality.

Although he was conflicted about vivisection, he decried the practice of making animals perform, the use of horses in war, animal fighting, the chaining of dogs, caged birds, and especially the cattle industry.[11] He allowed the journal of the Animal Friends' Society, *The Animals' Friend*,

---

[10] West's final chapter analyzes the contradictions within Hardy's animal welfare and animal–human relationships, such as the drowning of kittens. For other readings of Hardy's animal welfare and its relationship to his writing, see Jean Brooks, "The Place of the Animal Kingdom in Thomas Hardy's Works"; Michael Campbell, "Thomas Hardy's Attitude toward Animals"; Ron Morrison, "Humanity towards Man, Woman, and the Lower Animals: Thomas Hardy's *Jude the Obscure* and the Victorian Humane Movement"; and Christine Roth, "The Zoocentric Ecology of Hardy's Poetic Consciousness."

[11] West argues that Hardy saw the utility of vivisection, as he suggested it "might offer a trade-off of inestimable benefits from a minimum amount of inflicted pain" (West, *Hardy* 174). In his final entry for *Who's Who* in 1927, updated and edited by himself, he notes he was a member of the Council of Justice to Animals, and "is against blood-sport, dog-chaining, and the caging of birds" (*Public* 473). The first draft of this entry, from 1897, does not mention his commitment to animal welfare (142).

to print the pig-killing scene from *Jude the Obscure*, as he believed it "might be useful in teaching mercy in the Slaughtering of Animals for the meat-market – the cruelties involved in the business having been a great grief to me for years" (*Letters* II: 97). In 1924, Hardy wrote a poem for the RSPCA's centenary, in which he praised the humane movement but noted the cruelty that still exists, especially in private slaughterhouses: "Cries still are heard in secret nooks, / Till hushed with gag or slit or thud; / And hideous dens whereon none looks / Are sprayed with needless blood" ("Compassion" 21–24).[12] Indeed, Hardy was much affected by seeing a train of bulls and cows headed to Islington for slaughter, as he "thought of this sight for long after" (*Life* 468). He supported humane legislation that gave animals "A quick exit, with the minimum of suffering (mental and physical)" (*Public* 416), and became a member of the Council of Justice to Animals, which fought for humane slaughter, in 1911. In his will he left 50 pounds each to the RSPCA and Council of Justice to Animals "to be applied so far as practicable to the investigation of the means by which animals are conveyed from their houses to the slaughter-houses with a view to the lessening of their sufferings in such transit" (*Life* 468).[13] Hardy was never idealistic enough to believe that it was possible to stop killing animals for food, accepting instead that it "can only be mitigated" (*Public* 268). Thus part of Hardy's critique of the cattle industry stems from the objectification animals undergo at the hands of capitalism, a system that controls animal lives but neglects their status as feeling, thinking creatures. Hardy moves beyond economics to the realm of justice and morality.

This critique of economic exploitation is clear in Hardy's poem "Bags of Meat," which criticizes the capitalist nature of the cattle industry and its negation of an animal's subject status as it reduces them to a "bag of meat" (1). The poem's references to slave auctions – the auctioneer and jeering audience, the description of the animals' bodies and capacity for labor, and the sexualization of the animals – make clear Hardy's desire to instill a sense of personhood within a population objectified as property. The animals are made to stand and "turn about" (24), while the auctioneer and audience comment on their bodies and physical abilities. The auctioneer sexualizes the animals, as he exclaims, "'Now here's a heifer – worth

---

[12] West notes there are several variations of the poem (171).
[13] This money was also to investigate "condemnatory action against the caging of wild birds and the captivity of rabbits and other animals," and was originally to be called the Emma Hardy Bequest (*Notebooks* 101 n. 494).

more / than bid, were she bone-poor; / Yet she's round as a barrel of beer;' / 'She's a plum,' said the second auctioneer" (15–18), and emphasizes their fecundity: "'That calf, she sucked three cows, / Which is not matched for bouse / In the nurseries of high life / By the first-born of a nobleman's wife!'" (27–30). The poem highlights the different ways cattle are commodified and exploited by the meat industry: they are reduced to meat, sold for their ability to breed, described as possible Christmas gifts – "'He'd be worth the money to kill / And give away Christmas for goodwill'" (13–14) – and seen as ways to cultivate the land: "'Now this young bull – for thirty pound? / Worth that to manure your ground!'" (19–20). The behavior of the auctioneer and the objectification of the animals contrasts with Hardy's description of their emotional lives, as they are "timid" and "quivering" (3). The poem ends with their point of view, and offers a stark contrast to the auctioneer's objectification:

> Each beast, when driven in,
> Looks round at the ring of bidders there
> With a much-amazed reproachful stare,
>   As at unnatural kin,
> For bringing him to a sinister scene
> So strange, unhomelike, hungry, mean;
> His fate the while suspended between
>   A butcher, to kill out of hand,
>   And a farmer, to keep on the land;
> One can fancy a tear runs down his face
> When the butcher wins, and he's driven from the place.
>   (35–45)

As in his poem "Compassion," in which he calls the animal gaze "more eloquent / Than tongues of widest heed" (9–10), Hardy registers a Levinasian ethics that emphasizes animal subjectivity and morality, and posits the gaze of the animal as more powerful than human language. Hardy characterizes the bulls and cows as having the moral high ground, destabilizing the animal–human hierarchy that suggests animals lack social sympathies; rather, the animals in the poem "reproach" the unnaturalness of the humans. Indeed, elsewhere Hardy commented that humans are no more morally advanced than animals: "[I] think what an unfortunate result it was that *our* race acquired the upper hand," he wrote to Florence Henniker, "& not a more kindly one, in the development of species. If, say, lions had, they wd [*sic*] have been less cruel by this time" (*Letters* III: 74). Hardy emphasizes a natural connection between animals and humans, but by calling humans "unnatural kin" he shows their behavior as unethical. The cattle industry, Hardy suggests, disrupts the kinship between animals and humans, as it objectifies and commodifies animals instead of seeing them as subjects related to humans. The poem suggests that within the meat industry, animals cannot be objects of capital *and* subjects. In a liberal society where capitalism represents freedom, lack of government interference, and security for the nation, animals in the cattle industry will consistently be reduced to objectified capital.

Two well-known scenes from *Jude the Obscure* – when a young Jude lets the birds eat Farmer Troutham's corn, and the pig-killing scene – emphasize the difficulty of viewing animals as subjects worthy of justice under capitalism. While Jude sees both the birds and the pig as fellow creatures, for a capitalist society they are a means to either thwart profit or make it. When Jude gets tired of clacking and scaring the birds, for he "grew sympathetic with the birds' thwarted desires" (15), he speaks to them in collectivist terms, almost imagining a welfare state in which animals have positive liberties: "You *shall* have some dinner – you shall. There is enough for us all. Farmer Troutham can afford to let you have some. Eat, then, my dear little birdies, and make a good meal!" (15). What Jude doesn't realize is that even if Troutham could afford to let the birds have some corn, he would make more money if they had none. For Troutham, profit trumps a meal for the birds, whereas Jude decries capitalism's objectification of animals, bemoaning "the flaw in the terrestrial scheme, by which what was good for God's birds was bad for God's gardener" (17). As we saw above, animal welfare discourse perpetuated the opposite belief, whereas *Jude* highlights the incongruity between capitalism and animal welfare. Similarly, when tasked with killing the pig – "A creature I have fed with my own hands" (64) – Jude refuses to bleed him slowly and kills him quickly, even though it will result in the loss of twenty pounds. Arabella calls him a "tender-hearted fool" for thinking of fellow feeling over money (65), yet Jude realizes the impossibility of an alternate system in which animals can be killed for food yet treated as fellow creatures. After accidentally kicking the bucket of blood, Jude notes that "The white snow, stained with the blood of his fellow-mortal, wore an illogical look to him as a lover of justice" (67). The necessity of killing animals – Jude does not fault Arabella for needing the pig for food – conflicts with a just society.

Hardy's animal welfare thus emphasizes kin and community, destabilizing the animal–human divide much more than other writers in this study. Such ethics were inspired by a well-documented admiration for Darwin, giving credence to his belief that humans are no longer at the top of a great chain of being, and "all organic creatures are of one family"

(*Public* 306). For Hardy, Darwin's conclusions led to the obvious belief that humans should expand their sphere of morality to include animals, but "Few people seem to perceive fully as yet that the most far-reaching consequence of the establishment of the common origin of all species is ethical" (*Public* 311). Yet while Darwin saw elementary forms of morality and sociability in the animal world, and Hardy did too, Hardy ultimately saw nature in general as "*un*moral" (*Letters* III: 231), a belief Jude echoes in Hardy's last novel: "Nature's logic was too horrid for him to care for. That mercy towards one set of creatures was cruelty towards another sickened his sense of harmony" (*Jude* 18).[14] Scholars such as Gillian Beer, George Levine, Anna West, and Jean Brooks emphasize how Hardy's views on nature and animals are indebted to Darwin's belief in inter-species entanglement and dependence. Hardy's Darwinian impulses – his effusive descriptions of land, animals, and insects; his movement between different scales of life and time; and his descriptions of humans' intimate connection to the landscape and its creaturely inhabitants – mark his place as a writer to whom today's ecocritics and posthumanists can look for a decentralization of anthropocentrism. Although he has long been considered a nature writer, Hardy most fully details what Timothy Morton calls "the mesh," an "interconnectedness of all living and non-living things" (*Ecological Thought* 28), or "the ecological thought." Morton argues,

> Ecology shows us that all beings are connected. *The ecological thought* is the thinking of interconnectedness. The ecological thought is a thought about ecology, but it's also a thinking that is ecological ... It's a practice and a process of becoming fully aware of how human beings are connected with other beings – animal, vegetable, or mineral. Ultimately this includes thinking about democracy. (7)

Hardy's ecological thought led him to ask for equality and justice for animals, positing a more inclusive liberalism and broader representation. As seen through his views on animals, Hardy's liberalism emphasized the interdependence and cooperation that would be embraced by new liberals later in the century. As Willet argues, classic liberalism "displaced" older conceptions of animal and human communities (34), yet Hardy seeks to reemphasize kin and community, understanding animals as "kindred political agents in their own right with interlocking histories, cultures, and technologies" (Willet 38). Hardy saw the need for animals to be included

---

[14] See West and also Sumpter, "On Suffering and Sympathy: *Jude the Obscure*, Evolution, and Ethics," who discusses in detail how Hardy's views on animals, morality, and sympathy were influenced by Darwin.

within a moral and political community, but not with humans at the top of a great chain of being: "I fear that the human race has emerged so little as yet from a state of savagery that not much can be done" (*Public* 455), he wrote. In Hardy's animal politics, the human falls to the ground, only to be surrounded by animals gazing at him with astonished faces, asking as citizens ask their government, "Where is your justice, O man and ruler?"

Throughout his novels and poetry, Hardy imagines a multi-species democracy; he equalizes the representational sphere, giving voice to excluded animals and humans. Hardy brings the concerns of animals – their lives, perspectives, relationships, and epistemologies – into the public sphere, yet refrains from projecting anthropocentric viewpoints onto them. Importantly he argued for their inclusion not based on the belief that they desire to work for humans, or because they are lesser than humans, two claims cultivated by the RSPCA. Rather, Hardy believed in justice for animals, and thus takes liberal claims toward equality, justice, democracy, and equal representation to their most far-reaching conclusions. In his novels he expands the sphere of ethical and political concern beyond individualism and into interconnections, community, and alterity: an ecological thought. The result is a more democratic way of imagining animal–human relationships.[15] In the next section I describe how this representational sphere is articulated in Hardy's early novel *Far from the Madding Crowd*. Written during the height of concerns about the cattle industry, Hardy represents animals beyond the objectification as capital they faced through animal welfare and legal discourse. By focusing especially on animals whose lives are regulated in the cattle industry – a flock of sheep – I show how Hardy exposes biopower's pernicious effects and offers an affirmative biopolitics that enhances the lives of animals beyond their status as capital, including them in an imaginative multi-species democracy, the ultimate expression of ecological thought.

Biopolitical Realism in *Far from the Madding Crowd*

When working on revisions for *Far from the Madding Crowd*, Hardy was interested in the descriptive complexity of animal perspectives. Describing a scene in Celbridge Place, London, he writes, "Middle-aged gentleman talking to handsome buxom lady across the stone parapet of the house opposite, which is just as high as their breasts – she inside, he on pavement.

---

[15] I also explore these ideas, and what I call Hardy's "democratic impulse," in "Seeing Animals on Egdon Heath: The Democratic Impulse of Thomas Hardy's *The Return of the Native*."

It rains a little, a very mild moisture, which a duck would call nothing, a dog a pleasure, a cat possibly a good deal" (*Notebooks* 18). Hardy rejects a human-centered perspective, even in what seems a human-centered moment. Animal perspectives enhance description by representing a more inclusive viewpoint made up of difference; thinking about how other creatures experience the rain expands the sphere of subjectivity and offers perspectives that may differ from the human's. While *Far from the Madding Crowd* does not include many individualized animal viewpoints, his journal entry shows a desire to widen the sphere of representation and subjectivity to the animal world. The novel, which Hardy called a pastoral tale (*Life* 97), represents the life of Gabriel Oak, a shepherd who cares for his flock but refrains from constructions of subjectivity rendered in an anthropocentric liberal framework. The novel illustrates pastoral power, but critiques regulatory notions of animal conduct.[16] At the same time, however, Hardy's interest in the daily life of Gabriel's sheep, and his intricate, lyrical renderings of their lives merge pastoral power with a different form of power, one that controls not conduct, but the very lives of sheep.

The earliest reviewers of the novel praised its deep engagement with nature and animal life. In his 1874 review of the novel Henry James claimed that "Everything human in the book strikes us as factitious and insubstantial; the only things we believe in are the sheep and the dogs" (31), while the human characters are "artificial," "a shadow" and "an elaborate stage-figure" (31). Like George Gissing, who praises Grip's characterization over Barnaby's, James privileges animal representations as more life-like. Reviewers found the scenes where Hardy describes nature, the weather, and "the labours of beasts and men" the most realistic, "nearly perfect, and worthy of all praise" (Lang 36). An unsigned review in the *Athenaeum* explains that "we know of no other living author who could so have described the burning rick-yard or the approaching thunderstorm" ("Review" 20), while R. H. Hutton in the *Spectator* claimed that "at least so far as the physical forms of nature and the external features of the farm-work are concerned, it has been mastered by the author of the tale. The details of the farming and the sheep-keeping, of the labouring, the feasting, and the mourning, are painted with all the vividness of a powerful imagination, painting from the stores of a sharply-outlined memory"

---

[16] Foucault's concept of pastoral power is different from the pastoral literary genre. While pastoral power uses the image of the shepherd and his flock to describe power relations, pastoral as a genre is defined as positing an idealized rural against the urban. Michael Squires defines the pastoral novel as "a form which combines realism with the pastoral impulse" (2).

(21). Reviewers found the details of the sheep's lives worth quoting at length, as Andrew Lang explains in the journal *Academy*: "We prefer to quote the enumeration of the signs by which the hero detected the approach of a storm, because the quotation includes the sheep, whose birth and death, in this tale, are narrated with great minuteness" (36–37). More recently, Ivan Kreilkamp similarly locates the novel's realism in the lives of animals, but places it in opposition to the idealism associated with the pastoral genre. He explains, "Part of the 'realism' of the novel and its modification of any idealized pastoral lies in Hardy's insistence on the sometimes indecorous bodily life of the sheep in Gabriel's care. Hardy depicts the organic body, human or animal, as always at risk and susceptible to injury, a quality that is vividly embodied in these pathetic creatures" ("Pitying" 475). I suggest these connections between animal life and the novel's realism can be understood as biopolitical: an enhancement of life through description and narration, and a narrative emphasis on biological life over subjectivity. Understanding Hardy's interest in the animals' biological life and Gabriel's careful governance of it as biopolitical realism underscores Hardy's revision of pastoral power, critiques negative forms of biopower, and offers what Roberto Esposito labels an affirmative "politics of life," one that veers away from a drive toward death and moves toward a cultivation of life (15).

The novel's revision of pastoral power highlights animal welfare's uneasy connections to biopolitics and animal capital. Kreilkamp discusses Foucault's pastoral power in relation to the novel and the its investment in ethical animal–human relationships and animal perspectives, yet deemphasizes care's connections with unequal power relationships:

> For Foucault, much of the specificity of our Judeo-Christian inheritance ... may be traced to the vocation of the sheepherder and his ability to turn cross-species pity or empathy into the action of protective care and governance. *Far from the Madding Crowd* can be understood as an extended thinking through of these very topics. It teaches its readers, too, to pity the sheep and to push beyond an exclusively human-centered perspective.
>
> What interests me in Foucault's discussion of pastoral is less its emphasis on power through surveillance than its definition of the shepherd as one who treats the injured and the weak. ("Pitying" 475)

As we have seen, although "Pastoral power is a power of care" (Foucault, "Security" 127), it also regulates conduct in ways that reinforce inequality. Foucault further explains that "pastoral power – and this is one of its fundamental features, and one of its paradoxes ... is only concerned with individual souls insofar as this direction (*conduite*) of souls also involves a permanent intervention in everyday conduct (*conduite*), in the management of lives, as well as in goods, wealth, and things" (154). He also emphasizes that submission is central to how this power functions. Foucault argues that "The sheep, the one who is directed, must live his relationship to his pastor as a relationship of complete servitude. But conversely, the pastor must experience his responsibility as a service, and one that makes him the servant of his sheep" (179). We saw earlier how the Victorian animal-protection movement constructed animal subjects under this framework, as it imagined them as willingly submitting to humankind. Although the shepherd should also submit to his flock, as we saw earlier the shepherd ultimately gains from them; he is their shepherd only insofar as the sheep remain submissive and bring him profit. Animal welfare discourse reifies such drives for profit.

In *Far from the Madding Crowd*, Gabriel Oak is what Foucault would call a good shepherd. Foucault explains,

> The shepherd (*pasteur*) directs all his care towards others and never towards himself. This is precisely the difference between the good and the bad shepherd. The bad shepherd only thinks of good pasture for his own profit, for fattening the flock that he will be able to sell and scatter, whereas the good shepherd thinks only of his flock and nothing else. He does not even consider his own advantage in the well-being of his flock. (127–128)

In the scene where Gabriel loses his sheep – they are run over a cliff by his young sheepdog – and thus his livelihood, Gabriel epitomizes the good shepherd, as he feels pity not for himself but for his sheep:

> Oak was an intensely humane man: indeed, his humanity often tore in pieces any politic intentions of his bordering on strategy, and carried him on as by gravitation. A shadow in his life had always been that his flock ended in mutton – that a day came and found every shepherd an arrant traitor to his defenceless sheep. His first feeling now was one of pity for the untimely fate of these gentle ewes and their unborn lambs. (Hardy, *Far* 32–33)

The fact that Gabriel's first concern is for the dead sheep rather than himself suggests he always viewed these animals as more than capital. Indeed at this moment he is only leasing the farm and has "an advance of sheep not yet paid for" (10), suggesting the sheep have not been through the system of exchange value.[17] Gabriel's unease at the fact that shepherds are traitors suggests that killing sheep undermines the true role of the

---

[17] The sheep have also not yet been insured, suggesting Gabriel was not ready to place monetary value on their lives (33).

shepherd; one cannot be a good shepherd and kill the flock one has cared for. Indeed, the characterization of shepherds as "arrant traitor[s]" is similar to Hardy's narration of Jude's pig looking at Arabella, and "recognizing at last the treachery of those who had seemed his only friends" (66). It is also worth noting that, as Linda Shires emphasizes, Gabriel is more saddened by the loss of sheep than of Bathsheba (170). Thus the tenuous position of sheep – operating as both subjects of pity and objects of capital – emphasizes the ambiguous position Gabriel occupies between a shepherd who hopes to earn a living and a shepherd who takes good care of his sheep. He fits uneasily in the role of one who cares for a flock of animals with the knowledge they will soon be put to death, showing the incompatibility of shepherd and killer.

Not only does Hardy suggest that a good shepherd cannot exist in a society where animals are killed for meat – a shepherd who kills is, in fact, a contradiction in terms for Gabriel and Hardy – but he further critiques the regulation of animal conduct at the core of the liberal animal welfare movement. As Foucault explains, the historical model of the shepherd and his flock morphs when institutionalized by the church, becoming more invested in regulating conduct. Foucault explains, "the pastorate gave rise to an art of conducting, directing, leading, guiding, taking in hand, and manipulating men, an art of monitoring them and urging them on step by step" ("Security" 165–166). As I demonstrated in Chapter 2, this institutionalized form of the pastorate influenced constructions of animal subjectivity to align with liberal ideals of character and conduct. Hardy, however, critiques the idealization that results from such regulation. For it was Gabriel's young dog who ran the ewes over a precipice, "under the impression that, as he was kept for running after sheep, the more he ran after them the better" (Hardy, *Far* 33). Hardy phrases this in terms of conduct:

> George's son had done his work so thoroughly that he was considered too good a workman to live – and was, in fact, taken and tragically shot at twelve o'clock that same day – another instance of the untoward fate which so often attends dogs and other philosophers who follow out a train of reasoning to its logical conclusion, and attempt perfectly consistent conduct in a world made up so largely of compromise. (33–34)

The irony of young George doing his job too well, and of Gabriel – "an intensely humane man" – shooting the dog, demonstrates the limits of conducting animals and projecting onto them an idealized subjectivity, or "perfectly consistent conduct." While for Kreilkamp this moment shows "a spectacular collapse of the pastoral ideal of a shepherd who keeps vigilant watch over his flock" (478), it also shows a failure of the idealized sheepdog and the capitalist system in which animals are conducted. The scene demonstrates not a cultivation of life but a loss of life that results from institutions reinforcing an animal–human hierarchy through capital and conduct.

While the novel shows the failure of the pastoral power perpetuated by Victorian governmentality, it more forcefully envisions physical power over animal lives. Biopower does not signify a sovereign who controls life or death, but rather embodies the practices that "*foster* life or *disallow* it to the point of death," regulating and enhancing life in all its biological forms (Foucault, *History* 138). As a shepherd, Gabriel has control over not just the lives of his sheep, but *how* they live life; he fosters their lives, as we see in an early scene when he takes a newborn lamb and places it on a warm stove (Hardy, *Far* 11), and has the power to disallow it – as he almost does after the sheep eat too much clover (120–124). Gabriel alters their physical bodies as he marks them with Bathsheba's initials (101), and removes their warmth as he and the other farmers strip them of their wool in the famous sheep-shearing scene (125–129). Gabriel's veterinary books further suggest his role as cultivator of ovine health. Yet as a shepherd Gabriel is not the sovereign, for the farm itself – placed in a larger capitalist system – is a mirror of governmentality, "using overall mechanisms and acting in such a way as to achieve overall states of equilibration or regularity" as Gabriel and the other farm workers so often "tak[e] control of life and the biological processes ... ensuring that they are not disciplined, but regularized" (Foucault, "Society" 246–247). Although Foucault privileges "man-as-species" in his understanding of biopower (247), *Far from the Madding Crowd* illustrates how the biological lives of animals are also subject to biopower, how human control has "succeeded in covering the whole surface that lies between the organic and the biological, between body and population" (253), and how the cultivation of animal lives is primarily a drive toward their death. This biopower works for the economy: Gabriel cares for the sheep, regulates the population in order to foster it and make it live, and thus exposes how biopolitics, "a 'strategic' arrangement that coordinates power relations 'in order to extract a surplus of power from living beings' rather than 'the pure and simple capacity to legislate or legitimize sovereignty'" (Lazzarato qtd. in C. Wolfe, *Law* 33), cultivates animal life for the good of capital.

Yet I argue that Hardy's novel critiques how the lives of certain animals are cultivated only to be driven toward death. The most obvious scene is the moment where Gabriel feels pity for his dead sheep, and calls all shepherds "arrant traitor[s]." As a good shepherd, Gabriel finds a contradiction between his care for the sheep and his knowledge they are capital, commodities within the larger capitalist system in which he participates. Gabriel acknowledges his tenuous position as a good shepherd, and his role as traitor to his sheep and participator in the cultivation of life toward death. With its focus on the sheep, "whose *birth and death*, in this tale, are narrated with great minuteness" (Lang 37; emphasis added), the novel explores these tensions between pastoral power and biopower, between care for animals and the biopolitical regulation of their lives that cultivates them for the sake of capital. The novel charts the maintenance, regularization, and enhancement of the sheep population to emphasize the immense control humans have over animal lives, to show how they are cared for only to die for human consumption. Such logic is not far from what we have already seen: animal life is cultivated for the good of human populations. The novel represents biopower in an extreme form when the young dog, in an attempt to control the population as he has been trained, runs the sheep over a cliff. When Gabriel walks into Warren's Malthouse with "Four lambs hung in various embarrassing attitudes over his shoulders" asking, "'Neighbours, have ye got room for a few new-born lambs?'" (Hardy, *Far* 95), readers witness the precariousness of animal life and Gabriel's maintenance of it as he teaches "those of the helpless creatures which were not to be restored to their dams how to drink from the spout" (98). In a grotesque moment Gabriel and Bathsheba try to make a lamb "take,"

> which is performed whenever an ewe has lost her own offspring, one of the twins of another ewe being given her as a substitute. Gabriel had skinned the dead lamb, and was tying the skin over the body of the live lamb in the customary manner, whilst Bathsheba was holding open a little pen of four hurdles, into which the mother and foisted lamb were driven, where they would remain till the old sheep conceived an affection for the young one. (107)

Hardy carefully illustrates the sheep washing, which happens in a methodical fashion, almost like a pastoral assembly line:

> The meek sheep were pushed into the pool by Coggan and Matthew Moon, who stood by the lower hatch immersed to their waists: then Gabriel, who stood on the brink, thrust them under as they swam along with an instrument like a crutch formed for the purpose, and also for assisting the exhausted animals when their wool became saturated and they began to sink. (109–110)

And Hardy lyrically describes the great barn, giving it an aura of spirituality, wherein we see the sheep shorn in loving detail (125–130). Such moments emphasize the minute control humans have over the biological lives of animals, and the extent to which humans intervene in their daily lives. Gabriel's mothering care, and Hardy's lyrical narration, make more discordant the fact that the sheep are raised so carefully only to be killed for mutton.

For many critics, the famous sheep-shearing scene is exemplary of Hardy's realist pastoral as it illustrates his desire to show the life of the rustics around whom he grew up.[18] Yet it also represents the sheep as their lives are regulated, their bodies controlled and cared for. Indeed, it emphasizes a lack of pastoral ideal for animals, even if it exists for the human. Hardy's lyrical rendering of sheep shearing moves the reader back to an almost ancient pastoral, a mythologized life outside of an industrial modern world in which animals are driven into London for slaughter, sheared during the winter, and poorly transported to their deaths. At the same time, Hardy's lyricism is constantly juxtaposed with forms of power, as we see in the following passage of the shearers and the sheep:

> Here the shearers knelt, the sun slanting in upon their bleached shirts, tanned arms, and the polished shears they flourished, causing these to bristle with a thousand rays, strong enough to blind a weak-eyed man. Beneath them a captive sheep lay panting, increasing the rapidity of its pants as misgiving merged in terror, till it quivered like the hot landscape outside. (127)

The transition from the barn, described as spiritual, and the shearers, tan and shining in the sun, to the captive sheep, panting with terror, throws a discord into the scene as the focus moves to the subjected animal. Indeed, the entire scene moves back and forth between a lyrical rendering of control of the flock, what we might call an enhancement of the lives of sheep, to a more violent form of biopower, one seen in the sheep's physical reaction and terror. Even outside of industrial capitalism, animals are emotionally and physically traumatized by the regulation of their lives. At one moment, a newly shorn sheep becomes Aphrodite:

> The clean sleek creature arose from its fleece – how perfectly like Aphrodite rising from the foam should have been seen to be realized – looking startled

---

[18] See Sheila Berger, *Thomas Hardy and Visual Structures* (82); Lawrence Jones, "George Eliot and Pastoral Tragicomedy in Hardy's *Far from the Madding Crowd*" (408–415); and J. Hillis Miller, *Thomas Hardy* (57).

and shy at the loss of its garment which lay on the floor in one soft cloud, united throughout, the portion visible being the inner surface only, which never before exposed, was white as snow and without flaw or blemish of minutest kind. (128–129)

Soon after, however, Oak is distracted by Boldwood and Bathsheba, as his "eyes could not forsake them, and in endeavouring to continue his shearing at the same time that he watched Boldwood's manner he snipped the sheep in the groin. The animal plunged; Bathsheba instantly gazed towards it, and saw the blood" (130). The juxtaposition of lyricism and violence, between a description of care and an exposition of the frightened and injured sheep creates a telling alignment between pastoral power and biopower as they operate within animal–human relationships. While earlier chapters emphasized how Victorians grappled with animal subjectivity, here we locate the ways pastoral power is inseparable from forms of biopower that control animal populations in every way, from constructions of their minds to their physical lives, enhancing life while simultaneously subjecting them to human control. Thus in the scene just described, Hardy showcases his descriptive power and the care he takes in describing the minute details of the sheep shearing, the barn, and the very bodies of the sheep; at the same time, he exposes their subjection to a biopolitical system of animal capital.

Although for Victorian society sheep were capital, in the novel they are figured as subjects of a life and consistently refuse such objectification. Indeed, West outlines how the sheep too have their own plot in the novel, one almost as complex and tragic as the human plot:

> The novel opens with lambing season. A ewe dies; a lamb is offered as a courting gift; a dead lamb is fed to the dogs (old and young) George. Young George drives a herd of pregnant ewes over a cliff; the sheep and their unborn lambs perish. A new herd comes under the care of the first shepherd, a man who carries lambs out of the cold and teaches them to drink from kettles. An orphaned lamb is dressed in the skin of a dead lamb and placed into a pen with the grieving mother ewe. The flock is washed. The sheep stray into a patch of clover and suffer from gastrointestinal pain: four die, three recover, and 50 have an operation, of which 49 succeed. The sheep are shorn. One ewe blushes. Another is wounded. They huddle together through a storm. In the end, they are taken to the fair and sold for mutton. ("Rot" 388)

When taken on its own, the sheep plot emphasizes Hardy's investment in narrating animal lives as they exist on their own and alongside humans. The representation of the sheep's life story challenges their objectification;

by narrating their lives from birth to death Hardy brings them more fully into the sphere of moral and political concern. Throughout the novel Hardy consistently posits them beyond capital as sentient, emotional, and epistemological subjects. For example, the highly praised scene of the approaching thunderstorm demonstrates the text's positioning of animals as epistemological subjects, a subject status embraced by Gabriel as he looks to the animal world for knowledge of the weather. Finding "a large toad humbly travelling across the path" was a "direct message from the Great Mother," while in his house he spots a "huge brown garden slug, which had come indoors to-night for reasons of its own" (Hardy, *Far* 212). Yet the sheep most fully alert Gabriel to the approaching storm; when he walks into the barn, "they were all grouped in such a way that their tails, without a single exception, were towards that half of the horizon from which the storm threatened" (212). Gabriel extends his reading of animal epistemologies to a "voice in nature," and translates its signs: "The creeping things seemed to know all about the latter rain, but little of the interpolated thunderstorm; whilst the sheep knew all about the thunderstorm and nothing of the latter rain" (213). Gabriel's ability to recognize animal epistemologies, and understand animals as subjects rather than capital, allows him to save the ricks and the money they bring, not for himself but for "necessary food for man and beast" (213).

The novel's sheep plot, I suggest, is an explicit call for cattle industry reform; both animal lives and the industry are enhanced through Hardy's biopolitical realism, thus asking for alternate conceptions of animal capital altogether. Supporters of cattle industry reform such as the RSPCA asked for reform in three areas: sheep-shearing, transit, and slaughter, and in Hardy's novel the first two take place in a way that does not ask for better treatment on behalf of capital. Although Hardy will not articulate strong views on animal welfare until later in his life, the novel's representation of animals shows early signs of a concern with the lives of animals raised for capital. As we have seen, Hardy was critical of how the cattle industry objectified animals and valued them as profit rather than subjects, and desired to bring them into notions of justice and equality. Seeing animals as kin, he often posited his argument in specifically liberal language, envisioning them as members of a political community. He critiqued the lack of justice for animals, often positioning this from the animal's point of view, as if giving them a voice in how they are treated and, by extension, represented. *Far from the Madding Crowd* can thus productively be understood as showcasing Hardy's early animal welfare and political understandings of animal lives.

The sheep plot follows a life cycle of sheep up until their slaughter, and throughout they are consistently seen as subjects with their own lives and experiences that exist not for the human, but alongside them. Although considered capital by Victorian society, the animals are not figured as such. Throughout the novel and its early drafts, profit is never a concern for Gabriel. Even when learning that the previous shepherd under Bathsheba's uncle was able to keep the skin of dead lambs, "If they died afore marking ... the skin was the shepherd's ... And every live lamb of a twin the shepherd sold to his own profit" (99), Gabriel merely sighed, "which the deprivation of lamb skins could hardly have caused" (99). In the excluded sheep-rot chapter, Gabriel explicitly rejects the cultivation of sheep lives for the sake of profit.[19] Hardy explains that for a dishonest farmer, sheep rot is "an opportunity. The disease is a remedy: the blight of what is owned is the enrichment of the owner ... The end is readiness of stock for market, and consequent early profits from sales" ("Draft" 405). Yet Gabriel, after waiting by the swamp to see if Troy brings the sheep there to graze and catch the disease, is figured as a hero, telling Troy, "I came here to save the sheep" (409), rejecting the profit that could arise from selling them "rotted" (406).[20]

Instead of promoting animal capital, the novel cultivates animal life for its own sake. The sheep washing and shearing take place in May, and is narrated with a view toward the enhancement and fostering of life while exposing the injury and terror that can result in what, to the human, seems like a mundane and benign process. This emphasizes animal subjectivity without projecting ideals of liberal character or political ineligibility. The Greenhill sheep fair, held in late summer, features the possibility of a system wherein although being led to their deaths, animals are treated as fellow travelers, and cultivated along the way:

> Shepherds who attended with their flocks from long distances started from home two or three days, or even a week before the fair day, driving their charges a few miles each day – not more than ten or twelve – and resting them at night in hired fields by the wayside at previously chosen points

---

[19] As West explains, sheep-rot, "a dreaded nineteenth-century sheep illness ... occurred when flocks grazed in low-lying, swampy fields. While the condition was fatal, in the early stages it caused its victims to fatten quickly without showing other symptoms" ("Rot" 389). Hardy's familiarity with sheep rot – he even cites the statistic that "more than a million sheep and lambs die in Great Britain every year from this disease alone" ("Draft" 405) – and the possibility of farmers making money off the bigger diseased sheep, demonstrates his knowledge of mid-century cattle industry debates.

[20] Sanghee Lee analyzes the juxtaposition between Gabriel and Troy, arguing that the novel posits Gabriel as "an alternative hero to replace the conventional solider-hero as pillar of Victorian society" (100).

where they fed, having fasted all the day ... Several of the sheep would get worn and lame, and occasionally a lambing occurred on the road. To meet these contingencies there was frequently provided, to accompany the flocks from the remoter points, a pony wagon into which the weakly ones were taken for the remainder of the journey. (294)

As in the sheep-washing and shearing scenes, Hardy emphasizes the emotional lives of animals, challenging animal welfare discourses that claim these practices are good for them. When they get to the fair, "Men were shouting, dogs were barking, with greatest animation, but the thronging travelers in so long a journey had grown nearly indifferent to such terrors, though they still bleated piteously at the unwontedness of their experiences" (*Far* 295). Hardy's elements of the pastoral represent an alternative system in which animals are raised for food; while he never petitions for an end to the system – he believed it could never be abolished – he posits an enhanced system in which animal lives are fostered because they are kin, and their lives are intertwined with our own. He shows animal life, and by extension, nature, not as "a set of objects that humans act upon," but as "a web of life that human relations develop through" (J. Moore 33). By including animals in the political sphere through moral concern, *Far from the Madding Crowd* encourages a system that rejects the inhumane and objectifying effects of industrial capitalism. Yet for Hardy there can never be a truly good shepherd; there is treachery at the very heart of the system.

Hardy's biopolitical realism extends beyond an exposure of the biopolitics of animal capital and highlights his investment in the more radical politics of anti-capitalism and a multi-species inclusion that challenges liberal individualism. Given Hardy's beliefs that animals are kin, it is not surprising that the novel's politics are more-than-human. Its emphasis on narrating in detail the sheep's lives registers an inclusive community that destabilizes hierarchy and human exceptionalism, and imagines alternative relationships of capital and property that undermine the individualism undergirding liberal ideology and *homo economicus*. As Piers Hale argues in his analysis of the liberal politics of evolution, "over time an increasing number of people argued that evolution endorsed a collectivist politics" (156), and I suggest Hardy's novel gets us closer to this position. Indeed, *Far from the Madding Crowd* is essentially a story of Gabriel's social uplift: he moves from being "a shepherd only" (Hardy, *Far* 10) to owning two farms. Yet this social uplift is dependent on animals and Gabriel's good relationships with them; he can move up only insofar as his animals are treated well and conceptualized as knowing subjects. Further, his life is determined by their actions, as when young George chases the sheep and they run off a cliff, when George saves Gabriel from suffocation in his sheep hut, when the sheep eat a field of clover and cause Bathsheba to ask for his return, and when they hide in the barn in terror, alerting him to the storm. These are not moments of humans acting on nature but of animals acting in ways that change the direction of human lives and capital. Kreilkamp argues that "Hardy repeatedly submerges Gabriel Oak's individuality into a broader category that includes nonhuman animals" ("Pitying" 476), while Shires labels Gabriel's sheep "an extension of himself – his object of care, his livelihood, his companions" (170). Yet his very life is merged with animals, and by extension the life of the farm and its economy. Gabriel's careful fostering of the sheep, and the ways animals foster human lives, as in the case of the dog who helps Fanny get to the poorhouse, shows animals as kin whose lives shape and are shaped with those of the human.[21] The novel revises notions of community and the role of the individual within it; Gabriel's social uplift cannot be seen apart from the agency of animals with which he is surrounded. A good society – with a good economy – is multispecies. Just as Gabriel shapes their life, they shape his, and by extension, contribute to society as historical actors.

Animals and their treatment shaped liberal capitalism throughout the Victorian era. Concerns over their welfare structured legislation that directed the flow of capital, even if it did not necessarily better or save animal lives. Constructions of animal subjectivity influenced how animals were incorporated into a political community and how the state envisioned its governance of them. Capital and industry, which drove England's economy and its empire, was shaped not only by animal subjectivity but also by animal labor and their products, as I will show in Chapter 6.[22] Jason Moore suggests that "the capacity to make history turns on specific configurations of human and extra-human actors" (37), and that "Civilizations move *through*, not around, the web of life ... Capitalism does not develop upon global nature so much as it emerges through the messy and contingent relations of humans with the rest of nature" (44). In so carefully focusing on the life cycle of a flock of sheep, conceptualizing them as subjects and agents who take part, even if unwillingly, in the production of capital, Hardy shows animals as working for capitalism, not passively acted on. While animal welfare advocates also highlighted how

---

[21] West gives an extensive reading of this scene, and argues it demonstrates morality in the animal world and "the possibility of nonhuman animals as moral agents" (*Hardy* 67).

[22] For a discussion of sheep in relation to the expansion of empire and ecological imperialism in New Zealand, see Rebecca J. H. Woods, "From Colonial Animal to Imperial Edible: Building an Empire of Sheep in New Zealand, ca. 1880–1900."

animals work for the production of capital, Hardy emphasizes the injustice of such a system. For he does not suggest that recognizing animals as working for capitalism makes better the horrors of capitalism transforming England and the world, or even that animals should continue to be a part of such world-making. Throughout the novel Hardy consistently critiques self-interest and profit over the interest of the community. Multi-species economies highlight the interdependences between animals and humans and thus critique the core of liberal individualism and the speciesist exclusions on which it is based. By refusing to see animals as capital only, Hardy rejects the speciesism inherent in liberal capitalism, connected as it is to an individualism that prizes the human subject and views animals as capital. Human exceptionalism and the self-made individual are challenged by conceptualizing animals as taking part in history and world-making.

By focusing on sheep life in all its manifestations and interconnections, Thomas Hardy's affirmative biopolitics seeks a revision of how life is imagined in relationship to capital and governmentality. In discussing Esposito's biopolitics, Timothy Campbell explains that "The opening to an affirmative biopolitics takes place when we recognize that harming one part of life or one life harms all lives. The radical toleration of life forms that epitomizes Esposito's reading of contemporary biopolitics is therefore based on the conviction that every life is inscribed in *bios*" (16). Esposito moves beyond the *zoē/bios* distinction perpetuated by thinkers such as Agamben, wherein *zoē* stands for "life in its simple biological capacity" and *bios* refers to "qualified life" (Esposito 14). Conceptualizing animals outside of individualism – bound up as it is with regulatory notions of character and conduct – and along the lines of an inclusion based on an ecological ethic offers an alternate way to protect life. Esposito's claim that "The appeal to the impersonal as the only vital and singular mode isn't unrelated to the going beyond a semantics of the person that has been represented from the origin of our culture in its juridical status (at least insofar as the law was and continues to function in relation to the intangible individuality of the person)" (194) harkens back to Derrida's critique of the animal rights movement's dependence on liberal personhood. Expanding the political to include animals requires a revision of political categories and conceptualizations of democracy. Animals should not need liberal cognition for political inclusion, and one should be aware of the unequal powers that structure how animal subjectivity is represented. Animal lives should not be governed by economic and capitalist discourses, but posited within an ecological thought that destabilizes hierarchy, emphasizes interconnections, and spurs political action. Thinking ecologically requires an acknowledgment that what is good for human communities is not always good for animals.

Hardy's sheep are quite like Darwin's worms, which Jane Bennett analyzes to conceptualize a democracy including nonhuman actors. Bennett discusses Darwin's meticulous description of worm action in *Formation of Vegetable Mould through the Actions of Worms with Observations on Their Habits* and argues, "Darwin claims that worms inaugurate human culture and then, working alongside people and their endeavors, help preserve what people and worms together have made" (96). Worm actions and interactions offer a way for Bennett to describe how human societies and cultures are shaped by and with animals, leading her to suggest democracy should be expanded to take into account the nonhuman. "If human culture is inextricably enmeshed with vibrant, nonhuman agencies," she argues, "and if human intentionality can be agentic only if accompanied by a vast entourage of nonhumans, then it seems that the appropriate unit of analysis for democratic theory is neither the individual human nor an exclusively human collective but the (ontologically heterogeneous) 'public' coalescing around a problem" (108). For Hardy, including animals democratically means understanding them beyond the objectifying logic of capitalism and individualism.

The novel's intricate engagement with animals shows how interconnected animal and human lives are in the system of capital, and offers ways to understand the role of animals in the realist novel beyond individualized minor characters. The novel's sheep and dogs are minor characters, but do not necessarily align with Alex Woloch's two "existential states" of minorness in the nineteenth-century novel: the worker, a "flat character who is reduced to a single functional use," and the eccentric, a "fragmentary character who plays a disruptive, oppositional role within the plot" (25). Generally, the animals I have examined in earlier chapters have eccentric qualities, such as Grip, who consistently refuses a single function, or the Caterpillar, who badgers Alice. Hardy's animals, however, make claims on the reader's attention for alternative notions of animal subjectivity, liberal politics, and control over life. The novel's animals are indeed "*the proletariat of the novel*" (Woloch 27), as they emphasize not only class structure, but also the species structure of Victorian capitalism and the work animals do for human economies. The claims of the sheep and the dogs on the reader's attention – noticed by readers from the novel's initial publication – highlight the "democratic impulse" (Woloch 31) that informs Hardy's stance toward animals later in his life. Moving beyond the confines of individualism that Woloch's analysis privileges helps nuance the role of animals in the Victorian novel. Although sheep are not individualized in the novel, they still make claims on the reader's attention, as they did in Hardy's early life; getting down in the grass, he desired to see what animals thought. Hardy attempts the "Copernican 'humiliations' – coming closer to the actual dirt beneath our feet, the actuality of Earth" that Timothy Morton requires for "Politics in the wake of ecological thought" (*Ecological* 125). "It is too much to throw up one's hands and say that life is cruel," Morton continues, "like a character in a Thomas Hardy novel" (125). Yet *Far from the Madding Crowd*, while showing the cruelties that happen to both animals and humans, throws off human pretensions through its intricate focus on animal life. The humiliation should come from realizing that for too long humans have ignored animal kin, and continue to control their lives while simultaneously denying them. Hardy's animal politics suggests the possibility of doing otherwise.

CHAPTER 6

The Political Lives of Animals in Victorian Empire
Olive Schreiner's Anti-Colonial Animal Politics

> We now know that these non-European peoples did not accept with indifference the authority projected over them, or the general silence on which their presence in variously attenuated forms is predicated. We must therefore read the great canonical texts, and perhaps also the entire archive of modern and pre-modern European and American culture, with an effort to draw out, extend, give emphasis and voice to what is silent or marginally present or ideologically represented.
> – Edward Said, *Culture and Imperialism*

> Nothing in Australia, New Zealand or Canada can offer anything like the opening the Cape does to a young man, with only a few hundreds of capital, to set up for himself ... With ordinary luck at Ostrich farming, he is made a man.
> – Arthur Douglass, *Ostrich Farming in South Africa*

> The only thing that gives me any joy, is the sparrows & pigeons ... It's not only that my heart quivers with love when I see them ... but some person must be kind enough to throw crumbs out to them – though they are *not* of his nation. Nationality isn't everything!
> – Olive Schreiner, letter to Havelock Ellis, Dec. 13, 1914

In the introduction to her 1901 set of essays, *Thoughts on South Africa*, Olive Schreiner posits animals as resistant to imperial power. She explains how she was questioned about her statement that "if England made war on the Republics, she would have to send out at least one hundred and fifty thousand soldiers to attack these small states," rather than the twenty thousand speculated by British politicians (19). While her response is based on her knowledge of Boer men and women's strength and "resistile power," she suggests that even animals will not be defeated (20). For if the British did send out their soldiers, "even then there was a possibility that the red African mier-kat might ultimately creep back into its hole in the red African earth, torn and bleeding, but alive" (19–20). The meerkat, a member of the mongoose family native to southern Africa, was one of Schreiner's favorite animals, and throughout her adult life, she kept as pets the more mild and tame species.[1] As the above quote suggests, even if the meerkats are defeated, there is still the possibility they can again fight for their native land. Joyce Avrech Berkman has suggested that in such moments the meerkat represents Boer resistance and their ability to "resume a normal independent life at a later time" (114). But Schreiner's representations of rebel animals are not just metaphorical Boers; rather, they are sites of resistance to the racist, sexist, and imperial politics of late Victorian Britain, offering alternatives to oppressive forms of liberal subjectivity and governmentality that reify colonial practices. Schreiner's animal politics reexamines categories that have negatively defined animals and Indigenous peoples, and posits animals outside of an analytic that reduces them to a symbolic function. She takes seriously the political potential of animality, and removes animals from the forms of pastoral power and governmentality that regulate their conduct and keep them contained within a liberal anthropocentric framework.

Animals frequently appear on political and ethical levels throughout Schreiner's work, and it is no surprise, considering she wrote in 1884, "I am so one with animals & animal life" (letter to Havelock Ellis, Dec. 25). One of her major critiques of Christianity was its "scorn for the animal world," which led her to appreciate Buddha for seeing the divinity in plants and animals (letter to John T. Lloyd). Schreiner liked "big leopards" better than politicians (letter to Edward Carpenter), and felt that at one point, birds were her only comfort, helping her keep a "hold on life" (letter to Betty Molento, Aug. 22). But for her meerkats and her dog, she wrote in 1902, she didn't think she "could stand the loneliness of the life" (letter to Betty Molento, May 5). Gesturing toward the destruction of South African animals due to imperial violence, she commented more than once that she is "thankful I didn't come into the world in such a time as men had exterminated all the birds and wild beasties; as they will one day" (letter to Will Schreiner). Schreiner believed animals and relationships with them are constitutive of a national identity; that is, she saw them as part of her own imagined political community. Indeed, in general the British prided themselves on their relationships with animals, and believed

---

[1] Schreiner explains, "There are three species of mier-kat generally known in South Africa, two of which are mild and easily tamed, and the red mier-kat, a creature absolutely fearless and which no one has ever succeeded in taming" (*Thoughts* 250). The red meerkat thus resists domestication and human power.

they cultivated a strong sense of nationalism and civilization; but as we saw in earlier chapters, such relationships were often founded on violence and exploitation, functioning within forms of pastoral power and biopower that confined animals within oppressive liberal norms and capitalist practices.

In contrast, Schreiner conceptualized animals and relationships with them as a way to challenge hegemonic liberal norms such as patriarchy, the belief in forward-moving progress, and self-government. Schreiner wrote in *Thoughts on South Africa* that one can best understand the diverse regions of South Africa by learning about its land, animals, and multiple ethnic groups and races; she emphasized the importance of animals – alongside diverse landscapes and human groups – to South African identity. Appreciating such diversity was central to her politics; just as she thought one should embrace land, animal, and human, so she thought the human world should celebrate gendered, ethnic, and racial differences beyond a hierarchical view of liberal progress and social Darwinism. Animals thus hold an important role within Schreiner's oeuvre, as she included them in her politics and looked to them for relationship models. In her best-selling novel *The Story of an Animal Farm*, and other writings, she presents an animal politics that "*affirms a logic of mutual inclusion*" and denies "exclusive oppositions" (Massumi 45), thus offering alternatives to liberal dichotomies used to place the other in a subordinate position to a more "civilized" nation. Schreiner's animals are not to be read symbolically, as she includes them in the political sphere as resistant to governmentality, thus offering an inclusive and multi-species national identity.

Animals were essential to the British empire; animal capital drove the imperial project, while the construction of Indigenous subjects as animals legitimated the civilizing mission at the heart of liberal progress. Lisa Lowe argues that the "genealogy of modern liberalism is simultaneously a genealogy of colonial divisions of humanity" (7), and including notions of species into this genealogy nuances the oppressive logics of liberal imperial discourses.[2] Scholars across numerous disciplines have recognized that animals are "intrinsic components of the imperial world" (Roy 72), and call for increased attention to how imperial structures are imposed on animals. As Shefali Rajamannar argues, "a systematic – and systemic – acceptance of the hierarchization of living beings undergirds the mind-set and worldview that work in a symbiotic relationship with a phenomenon

---

[2] Rajamannar similarly suggests that our understandings of British imperial ideology can be expanded and nuanced by recognizing species as another part of the race–class–gender triumvirate.

such as imperialism" (2). She also emphasizes that animals were figured in myriad ways within imperial discourses: "dominant and sadistic, extravagant and moralistic, sensual and playful" (157). Examining the "material and metaphorical significance" of animals for humans throughout imperial discourses (Roy 66) alongside non-metaphorical readings of animal subjectivity and epistemology highlights the nuanced and pervasive function of liberal-imperial logics. Especially in the latter half of the nineteenth century, animal populations were decimated across Africa and India, as hunters killed record numbers of elephants, antelopes, and lions, among other species, inflicting so much carnage that one famous hunter, William Charles Baldwin, simply sank animal carcasses in St. Lucia Bay when he had too many dead bodies (MacKenzie 105). Harriet Ritvo reads animals in zoos or circulating as trophies as symbolic of imperial conquest, while John Miller describes in detail how adventure fiction reinforced hunting as part of imperial conquest. Animal bodies thus emphasize the strength of the British imperial project while reinforcing both the animal–human divide and the colonized–colonizer hierarchy.

While across the empire animal lives were most often controlled in ways similar to colonized subjects, this is not their only story. As Rohan Deb Roy argues, animals "were not merely victims of imperial violence ... but also agents who were marginalized by imperial historiography" (72). Extending Edward Said's call for reading colonized voices in nineteenth-century British fiction to animals helps uncover the myriad ways animals emerge within imperial and colonial histories. I suggest that Schreiner views animals as subjects outside the constraints of liberal imperial discourses, as they offer alternative epistemologies and subjectivities to those cultivated by liberalism. Through conceptualizing animals outside of liberal discourses of animality – those emphasizing their negative difference from the human, often in terms of instinct, savageness, or stupidity – Schreiner disputes liberal conceptions of animality. Schreiner's work registers a counter animal politics that resists imperial hierarchies and highlights the speciesism of Victorian liberalism that perpetuates imperial dominance. While conceptions of the non-Western other frequently relied on negative conceptions of animality, in Schreiner's thought animality offered alternative forms of political resistance and inclusion. As such, Schreiner's work helps us analyze domestic animals whose lives were fostered rather than extinguished, and reveals how animal welfare discourses functioned in colonial contexts.

In this final chapter I extend analyses of animals across the British empire to domestic animals to understand how animal lives inform narratives of settler-colonialism. I suggest that the physical and philosophical oppression of animals – especially through forms of biopower and pastoral power – serves as a justification for colonial practices, making the construction of animal subjectivity an important site for uncovering imperial logics. Instead of focusing on decimated animal populations, I examine domesticated animals whose lives were fostered by British colonists, and whose treatment was a concern of animal welfare advocates. I focus on the story of the ostrich, an animal native to southern Africa who offers another layer to the social and cultural history of colonized animals. While the logic cultivating the governing of animals was similar to the logic used to oppress Indigenous peoples – ostriches were seen as stupid and ungovernable, as some Africans were seen, for example – their lives were fostered by the British, as their beautiful plumes became part of the world economy after the 1860s. Ostriches emphasize the importance of living animals to the British imperial economy and demonstrate how liberal discourses articulated animal subjectivity in ways that encouraged and justified the physical control of humans over animals. As I will show, both animal bodies and minds were controlled under the restraints of a biopolitical imperial discourse.

I then demonstrate how Olive Schreiner conceptualized animals outside of liberal subjectivity and offered alternative formulations of animality. Within *The Story of an African Farm*, in which the ostrich plays an important role, Schreiner's realism represents a colonized animality that exposes the oppressive nature of liberal subjectivity in its relationship to settler-colonialism. Her animal politics was an integral part of her anti-imperial politics, which is admittedly often limiting. Although at times radical, Schreiner is imbricated within practices of settler-colonialism, animal husbandry, and racism; her politics highlights complicated and oppressive relationships between Indigenous subjects, domesticated animals, and Boers. Through examining Schreiner's often contradictory politics, and animal–human relationships within settler-colonies, this chapter extends our understanding of the role of animals in Victorian colonial discourses, addresses the political valence of animality and imperial animal–human relationships, and uncovers the role of the realist novel in presenting an anti-colonial animal politics.

Victorian Empire's Animal Capital: The Case of the Ostrich

In *Principles of Political Economy*, John Stuart Mill legitimized the imperial project by arguing that colonization was essential to building the nation's wealth. This belief was predicated not only on the vast amount of what the British saw as uncivilized and uncultivated lands but also on the character of the land's inhabitants. Mill's rationalization for imperialism is hinged to the construction of others as lacking self-government, and thus as primitive or uncivilized. He explains,

> As civilization spreads, and security of persons and property becomes established, in parts of the world which have not hitherto had that advantage, the productive capabilities of those places are called into fuller activity, for the benefit both of their own inhabitants and of foreigners. The ignorance and misgovernment in which many of the regions most favoured by nature are still grovelling, afford work, probably, for many generations before those countries will be raised even to the present level of the most civilized parts of Europe. (72)

For Mill, many fertile lands are misgoverned; those blessed with abundance are the least qualified to know what to do with it and how to govern it, to the detriment of the world economy. Following this logic, human dominance over nature – what Mill called "the unlimited, growth of man's power over nature" (66) – enacts a civilizing process over both nature and non-Western subjects, helping the "progressive economical movement of civilized nations" (66). The cultivation of non-British lands is a civilizing mission of nature, implying the free use of natural resources. Reflecting Lockean beliefs that land becomes property once cultivated, Mill suggests that supposedly uncultivated land across the world is up for grabs, waiting to become the property of the British national economy. Thus positing colonization and cultivation as essential to British progress, and aligning this with notions of ungovernability, Mill encourages a civilizing mission of land, animal, and non-Westerner. Through such philosophies, as Lowe has argued, Mill is able to "manage *colonial difference*" within Victorian empire (106), while offering "the terms, logics, and powers through which older colonial domination was rationalized and new forms of imperial domination were innovated and executed" (113).[3] Colonial difference and its management occurs not just within constructions of human communities, but also within the intricate relationships between species and environment.

Animal studies offers a productive framework for analyzing environmental destruction across the empire, as John Miller has suggested, particularly given the speciesism of liberal imperialism and the hierarchical thinking it encourages ("Postcolonial"). Especially in hunting narratives

---

[3] For an in-depth analysis of the inconsistencies of liberal imperialism in the second half of the century, see Goodlad, *The Victorian Geopolitical Aesthetic*.

popular toward the end of the century, representations of animals frequently conform to beliefs in British dominance over imperial subjects and spaces. Throughout imperial texts such as Haggard's *King Solomon's Mines*, animals are destroyed without any moral qualms. As Allan Quatermain says on stumbling onto a herd of elephants, "it went against my conscience to let such a herd as that escape without having a pull at them" (39). Further, animal subjectivity frequently aligned with the constructed subjectivity of colonized subjects in ways that posited both beneath the white male British subject. In such representations, Miller argues, the "supposed gulf between colonizer and colonized" opens "a range of violent and repressive possibilities for colonial rulers as racial others are emptied of their human status" (*Empire* 2). Yet while critics often focus on the "exotic" animals found throughout hunting narratives, and whose bodies, both alive and dead, were sent home to England, domestic animals offer a fruitful subject for nuancing the extent to which animal subjectivity reinforced alignments between animals and colonized subjects. Animal representations can disrupt ideologies that associate animals with the colonized, and expose the restrictive nature of liberal subjectivity more generally. As the case of African ostriches shows, the British also tried to civilize indigenous animals in the lands they colonized. Domestication functions as a civilizing mission that tames not unruly humans, but wild and uncooperative animals, and is intricately tied to capitalist ideologies.

The domination of animals supported imperial economies and the social movement central to liberal individualism; British subjects were encouraged to pull up their bootstraps, set off in search of uncultivated land, and contribute to the nation's wealth.[4] The ostrich, who like the meerkat is native to Africa, was an integral part of the British imperial economy, and responsible for a large influx of eager British colonists to the Cape. In fact, British colonial ostrich farmers credited themselves with first domesticating the bird around 1867, even though Boers had been trading in ostrich feathers for decades, and the San depended on them for everything from kitchenware – using eggshells for bowls – to meat (Nixon 48).[5] In his 1881 guide for interested ostrich farmers, *Ostrich Farming in South Africa*,

---

[4] Although I focus on ostrich farming in South Africa, the domestication and cultivation of sheep in Australia and New Zealand was also an important part of the imperial economy. See the works of Philip Armstrong and Rebecca J. H. Woods.

[5] Beinart and Hughes emphasize that the ostrich was one of the few animals newly domesticated in the nineteenth century (72). See also Rob Nixon's *Dreambirds: The Strange History of the Ostrich in Fashion, Food, and Fortune*, and Nathalie Saudo-Welby, "Learning from Nature: Feminism, Allegory and Ostriches in Olive Schreiner's *The Story of an African Farm* (1883)."

Arthur Douglass explains that although some may debate the British claim to domestication of the bird, "no one disputes that we were the first to make it our sole occupation, and to bring it before the world as the extraordinarily lucrative and great industry it has now become" (2). Douglass argues that ostrich farming was a purely British affair, emphasizing it was mostly done in British colonies: "Birds as yet are only being farmed to a small extent in the Free State," he claims, "and scarcely at all in the Transvaal and Natal" (19). Indeed, the ostrich becomes a tool of colonization and contributes to the British domestication of land, as ostriches have "now been introduced into every part of the Cape Colony" (18). Douglass's text attests to the popularity of the ostrich for colonial endeavors, and the desire for advice on how to enhance ostrich life. As Douglass notes, "Nothing in Australia, New Zealand or Canada can offer anything like the opening the Cape does to a young man, with only a few hundreds of capital, to set up for himself . . . with ordinary luck at Ostrich farming, he is made a man" (26, 28). The ostrich drove many to set up farms in the Cape Colony, and when dominated stood as an example of liberal individualism, British capitalism, and the domesticity that Ann McClintock identifies as formative to imperial practices (32). The domestication of South African animal subjects highlights the biopolitical fostering of animal lives as essential to the imperial economy.

Ostriches were prized for their beautiful plumes, a high-end fashion accessory toward the end of the nineteenth century, the craze for them lasting until the beginning of World War I. They were a large part of the British imperial economy thanks to upper-class Victorian women in England and other Western nations who wore them, most often on top of elaborate hats. Such fashion drove the feather trade and thus colonization; it reassured aspiring colonists that the demand for ostrich feathers would be long lasting. They are "part of the Court dress," Douglass emphasizes, "and as long as it is so it will always be fashionable" (4). Although ostriches were not as exotic as lions and tigers, their plumes were considered "Africana refined" (Stein 22). Sarah Stein even suggests ostrich plumes symbolized the growing feminist movement: "Fashion critics called the feathers sinuous and sensual and noted that, when moored to the hat, fan, or boa, they lent their wearer the impression of movement and freedom. Like the modern woman, who moved and encountered space in new ways, the plume embodied emancipation and mobility" (22). Thus although "imperial domesticity is a domesticity without women" (McClintock 32), they were a core market of its productive output. Yet the "freedom" they symbolized in the wearing of feathers was hinged to oppressive colonial practices, showing the racism inherent in white liberal feminism. Indeed, the plume signifies support for the British empire. Especially when worn by "the Court" and the upper class, the plume exemplifies British domination of colonized spaces and their animal and human inhabitants.

Unlike other exotic animals brought to Britain or massacred throughout the empire, colonists fostered the lives of ostriches, a point many supporters of the plumage trade emphasized once animal welfare advocates began protesting against cruelty toward the birds in the 1860s. Ostrich feathers were such a boon to the British economy that when advocates protested their cultivation, supporters of the plumage trade in parliament decried that abolitionist bills would not only "destroy the *whole* trade," but would not even be beneficial to the bird; for if the British didn't kill them, the French would (Moore-Colyer 63). Earlier campaigns against cruelty to birds targeted the threat of extinction and emphasized the effects it could have on the British economy, and through focusing on the feather trade, later anti-plumage campaigns more fully emphasized the world market. *Animal World* published numerous articles debating the levels of cruelty involved in collecting ostrich feathers. An 1886 article titled "Ostriches and Their Feathers" argues against those who compare the taking of feathers to the cutting of human hair or nails, as Stein describes the process (23), yet reifies ostriches in colonial practices that turn them into objects of capital. The author notes that even "If ripe feathers only can be 'plucked' without cruelty, is it not likely that mistakes are often made by the pluckers, or that occasional carelessness or recklessness occurs ...?" (100). They emphasize, however, that the trade itself should not be abolished – "We do not ask ladies to renounce the wearing of ostrich feathers *because* farmers are stupidly indifferent to animal suffering" (100) – but that "ostriches who are fated, in the time to come, to live and produce feathers for the use of the gentle and good of mankind, may fall into the hands of intelligent and humane owners, whose study it will be to save them from unnecessary suffering" (100). The proposed goal was to foster ostrich lives to such an extent that they were fully inscribed in colonial practices, and that these practices had the support of humane advocates. Indeed, a letter to the editor in the next issue of *Animal World* emphasizes that "The ostrich farmers have positively declared that as the present system of ostrich farming is devoid of cruelty, and that they, as important colonists, deserve every encouragement from the mother-country" ("Ostriches and the Selborne Society" 126). Animal welfare discourse thus promoted the fostering of ostrich lives and their domestication, believing it contributed to larger colonial practices that benefited the expansion of the British economy.[6] Here biopolitical regulation fosters animal life only to keep it within an exploitative capitalist system; just as we saw in Chapter 5, capital is often the motivation for treating well animals whose bodies are destined for consumption.

At the same time, Victorians debated ostrich character, and used it as evidence for or against better treatment. Often such reports focused on maternal affection. "It has been said for ages that the ostrich is a bad mother," notes an 1883 article from *Animal World*, "laying her eggs in the sand, and leaving them to chance and sunshine; but this is very false, as every farmer who has tamed them knows. Both the parent birds watch over their young with the tenderest love" ("The Ostrich and Its Wings"). Other representations, however, construct ostrich subjectivity to mirror British perceptions of South Africa: ungovernable and in need of domination. This is clear in British colonist Annie Martin's 1890 *Home Life on an Ostrich Farm*, a memoir of her and her husband's attempts at ostrich farming in the Cape Colony. Her text is a narrative about the animals of South Africa, the character of the ostrich, and her personal struggles and successes at the colonial enterprise. According to a review in *Animal World*, this "amusing book" gives "a more accurate idea of the manners and customs of this strange bird," "too often strangely misrepresented and misunderstood," and places the ostrich in a "far more human light that we have yet seen him" (Fletcher 99–100). The reviewer argues that Martin's anecdotes show the ostrich as a liberal creature: "he is a bird of strong affections and much individuality of character" (102). Yet Martin's memoir largely presents a disdainful picture of the birds, painting them as troublesome precisely because they do not adhere to liberal norms. Overall Martin preferred the more easily tamed meerkats and secretary birds to the ostrich, of whom she said, "There surely does not exist a creature – past earliest infancy – more utterly incapable of taking care of itself than an ostrich" (147). Lacking the self-government reinforced by liberal governmentality, the ostrich requires domination. Indeed, the need for domination was projected onto their physical bodies, as Martin explains, "The very necessary operation of branding is performed on the ostrich's large, bare thigh, which seems just made for the purpose" (145). She writes that the ostrich possesses "even less

---

[6] The plumage trade became such an important part of the colonial economy that, as Moore-Colyer notes, in the first part of the twentieth century the trade in ostrich feathers was worth two million pounds annually (63). The anti-plumage campaigns were ultimately successful, and together with the outbreak of the war, they lessened the power of the plumage trade that drove the colonization of South Africa.

intelligence than a common fowl ... not recognizing the man who has fed him every day for years" (146). Far behind the scale of animal progress, unlike the meerkats, who "were surely created for the express purpose of being made into pet animals" (157), even if an ostrich was tame, they were "absurdly and often inconveniently tame" (119). While the tame meerkat's only role was pet companion, as capital the ostrich did not belong in the home, and could not occupy positions of both pet and capital. The meerkats who could be tamed represented liberal animal subjectivity through recognizing human superiority. Ostriches, however, denoted animal subjectivity that needed control, as they could not obey the rules of the house and, by extension, the workings of governmentality. Indeed, as Barbara Gates suggests, ostriches "became for her [Martin] the epitome of otherness, the things that trapped her in South Africa" (11).

According to Martin, ostriches were also racist, a belief that shows how racialized subjects helped to define not just white, liberal subjectivity, but forms of animal subjectivity as well. Indeed, the construction of racist ostriches illuminates how deeply representations of animals were projections of imperial ideologies. Martin writes that ostriches "appear to have a strong aversion to all the negro race. They attack Kaffirs and Hottentots much more readily than they do their white masters," and "stand in some sort of awe of a white man as compared with the 'niggers,' for whom they have the deepest contempt" (115). Like the Boers, whom the British believed were more racist and less civilized than themselves, ostriches were seen as low in the scale of evolutionary progress, thus legitimating their status as objectified capital. Tellingly, they carry qualities of liberal subjectivity only when they stand in "awe of a white man." These constructions follow the needs of the humans who describe them; racist ostriches are a projection of British racism. Indeed, the imagined contempt for Africans places ostriches in a hierarchical position above, rather than below Indigenous peoples, complicating narratives that align animals with colonized subjects. Here, racialized humans are below the animal, suggesting blackness could be associated with qualities of liberalism only insofar as it was used as a negative to constitute its borders. The subjection of animals thus further contributed to the racialization of Indigenous peoples.

Ostriches present something of a paradox among colonized animals: they are nurtured and raised with care, yet representations of their subjectivity oscillate between liberal character and savage animality. The biopolitical tactics regulating ostriches objectify them as capital, yet depending on the context – animal welfare, for example, or colonist memoir – manipulate their subjectivity to achieve desired political ends. Most often, however, these representations of ostrich subjectivity keep animals confined within regulatory imperial practices and animal husbandry. Even when liberal qualities are noted in the ostrich, they are undercut by negative descriptions. *The Settler and the Savage*, R. M. Ballantyne's novel of colonization in South Africa, for example, registers these tensions between liberal and savage qualities. In the chapter titled "Adventure with an Ostrich," Hans and Charlie come upon an ostrich sitting on a nest of eggs, whom they note is a "gallant bird," who "guards his wife most faithfully, and shares her duties" (186). They then view the bird with a capitalist's eye and discuss the possibility of farming ostriches for their feathers; they decide to steal an egg and try it. At first the ostrich is constructed as an ideal father, one who lovingly cares for both the eggs and his "wife." The narrator explains, "Hans did but bare justice to the cock ostrich when he said he was a gallant bird. It is within the mark to say that he is not only a pattern husband, but a most exemplary father, for, besides guarding his wife and her nest most jealously by day, he relieves her at night, and sits himself on the nest, while his better-half takes food and relaxation" (187). However, as soon as Hans and Charlie get close to the ostrich, this "gallant bird" is quickly transformed into one described with adjectives such as "ferocious" and "vicious," who reacts to the two men with "a hiss and a furious rush," running toward them with "furious rage," ready to "danc[e] on its prostrate foe" (187–189). As soon as he challenges the capitalist, the ostrich's gallantry becomes a mark of wildness. Resisting Hans and Charlie's attempts at turning himself and his family into capital, the ostrich is killed for his efforts, while Hans and Charlie's status as capitalists is affirmed through a literal erasure of his resistance. The egg, however, is taken and nurtured by Hans's wife, who "opened the door to a great colonial industry when she held that infant ostrich between her knees, and stuffed it with minced eggs and liver" (193). As such, future generations of ostriches are nurtured within a domestic space, where they can be more controlled and, ideally, nurtured to submit to the liberal human subject. Attempts at resistance to the capitalist enterprise and domestication are, however, labeled savage and wild. The frontispiece to *The Settler and the Savage* highlights this scene (Figure 6.1), suggesting that the ostrich is "the savage" that needs domination, and battles with the colonist who comes to South Africa for moral and economic ends.

Ostriches nuance our understanding of animals in imperial spaces through their domestication; they embodied British liberal individuality, power, and progress insofar as British colonizers dominated and objectified them as capital. They are included in domestic and economic spaces only to be excluded, incorporated to the extent that their alterity is regulated, or

Figure 6.1 "Attacked by an Ostrich." Frontispiece to R. M. Ballantyne, *The Settler and the Savage*.

their liberalized qualities emphasized. They are dominated like other indigenous animals, but instead of facing extermination, they flourished under a biopolitical governance in which farmers strove to foster their lives by keeping them healthy, breeding them, and ensuring they lived as long as possible. Part of this fostering, however, involved a construction of their subjectivity that reinscribed them into colonial practices and ideologies. Ostriches were exotic, but could be tamed and contribute to the nation's wealth. However, for Martin and Ballantyne especially, the ostrich carried too many negative qualities, one of which was their resistance to liberal subjectivity and the animal–human hierarchy.

The above examples expose the extent to which constructions of animal subjectivity vary based on political ends, and highlight that by their very nature such constructions are always political. Whether the above writers desired a continuation of the plumage trade, better treatment of ostriches, or positive images of colonization, representations of ostrich subjectivity align with their political goals. Their specific imbrication within a variety of colonial practices, such as capitalism, animal husbandry, racism, and animal welfare, affects how their subjectivity is represented, as it is filtered through the ideological makeup of these practices and the strategies of governmentality that regulate them. Throughout *The Story of an African Farm*, Schreiner challenges this embodiment of imperial ideologies, instead using animals to reflect her own anti-colonial politics. For when inserted into discourses of British colonial politics as capital, ostriches exemplify a speciesist form of liberal progress; part of this oppression was reliant on the treatment of and construction of indigenous animals and their subjectivity, and thus speciesism more broadly. Yet they can also embody an animal politics that critiques imperial logic.

Olive Schreiner's Animal Politics

In her preface to the second edition of *The Story of an African Farm*, Schreiner emphasizes the lack of realism within cultural representations of African animals. In a famous statement demonstrating her commitment to realism, Schreiner writes,

> It has been suggested by a kind critic that he would better have liked the little book if it had been a history of wild adventure; of cattle driven into inaccessible "kranzes" by Bushmen; "of encounters with ravening lions, and hairbreadth escapes." This could not be. Such works are best written in Piccadilly or in the Strand: there the gifts of the creative imagination, untrammelled by contact with any fact, may spread their wings. (41–42)

For Schreiner, adventure novels such as *The Settler and the Savage* and *King Solomon's Mines* present an unrealistic view of non-Western spaces and their multi-species inhabitants. In contrast, Schreiner aims to avoid exaggerations and show "the method of life we all lead" (41), filled with empty spaces, moments of unknowability, disappointments, and a lack of closure. Unlike masculine depictions of Africa circulating among the British populace, Schreiner aimed to represent the daily life of colonized spaces. Her realism reflects her belief in the importance of diversity to a South African national identity. She takes pains to represent all its aspects, from the Karoo and insects, to the Kaffirs and state officials wandering through the countryside. The novel's project is similar to *Thoughts on South Africa*, in which she hopes to show the Boer "to the world as he is" (10). Schreiner's realism is a fictional representation of her political philosophy, particularly in her desire to bring the marginalized into the political sphere, even though critics such as Zarena Aslami have pointed toward the novel's "refusal to allow the reader to imagine that a harmonious South African social body exists" (28). Schreiner's project thus aligns with those of other realists such as George Eliot; both have a democratic impulse to represent daily life and subjects who are poorly represented throughout popular depictions.[7] Part of such corrections involve the representations of animals found throughout the empire.

Previous critics have emphasized that Schreiner's politics are often contradictory, at times radical, and at others conservative and racist. Joyce Berkman suggests Schreiner hoped to "create organic democratic communities that accommodated cultural differences, interaction, and change," and "envision[s] alternatives to the social and symbolic order of oppositional and deferential patterns embedded in colonial Victorian views of human differences" (6). Indeed, Schreiner's characterization as a new woman posits her politics against those of patriarchal colonial adventure fiction, even if her racism conflicts with her claims toward a universal feminism, as McClintock and LeeAnne Richardson have demonstrated.[8] At the same time, Schreiner's new woman politics often align with her anti-colonial politics, as both expose the oppressive hierarchies of a patriarchal imperial

---

[7] The project of speaking for the other is not without its own set of complications, as Gayatri Spivak has shown in "Can the Subaltern Speak?" As I have demonstrated throughout this book, attempts to speak for animals often result in a perpetuation of their oppression and subjection to violent forms of human control. Similarly, attempts to speak for marginalized groups often perpetuate racism, sexism, and classism.

[8] Both McClintock and Richardson point to Schreiner's negative depictions of African women in her *The Story of an African Farm* and *From Man to Man*.

society and its culture. Laura Chrisman has demonstrated how Schreiner aimed to critique "economic rationality as sovereign" and place more value on an affective ethics, seen especially in her critique of Cecil Rhodes in *Trooper Peter Halket of Mashonaland* (9).⁹ In her reading of state fantasies, Aslami suggests *African Farm* demonstrates how biopolitics, as a "new mode of liberal governance," is "more difficult to resist and in some ways more insidious because of the fantasies of wholeness and recognition that it inspires in colonial subjects" (28). Indeed, the novel is a stark portrayal of oppression and the lack of power faced by numerous social groups: children, the poor, women, animals, and the non-British. Tant Sannie, a highly unlikable yet financially independent character, is the only one who wins in the novel. Liberal ideologies – seen in the belief that Waldo can go out into the world and become a self-made man, that Lyndall can break free from patriarchy through education, and the larger understanding that colonial subjects can strive in a new land of opportunity – fail most characters. As LeeAnne Richardson points out, "Schreiner's characters do not necessarily identify with the British public and British pride" (80), yet they remain affected by the wide reach of its politics. The kind of subjectivity nurtured by liberal governmentality and British imperial ideologies is ultimately another form of oppression the main characters are unable to resist.

Adding animals into critical accounts of Schreiner nuances her critique of British imperialism, while adding a counter-narrative to the role of animals and animality across the British empire. Indeed, it is striking how often Schreiner's dissatisfaction with British imperial politics and its patriarchal society is articulated through representations of animals, whether these critiques are of British conceptions of animality or instinct, or of violent and oppressive forms of contemporary animal–human relationships. For Schreiner, animal life offered alternate models for human relationships; while animality was often defined in negative ways against the human, Schreiner suggests that some animal relationships were perhaps more moral and progressive than human ones, significantly reworking narratives of liberal progress, especially those based in evolutionary science.¹⁰ Schreiner reads animal actions outside of liberal hierarchies, and shows how animal epistemologies and relationships offer alternatives to those influenced by

---

⁹ For further discussion of the role of economics within colonial South Africa, see Spillman, *British Colonial Realism in Africa*.
¹⁰ Valerie Stevens has recently argued that Schreiner's representations of women and pets offer progressive maternal relations beyond the social confines of patriarchy. See works by Dirk Klooper and Robert Young for detailed accounts of evolutionary logic and racialization.

governmentality. For Schreiner, alternative views of animality challenge the hierarchies and mutual exclusions regulated by liberal imperial discourse. Reading Schreiner's politics through animals elucidates liberalism's failures, as well as the political potential of animality. A reading of her animals also highlights where Schreiner's own politics risk falling back onto liberalism's racist ideologies.

Kathleen Frederickson suggests that in the second half of the nineteenth century instinct became an important and privileged category for liberal governance. She explains that Lamarck's understanding of instinct as adaptable makes it "more consistent with the precepts of liberal bootstrapping and the promise of class mobility" (19). She highlights a relationship between this Lamarckian adaptability of instinct and self-possession:

> In the Lockean models adapted by the late Victorians, "free" choice was a condition of liberal contract through which a person might suspend part of his or her self-ownership. Instinct worked as a palliating corrective to this alienation because it offered a model of self-continuity that could not be alienated, being safeguarded against the alienation of contract precisely because it exists outside of reason and rational choice. (23)

In this understanding, instinct can*not* be a part of the social contract, and is out of reach of the long arm of government. However, Frederickson argues that when applied to Indigenous peoples instinct took on a different meaning: "savage social institutions express the instincts of a collectivity of individual savages" (106), rather than the self-possession essential to liberal ideology. In the context of Victorian empire, instinct is often read as wildness or irrationality, not as a desired quality for inclusion in a political community. Frederickson's astute reading of instinct, however, does not explain how political understandings of instinct reflect back on the animals from which scientists and evolutionary theorists first formulated it, especially in opposition to reason, culture, and civilization. If instinct was outside the reach of governmentality, there were many attempts to reign it in and reform it. Schreiner, however, takes animality, what can be read as instinct, intuition, or reaction – indeed, its very opacity and ambiguity is telling – and uses it to demonstrate where liberal thought fails in its relationship to and construction of alterity. Instinct, which I read here as animal epistemology, counteracts the Lockean belief in ownership through cultivation of "uncivilized" land, prohibits the promise of class mobility through colonial ventures, and disrupts liberal self-possession. Indeed, in Schreiner's hands, animality unsettles the very workings of liberal governmentality within a colonial context.

The Story of an African Farm reworks negative conceptions of the ostrich to represent an animality that resists illegitimate colonial power, exposing the weak points of liberal ideologies such as self-government and individualism. Although Waldo's dog Doss is represented with more subjectivity, the ostrich Hans functions more fully within Schreiner's anti-imperial politics. Wendy Woodward and Deborah Shapple Spillman have discussed Doss in some detail, linking him to Schreiner's animal ethics. For Woodward, Doss represents Schreiner's desire to show animals as thinking, feeling subjects. Indeed, the scene in which the oxen call to God as they are beaten also shows animal emotion. Similarly, Spillman emphasizes that Doss's perspective removes the reader from reason and emphasizes Waldo's emotional state (194–195). I read Doss as representative of British pet-keeping and constructions of canine loyalty, even though he is associated with Lyndall, the novel's most radical character. While Doss and the oxen are important to Schreiner's animal ethics, and, as Stevens argues, Doss is connected to Schreiner's critique of wifehood and motherhood, I suggest the native ostrich more fully registers her anti-liberal propensities. While the above representations of ostriches justified capitalist ideologies in relation to colonialism, Schreiner's representation shows the illegitimacy of the colonial project. Although she does not, as one reader of *Animal World* admits, point out the cruelty ostriches experience – "Olive Schrimer [*sic*] in her sad story of 'An African' farm, though drawing the most lamentable picture of human life in that country never speaks of the cruelty your February number mentions" (S.K.H.) – she does show the hypocrisy and illegitimacy of the settler-colonial project, precisely through the domesticated ostrich. Indeed, she neglects animal welfare discourse altogether when it comes to the ostrich. Although we could read this as a removal of ostriches from the sphere of moral concern, I suggest it gives them more political power. By removing them from a liberalizing discourse of animal welfare, the ostriches offer a more radical politics outside of a regulatory pastoral power.

Through his interactions with Bonaparte Blenkins, the novel's sleazy representation of a colonist, Hans, the native ostrich, is the only character who physically resists manifestations of liberal ideologies within a settler-colony. While Hans's actions toward Bonaparte do not cause his removal from the farm, which happens only after Tant Sannie catches him with her niece, they do expose the limitations of Bonaparte's liberalism, and by extension those of the settler-colonist. Indeed, Hans turns Bonaparte's colonial mimicry into a form of mockery that destabilizes the authority of British colonial practices. For although Bonaparte is a colonist who comes to a farm and tries to take it over with no authority to do so, he is also Irish, and thus himself a colonized subject.[11] Through his actions on the farm he mocks the British colonists; Bonaparte is "*almost the same,*" as the British colonist, "*but not quite*" (Bhabha 126), for he does not have the self-possession and character that exemplified the liberal subject. For Homi Bhabha, mimicry "raises the question of the *authorization* of colonial representations" (131). Yet the mockery Hans creates questions not just colonial authority, but human superiority as well. As Saudo-Welby argues, the novel's chapter titles animalize Bonaparte, thus further destabilizing his superiority as both a colonist and a human.

The first scene with Hans reworks the ostrich scene from *The Settler and the Savage*, as Schreiner revises representations of animals in adventure fiction. Here the ostrich's reaction to a capitalist-colonist is valued rather than ended by death; instead of reinforcing colonial power, Hans exposes it as illegitimate. The first morning Bonaparte is on the farm he is horribly frightened by Hans. Lyndall looks on with satisfaction as Bonaparte runs to Otto's cottage screaming, "'Oh, God! my God! I am killed!'" as with "shaking flesh," he "fell into the room, followed by a half-grown ostrich, who put its head in at the door, opened its beak at him, and went away" (73). Overly apologetic, Otto explains, "I never knew so young a bird to chase before; but they will take dislikes to certain people" (73). The ostrich seems to immediately sense – almost on an instinctual level, spontaneous, perhaps without forethought – that Bonaparte is an outsider with plans to illegitimately take over the farm. While Bonaparte dupes Otto, Lyndall recognizes he is a liar, yet her age prohibits her from convincing the adults. Due to his freedom from the constraints of liberal subjectivity, Hans actively resists and challenges the colonial mindset. In doing so, he exposes Bonaparte's lack of character and mocks his authority as a colonist and a human. For this scene comes the morning after Bonaparte bragged about killing ten bears, a much more frightening animal than an ostrich. While Bonaparte professes himself unafraid to die in his encounter with the bears, here his face turns "blue and white, with a greenishness about the mouth" (73) from fear of the large bird. Hans further reveals Bonaparte's physical weakness – "my nerves ... always delicate – highly strung – are broken – broken!" (73) – not a desirable quality for a colonist who should embody British masculinity.

---

[11] I thank Isaac Wang for this insightful suggestion of Bonaparte performing a mimicry that turns into mockery.

After Bonaparte has effectively usurped Otto's role as overseer of the farm, Hans again challenges Bonaparte's claim to power, this time through a resistance that, for Bonaparte, manifests as a power beyond reason, what Saudo-Welby labels an act of divine justice. While the earlier scene exposes Bonaparte's lack of character and masculinity, this moment further disrupts Bonaparte's self-possession. Making himself comfortable in Otto's cabin and searching for a stack of money he is confident must be there, Bonaparte comes across Otto's dead wife's wedding ring. Singing to himself that he will not only possess Tant Sannie but also her "money-bags" (106), Bonaparte feels "a slow and distinct rap ... on the crown of his bald head." He looks around and notices the wedding ring is missing, and he again feels "three slow and distinct taps" on his head, and then finally, "a resolute tug at the grey curls at the back of his head" (106–107). This last tug causes him "to leap up, yelling wildly. Was he to sit still paralysed, to be dragged away *bodily* to the devil? With terrific shrieks he fled, casting no glance behind" (107). We learn later this had been Hans, and that Lyndall let him out of the ostrich-camps in the hopes he would kill Bonaparte. While he failed in this regard, Lyndall observes that Hans "frightened him horribly," and that perhaps now Bonaparte will leave Waldo's things alone, as indeed he does (107). In both moments Bonaparte is, more so than the ostrich, unable to control himself, lacking self-government and liberal character. Hans has made a mockery of colonial bootstrap ideology – "with only a few hundreds of capital, to set up for himself ... With ordinary luck at Ostrich farming, he is made a man" (Douglass 26, 28) – and shows the illegitimacy of colonial power.

Schreiner thus offers two productive moments where Hans has the most power over Bonaparte. He first manifests an active resistance, literally chasing Bonaparte down, while the second encounter functions as an animal power or logic Bonaparte cannot comprehend, an alternative mode of challenging illegitimate power. The second encounter is also a relational form of resistance, involving cooperation between Lyndall and Hans, which demonstrates her own valuation of his animality. In Lyndall's understanding Hans's animality offers her and the farm's other oppressed inhabitants a way out from colonial rule, or at least a means of exposing its falsehoods. Whereas other cultural representations of ostriches depict them as the colonist's gold ticket to a successful life abroad or as stupid birds lacking self-government and in need of domination, Schreiner privileges these colonized animals, thus reworking British conceptions of South Africa. The ostrich suggests that perhaps what alternative subjects ostensibly lack is what gives them power, or that animality need not function in a hierarchical manner below a more civilized, liberal reason. For Leela Gandhi, the most pertinent resistance to imperial logic is in "the rehearsal of unmediated or immediate and extreme forms of relation between beings with 'vastly different phenomenologies and ontologies,' that is, across genders, races, classes, and paradigmatically across the species barrier" (86), and Hans illustrates this well. He exposes the lack of character in someone like Bonaparte and the illegitimacy of settler-colonialism. Here, animals seen as stupid or in need of human governance actually have power over humans both physically and morally. While Hans's charging at Bonaparte could be read as "savage" behavior, in the larger context of the novel it is valued, rather than seen negatively. Hans has a power that Lyndall, Waldo, and Otto do not; indeed, it is a power Lyndall admires and wishes she had. Hans ultimately destabilizes Bonaparte's liberal subjectivity and his control over the farm, foreclosing a natural hierarchy between the uncivilized and the civilized, the colonized and the colonizer, and even the animal and the human. The ostrich is valued by Schreiner, Lyndall, and, ideally, the Victorian reader.

Interactions between Hans and Lyndall – the novel's most political character and figure of new woman feminism – link Schreiner's anticolonial and feminist politics, and highlight how she posits animal relationships and epistemologies as alternatives to liberal ideologies. Lyndall's valuation of animals highlights the political potential of their resistance to liberal governmentality and its more material manifestations. For example, before Lyndall goes into her first speech about the condition of women, as she and Waldo watch the birds, "an ostrich hen came bounding towards them . . . while far away over the bushes the head of the cock was visible as he sat brooding on the eggs" (183). Lyndall says, "I like these birds . . . they share each other's work, and are companions" (184). Unable to see non-patriarchal relationships within the human world, Lyndall locates them in the animal world. She takes the opposite view of liberal discourses of civilization and progress, suggesting that the animal world offers models to aspire to, not move away from. While imperial and animal welfare discourses on the ostrich focus on stereotypical gender roles to align with liberal character, emphasizing the care and tenderness with which mothers watch their eggs, Schreiner focuses on the companionability and equality of the birds. She asks for better treatment not of ostriches but of women, especially when it comes to work and marriage. Schreiner views animals as subjects from whom the human world can learn.

Women and Labor and *From Man to Man* also locate alternate relationship models in the animal world. The majority of the chapter "Sex

Differences" in *Women and Labor* is composed of non-patriarchal models of animal relationships, where women and men work together to raise their young. Schreiner privileges birds, writing, "It is among certain orders of birds that sex manifestations appear to assume their most harmonious and poetical forms on earth" (73). In *From Man to Man*, Schreiner uses the ostrich as her model of an equal partnership, asking, "Could the ostrich breed out its eggs in the wastes, where long journeys for food are needed, if the male did not daily take his hours of brooding on the nest to keep the eggs warm and care for and watch over the young with a tenderness even greater than their mother's while she goes afar to seek for food?" (186). While colonist Annie Martin reads the male ostrich who sits on eggs as a "poor husband, determined not to be disappointed of his little family ... sitting bravely and patiently day and night, though nearly dead with exhaustion" (117), and Hans and Charlie in *The Settler and the Savage* disavow these gender politics for capital gain, for Schreiner ostrich couples represent a non-patriarchal animal politics in which shared labor leads to evolutionary progress beyond liberal norms. In a similar fashion, Waldo sees "a certain harmony" and beauty in the lives of pigs, even with all their mud and "rotten pumpkin" (116). His absorption in pig life is, however, disrupted by Bonaparte pushing him over the gate into the pigsty, as if reminding him that such harmony does not exist in a colonial setting. The belief that imperialism promotes liberal progress is rejected in favor of Waldo's fall into an animal setting of mud and rot, and Lyndall's attempt to have an ostrich-like relationship. Throughout her writings, Schreiner suggests that because of their desire to move away from and renounce animality and the animal world, British imperial ideologies such as liberal progress impede real political and social reform.

From Man to Man further brings together connections between speciesism, sexism, and imperialism through a critique of hunting, the imperial adventure prized by male colonists. Rebecca describes the differences between Frank's relationships with animals and her own, contrasting his desire to hunt, which is mere sport, competition, and the thrill of the chase, with her desire for intimate connection: "The supreme moment to me is not when I kill or conquer a living thing, but that moment its eye and mine meet and a line of connection is formed between me and the life that is in it" (269). Here hunting links patriarchy and imperialism, as both are forms of possession. Indeed, Schreiner's suggestion that men view women as animals – "that somewhat quadrupedal posture is for him truly feminine," she argues (*Women* 80) – solidifies the patriarchal logic of hunting. For Rebecca, on the other hand, the animal gaze registers a

Levinasian and Derridean ethics prohibiting human domination, revealing a sense of equality, or at least an acknowledgment of the animal point of view.

Schreiner further links feminism and a disdain for hunting in *Women and Labor*, writing, "The relations of the female towards the production of human life influence undoubtedly even her relation towards animal and all life" (67). As opposed to the masculine desire for hunting, "There is no light-hearted, careless enjoyment in the sacrifice of life to the normal woman; her instinct, instructed by experience, steps in to prevent it. She always knows what life costs" (68). Similarly, in *Thoughts on South Africa*, Schreiner uses the contrast between Boer and British attitudes toward hunting to critique imperial discourses, and what Leela Gandhi identifies as a link between animal cruelty and conspicuous consumption (105). In the chapter "The Psychology of the Boer," Schreiner writes that Boers will hunt only when necessary, and view British fox and trophy hunting as incomprehensible. Importantly, this relationship with animals reflects their relationships with other humans; for them hunting is the same as war, as Schreiner notes that "after a long and intimate knowledge of the old-fashioned Boer ... never, in one instance have we heard man or woman speak of war with joy, desire, or elation" (254). If Boers were seen as uncivilized by the British, Schreiner suggests they are morally superior, as hunting for sport is a form of degeneration (*Women and Labor* 36). Indeed, Schreiner scorned hunting because she saw how much it decimated the animal populations constituting her conception of South African identity.[12] Thus instead of reifying regulatory liberal-imperial strategies, Schreiner's valuation and conceptions of animals show a desire for an anti-imperial feminist politics that resists the speciesist discourse perpetuated by the empire.

Animality, Racism, and Speciesism

To what extent does Schreiner's reworking of animality align with the animalization of Indigenous humans? While Hans's animal politics rejects beliefs that non-Western spaces and their inhabitants were, like the ostrich, incapable of self-government and in need of domination, this does not suggest that Schreiner believes treating animals differently will lead to better treatment of animalized human subjects, or that Indigenous peoples

---

[12] Schreiner discusses animal extinction most fully in her 1891 essay "Our Waste Land in Mashonaland," where she details animal extinction and the need for a nature preserve.

should embrace the animality projected onto them by colonial discourses. Rather, Schreiner demonstrates how speciesism functions as part of liberalism's imperial logic and mode of constructing racial difference. As is well known, projecting animality onto non-British human subjects was common in late nineteenth-century discourses of anthropology, ethnology, and travel writing. Dirk Klooper discusses this animalizing process in South Africa and argues that both "the Bushman [San] and the Boer were ambiguously located on the boundaries of culture and nature, human and animal" (5). Missionaries, travel writers, anthropologists, and ethnologists detailed how closely both groups were aligned with animals, especially the San, who, some argued, believed baboons were people (13). McClintock similarly notes that the Khoekhoe and San "were located at the very nadir of human degeneration, just before the species left off its human form and turned bestial" (55). As numerous critics have discussed, Schreiner frequently perpetuates racist depictions of Indigenous Africans.[13] In *The Story of an African Farm*, for example, she has unsympathetic views of the Xhosa, describing them as "star[ing] stupidly" (62) and "howling horribly" (63), with "lips hideously protruding" (94). As such moments make clear, Schreiner seems to privilege domestic animals above the animalized human, illuminating more limitations to her politics and showing how she still perpetuates racist liberal ideology. However, we are not to support Tant Sannie's polygenesis view that "they were descended from apes, and needed no salvation" (79). Schreiner, rather, rethinks animality and gives it political potential, while separating it from human animalization. That is, Schreiner does not equate animal animality with human animality, yet the two are still intimately connected by larger structures of violence, and still coexist in her own liberal politics.

Schreiner's progressive *and* problematic politics demonstrates that connections between racialized animality and violence against animals must be nuanced to avoid reinscribing Indigenous peoples into animalizing discourses *and* to take into account the varying layers of violence colonized animals and humans experienced. Christopher Peterson argues that speciesism contributes to human animalization, as it "engenders the bestialization of social and political others. That the human/animal

---

[13] Paula Krebs argues that through Anglicizing Boers and seeing Africans as a "class" who can contribute to the economy, Schreiner "is incapable of envisioning a truly multi-racial or non-racial future for South Africa" (428). Bart Moore-Gilbert takes an alternative view, and suggests that Waldo is a stand-in for a colonized subject, and as such the novel is both feminist and anti-imperialist. I agree that Schreiner's racial politics are limited at best, and that she privileges animal politics at the expense of a more liberating and inclusive multi-racial politics.

opposition makes the abjection of *human* others possible means that insisting on their humanity as a mode of resistance can only reinscribe the speciesist logic that initiates their exclusion" (2). Yet, as Neel Ahuja emphasizes, we must be cautious when analyzing animality and racialized subjects together, and not immediately align the two. Ahuja emphasizes the limitations of conflating race and species:

> Unfortunately extending the conflation of race and species, "animal studies" often assimilates racial discourse into species discourse, flattening out historical contexts that determine the differential use of animal (and other) figures in the processes of racialization. Even some of the field's more nuanced accounts of racialization assimilate race critique into species critique, taking animalization as the generic basis of racism. (557–558)

While I have outlined alignments between animals and Indigenous peoples, they should not be assumed, as such assumptions can reinscribe an animalizing logic. At the same time, nuancing these alignments leads to fruitful analyses of the larger power structures that construct such subjects in the first place. For example, Sujit Sivasundaram insightfully discusses "the disciplinary genealogies of race and animality" through discourses of aboriginiality, criminality, and nature versus nurture (157), to show how these guiding discourses of empire align racialized humans and animals, especially through material practices. For Schreiner, speciesism, alongside racism and sexism, structures relationships between colonizers and colonized animals and humans. I would argue that at times it also structures some of her own relationships. Yet offering new articulations of animality and writing against speciesist discourses challenges the animal–human distinction that legitimates the multi-layered forms of violence existing within imperialism, from the subjection of animals to the oppression of Indigenous peoples. As Sivasundaram emphasizes, "Nonhuman empires may be differently nonhuman" (170).

As in her racist moments, the privileged animal–human relationship Schreiner presents is not without its own limitations. The fact that Hans is useful to Lyndall only insofar as he is subjected to animal husbandry shows the many layers of violence taking place in settler-colonies. Schreiner herself is a second-generation settler-colonist; her valuation of other South African subjects such as the Boers rests on this position. Like privileged forms of animal–human relationships such as pet-keeping and domestication, relationships among settler-colonists and Indigenous peoples can rarely be ones of equality. The forms of violence among animals and humans taking place within animal husbandry are reflective of more intense forms of imperial violence, connected as they are to colonial practices. Not only is animal husbandry a form of violence against animals, but the land colonists grabbed to create their ostrich farms affected the livelihood of the colonized. For example, an 1870 Act for the preservation of wild ostriches in the Cape Colony basically made ostrich hunting illegal, fining those who killed a wild ostrich without a license between 30 to 50 pounds (Saudo-Welby). Of course, such a law would mostly affect the Indigenous Africans who hunted the wild ostrich for crucial resources.[14] And as I have shown throughout this book, speaking for animals perpetuates many forms of oppression, and reinscribes them into Western, liberal, anthropocentric frameworks that most often perpetuate speciesism. Similarly, Schreiner's move to *speak for* the Boers and Indigenous Africans is also a form of intimate violence, based as it is on relationships that could take place only as a result of settler-colonialism. In this sense, Schreiner's politics can be only so radical. Just as she grappled with her national identity throughout her life, so her politics struggle to offer alternative possibilities of relating within the violent structures of settler-colonialism *and* the domestication of animals. She exposes the hypocrisies and contradictions within liberal ideologies, but remains within their larger power structures.

Looking at animals within colonized spaces thus uncovers the intimacies taking place within unequal power relations. Within the novel, Schreiner props up animal epistemologies when contained within human structures of violence; similarly, she argues for an anti-colonial politics from the position of settler-colonist. The intimate relationships that Schreiner cultivates with Boers, Indigenous Africans, and animals shows how, as Lowe has suggested, intimacies become hierarchized and divided within colonial relationships. Lowe argues that "intimacies of desire, sexuality, marriage, and family are inseparable from the imperial projects of conquest, slavery, labor, and government" (17), and "Just as we may observe colonial divisions of humanity, I suggest there is also a colonial division of intimacy, which charts the historically differentiated access to the domains of liberal personhood, from interiority and individual will, to the possession of property and domesticity" (18). Analyzing animal–human colonial intimacies highlights the numerous and often contradictory positions animals occupied. Offering the possibility of liberation from liberal-imperial forms of subjecthood and subjectivity, Schreiner's animals highlight the

---

[14] See also David Nibert, *Animal Oppression and Human Violence: Domesecration, Capitalism, and Global Conflict*.

deep imbrication of animals within colonial discourse and practices, and reveals how they served as sites of both subjection and resistance within a South African settler-colonial context. Although working on different levels with varying forms of violence, the intimacies Schreiner represents are connected by the liberal governmentality that structures difference across speciesist lines. Even as she tried to escape such ideologies, she was still implicated in their perpetuation.

Thus, Schreiner's animal politics counters the liberal ideologies – the self-made man, individualism, capitalism, and patriarchy – that contribute to the exclusionary practices of imperialism, while highlighting the pervasiveness of speciesist logic. Her animal politics demonstrates the restrictiveness of Victorian liberal thought through its oppression of animal and human others, its obsession with reason and narratives of progress, and its construction of the animal–human divide. Hegemonic views toward animals were intimately connected to racist narratives of civilization and evolutionary progress, showing how integrally speciesim was imbedded in Victorian racism and the imperial project. If the British aligned animals and non-Western humans as justification for colonization and evidence for white superiority, Schreiner suggests that views toward animals reflect how little the British have accomplished on their own in terms of civilization. In *From Man to Man*, for example, Rebecca thinks to herself, "It ill becomes us, who are but the tamed children of yesterday, to talk of primitive savages. Even to-day, when we have inherited all, is it so certain that our vaunted civilization is so much statelier and on all sides wider and with nobler elements of truth lying at its foundation than the older civilizations of the yellow and brown races?" (178). Schreiner compares this to Buddha's valuation of animal life, which throughout her letters she contrasts with the "brutal doctrine of Christianity in its scorn for the animal world" (letter to John T. Lloyd), and critiques common narratives about civilization that cultivated racist discourses:

> Did not the deep-seeing eye of the Buddha, hundreds of years before the Jewish teacher walked in Syria, perceive clearly beneath all the complexities of form and individuality the unity in life upon the earth? He did not get at it as the modern man of reason, slowly, by measurement and calculation; by deep perception he knew that our little brothers look out at us from the eyes of animals, that the life of no beast and bird or insect is alien and unconnected with ours. (*Man to Man* 178)

As Robert Young argues, non-Western cultures were understood as behind the British in terms of civilizational progress, or as in the case of ancient

Egypt's civilization, were whitened (127). Instead of looking to racial theories based in zoology and anatomical differences, Young argues that "From the 1840s onwards these comparative forms of racial description were increasingly augmented by evaluations based on a presupposition of cultural hierarchy" (121). Schreiner reworks such racist doctrines by suggesting that other races and cultures were "civilized" before the British. Schreiner further removes evolution from racist and speciesist discourses, placing it within an inclusive philosophy that values all life and sees more connections than differences.

Schreiner's animal politics critiques Enlightenment logic and privileges animal epistemologies, agencies, and relationships. She suggests that the rationality vaunted by speciesist and racist liberal discourses creates the hierarchies essential to imperial logic. As such, valuing animals becomes political in ways not seen within liberal animal welfare discourse; her animal politics shows how deeply speciesism, alongside racism and patriarchy, was part of the narrative of British imperialism, capitalism, and liberal progress. If instinct was valued in liberal discourses of governance, as Frederickson argues, it was valued only insofar as it separated animals and humans. Yet Schreiner suggests that the animal world has much to offer a liberal society in need of progressive and radical change. Animals disrupt liberal subjectivity and offer progressive models for new relations. If evolutionary discourses argued that human evolution away from animal life was a good thing, Schreiner suggests this was perhaps a devolution, as her animal politics shows humans may want to be closer to the animal world, rather than separate from it. Yet, her very articulation of this view from her position as a white, British settler-colonist signals her own position of privilege, and thus the limitations of her politics.

Throughout her later life, Schreiner was increasingly frustrated by liberal politics, especially once she became more concerned with South African politics in the 1890s. As Berkman explains, Schreiner no longer thought England offered a paternal model of civilized and moral progress, and wanted to "envision alternatives to the social and symbolic order of oppositional and deferential patterns embedded in colonial Victorian views of human differences" (6). This involves rethinking animality and the kinds of animal–human differences that proved destructive to colonized animal and human subjects. In looking to South Africa as a model for diversity, Schreiner found within animal life alternatives to speciesist and racist liberal ideologies that reinforced England's belief in its superiority and justified imperial expansion. As Uday Singh Mehta has discussed, nineteenth-century British imperialism legitimated itself through beliefs in liberal progress, seen, for example, in Mill's claims that not all human societies were yet capable of representative government, and needed to be moved "along the ascending gradient of historical progress" (*Liberalism* 82). Among other liberal justifications of empire was, according to Mehta, the belief that territory is not "a symbolic expression and a concrete condition for the possibility of (or aspirations to) a distinct way of life," as "Liberals have failed to appreciate that territory ... gathers together many of the associations through which individuals come to see themselves as members of a political society" (*Liberalism* 119). For Schreiner, the physical geography of South Africa and *all* its inhabitants was essential to her belief that its diverse regions could form a national identity, and through its difference and mutual inclusion, served as a better example of progress.

Schreiner provides alternative representations to colonized spaces, presenting a counterpoint to narratives that told of hunters, exotic animals, and violent African goddesses. Her animal politics offers a counterpoint to dominant conceptions of liberal subjectivity that guided British beliefs about non-Western spaces. For although she paints her main characters with the utmost sympathy, showing how they are fooled or oppressed by liberal ideologies, the last line of *The Story of an African Farm* reminds us that "the chickens were wiser" (283). And while she includes animals in national belonging – wherein they are valued above objectification and understood outside of purely economic discourses – she also examines how animal–human interactions can allow for moments that move beyond a contentious political category caused by imperialism and inciting war and violence. For in a letter from 1914, Schreiner again privileges birds as a model for human relationships, as they invite a form of animal politics: "The only thing that gives me any joy," she wrote, "is the sparrows & pigeons ... It's not only that my heart quivers with love when I see them ... but some person must be kind enough to throw crumbs out to them, though they are *not* of his nation. Nationality isn't everything!" (letter to Havelock Ellis, Dec. 13). Under imperialism and settler-colonialism, there will always be fractured identities and contentious relationships. Alternative relationships with animals, however, reflect possibilities for new and more compassionate human relationships that accept others as fellow creatures beyond arbitrary national borders. Schreiner uses animals to both articulate a national identity and transcend the limitations of international relationships structured by a liberal framework and governmentality's regulation of alternative subjectivities.

Coda

Through its analysis of how Victorian animal subjects were constrained by liberal governmentality yet offered ways out of its more oppressive aspects, *The Political Lives of Victorian Animals* aims to open a conversation about how animals intersect with Victorian studies' more foundational and dominant conversations, and how animals operate politically across multiple discourses. Bringing animals into discussions of Victorian liberalism can, I hope, both nuance the field of Victorian animal studies and show how intimately animals were connected to formative discourses and practices of the Victorian age. I also hope that this book offers ways to think more deeply about the forms of power humans have over animals, and how animals can be envisioned outside of them. Although focused on nineteenth-century Britain, this book asks animal studies and other posthuman scholars to look more closely at the forms of power guiding constructions of animal subjectivity. It also shows the limitations of liberalism as a political framework for animal rights and progressive animal–human relationships.

Reading animals as political subjects in their own right, and with political agency, can fundamentally upset and challenge our anthropocentric and exclusionary human politics. It can revise some of the foundational discourses still with us today – such as liberalism and animal welfare – and locate more inclusive and democratic ways to move beyond them. Human power over animals is almost always present in any animal–human relationship, even in assumingly benign places such as pet-keeping. Without ignoring the physical forms of biopower humans have over animals' lives, this book emphasizes how animals are almost always constrained by human discourses, and most especially, that we can only ever imagine animal subjectivity. Certainly, animals have multiple ways of communicating with humans, yet there is still an element of undecidability that humans must fill in with their own projections. One of the questions this book raises is how to acknowledge animal communication and agency while remaining cautious of projecting our own beliefs and desires onto them. How do we recognize the human power in articulating animal subjectivity while not reducing it to such? As Cynthia Willet reminds us, "Animals are not vulnerable sites of protection and recipients of human sympathy, but kindred political agents in their own right with interlocking histories, cultures, and technologies" (38). When engaging with animals we must acknowledge these histories and cultures, and I would add, emotions, thoughts, and desires, yet look out for the moments of speciesism and anthropocentrism that can all too easily come creeping in, and can affect humans as well as animals.

Thus while this book has emphasized many forms of power over animals, it does not claim animal–human relationships should always be reduced to them. And indeed, my exploration of an animal politics has been an attempt to counter human power with the possibility of a powerful animal agency, autonomy, and a set of epistemologies that ask the human to envision alternate ways of being in the world, and to take part in a more inclusive multi-species world. While animal politics may always only ever be a thought experiment, this does not mean we cannot imagine ways to make our human politics more animal-like, to move beyond exclusionary frameworks that result in the physical subjection of others, or the regulation of their lives on a daily level. Envisioning animal politics allows us to seek alternate frameworks for engaging with alterity, and take more care to allow for the multiple subject positions that compose our public and private spaces. If, as Chantal Mouffe so succinctly puts it, pluralism should be acknowledged as "constitutive of modern democracy" (104), we must move beyond a liberal-individualist framework, and a homogenous conception of "the people" or "consensus," and imagine alternate publics and forms of democracy that allow for multiplicity. *The Political Lives of Victorian Animals* has shown how we might begin to think through what a radical democracy that includes animals may look like. If nothing else, I hope it has shown that liberal frameworks are too restrictive for taking animals seriously as political subjects.

Our contemporary animal–human relationships were forged throughout the Victorian era. Animal–human relationships and practices such as anti-cruelty legislation, animal welfare societies, vegetarianism, the meat industry, animal experimentation, zoos, the trade in exotic animals, big-game hunting, pet-keeping, and more all intensified in the nineteenth century. Thus, examining how such practices formed, the political contexts in which they operated, and most especially how they imagined the inner lives of the animals affected by them can help us think about how they function today, how they encourage citizens to conceptualize animal subjects, and to see the contradictions that arise from caring deeply for some animals, while continuing to exploit them for the benefit of human pleasures and economies.

Works Cited

Primary Sources

"Abolition of Private Slaughter-Houses." *Animal World*, vol. 5, no. 63, Dec. 1874, p. 180.
"Adjourned Conference." *The Healthian Journal*, Oct. 1847, p. 29.
"The Animal World." *Animal World*, vol. 2, no. 24, Aug. 1871, p. 207.
"Annual Meeting." *Animal World*, vol. 2, no. 23, Aug. 1871, pp. 172–179.
"Another Great Cat Show." *Animal World*, vol. 3, no. 27, Dec. 1871, pp. 40–42.
"An Appeal from a Brute to Road-Makers." *Animal World*, vol. 1, no. 9, June 1870, p. 157.
Arnold, Matthew. *Culture and Anarchy and Other Writings*, edited by Stefan Collini. Cambridge University Press, 2010.
"The Autobiography of Another Cat. By Mow Wow." *Animal World*, vol. 4, no. 49, Oct. 1873, pp. 146–147.
"The Autobiography of a French Partridge." *Animal World*, vol. 6, no. 73, Oct. 1875, pp. 153–154.
Barmby, Goodwyn. "A Testimony against the Butcher Class." *The Healthian Journal*, Nov. 1846, p. 48.
Bentham, Jeremy. *A Fragment on Government*. Cambridge University Press, 1988.
— *An Introduction to the Principles of Morals and Legislation*. Dover, 2007.
"Birds without Friends in Parliament. – No. 3." *Animal World*, vol. 4, no. 46, July 1873, p. 100.
"Birds without Friends in Parliament. – No. 4." *Animal World*, vol. 4, no. 46, July 1873, p. 101.
Bray, Cara. *Our Duty to Animals*. S. W. Partridge, n.d.
Carlyle, Thomas. *Chartism*. John Alden, 1885.
Carroll, Lewis. *Alice's Adventures in Wonderland*, edited by Richard Kelly. Broadview, 2000.
— *The Diaries of Lewis Carroll*. Vol. II, edited by Roger Lancelyn Green. Greenwood, 1954.
— "Some Popular Fallacies on Vivisection." In *The Complete Works of Lewis Carroll*. Modern Library, 1936, pp. 1189–1201.
Carroll, Lewis, and Martin Gardner. *The Annotated Alice*. Norton, 2000.

"Cat Shows and Beautiful Cats." *Animal World*, vol. 4, no. 49, Oct. 1873, pp. 145–146.
"Cats at the Crystal Palace." *Animal World*, vol. 3, no. 33, June 1872, p. 131.
Chater, F. J. Talfourd, and H. F. Lester. "Slaughter-House Reform." *Animal World*, vol. 13, no. 154, July 1882, pp. 99–100.
Cobbett's Parliamentary Debates. Vol. XIV. Hansard, 1809.
"Constitution of the London Vegetarian Society." *The Vegetarian*, vol. 1, no. 17, April 28, 1888, pp. 51–52.
"Contagious Diseases (Animals) Act, 1869." *Animal World*, vol. 1, no. 1, Oct. 1869, p. 16.
"Correspondence." *Animal World*, vol. 1, no. 6, March 1870, p. 110.
Coutts, Angela Burdett. "Systematic Education for the Humane Treatment of Animals (Miss Coutts's Letter to the Editor of "The Times")." *Animal World*, vol. 1, no. 1, Oct. 1869, p. 11.
"Cruelty to Animals." *London Times*, June 2, 1821.
"The Cruelty of Preserving Ferocious Wild Animals." *Animal World*, vol. 5, no. 54, March 1874, pp. 40–41.
Darwin, Charles. *The Descent of Man*. Penguin, 2004.
  The Expression of the Emotions in Man and Animals. Penguin, 2009.
Dickens, Charles. *Barnaby Rudge*. Oxford University Press, 2003.
  "From the Raven in the Happy Family." In *Miscellaneous Papers*. Vol. 1. Kraus, 1983, pp. 203–207.
  Hard Times. Penguin, 1995.
  The Letters of Charles Dickens. Vol. II, 1840–1841. 12 vols., edited by Madeline House and Graham Storey. Clarendon, 1969.
  The Letters of Charles Dickens. Vol. X, 1862–1864. 12 vols., edited by Madeline House and Graham Storey. Clarendon, 1969.
  Oliver Twist. Penguin, 2003.
  "Perfect Felicity in a Bird's-Eye View." In *Miscellaneous Papers*. Vol. 1. Kraus, 1983, pp. 199–202.
Dickens, Charles, and W. H. Wills. "The Heart of Mid-London." In *The Uncollected Writings of Charles Dickens: Household Words 1850–1859*. Vol. 1, edited by Harry Stone. Indiana University Press, 1968, pp. 101–111.
Disraeli, Benjamin. *Sybil*. Oxford, 2009.
"A Dog's Appeal." *Animal World*, vol. 14, no. 171, Dec. 1883, p. 186.
Douglass, Arthur. *Ostrich Farming in South Africa*. Cassell, Petter, Galpin, 1881.
Drummond, William H. *The Rights of Animals and Man's Obligation to Treat Them with Humanity*. John Mardon, 1838.
E.A.W. "Our Pets – III. 'Oberon and 'Titania.'" *Animal World*, vol. 4, no. 43, April 1873, pp. 51–52.
"The Education of Animals." *Animal World*, vol. 3, no. 33, June 1872, p. 134.
Eliot, George. *Felix Holt, the Radical*. Penguin, 1995.
Engels, Friedrich. *The Conditions of the Working Class of England*. Oxford University Press, 2009.

Erskine, Thomas. "The Liberated Robins." *Animal World*, vol. 1, no. 5, Feb. 1870, p. 87.

"Extracts from Essays." *Animal World*, vol. 3, no. 36, Sept. 1872, pp. 195–198.

Fairman, Frank. *The Principles of Socialism Made Plain*. W. Reeves, 1888.

"First Annual Report of the Vegetarian Society." *The Vegetarian Advocate*, vol. 1, Sept. 1848, pp. 5–20.

Fitzgerald, Percy. "Dickens's Dogs; or, the Landseer of Fiction." *London Society: An Illustrated Magazine of Light and Amusing Literature for the Hours of Relaxation*, vol. 4, July 1863, pp. 48–61.

Fletcher, Evelyn. "On Some of Our Earth-Born Companions – II. The Ostrich." *Animal World*, vol. 22, no. 262, July 1891, pp. 99–102.

"A French Schoolmaster on Humane Education." *Animal World*, vol. 1, no. 1, Oct. 1869, p. 7.

Gaskell, Elizabeth. *Mary Barton*. Penguin, 1996.

Haggard, H. Rider. *King Solomon's Mines*. Oxford University Press, 2008.

Hansard's Parliamentary Debates. Third Series. Vol. II. Hansard, 1831.

Hansard's Parliamentary Debates. Third Series. Vol. XLVIII. Hansard, 1839.

Hansard's Parliamentary Debates. Third Series. Vol. LXXVI. Hansard, 1844.

Hansard's Parliamentary Debates. Third Series. Vol. CXCIV. Cornelius Buck, 1869.

Hansard's Parliamentary Debates. Third Series. Vol. CCXI. Cornelius Buck, 1872.

Hansard's Parliamentary Debates. Third Series. Vol. CCXV. Cornelius Buck, 1873.

Hardy, Thomas. "Appendix II: The Surviving Draft-Fragments of *Far from the Madding Crowd*." In *Far from the Madding Crowd*, edited by Rosemarie Morgan. Penguin, 2003, pp. 396–412.

———. "Bags of Meat." In *The Complete Poems of Thomas Hardy*, edited by James Gibson. Macmillan, 1976, pp. 807–808.

———. *The Collected Letters of Thomas Hardy*. 7 vols., edited by Richard Little Purdy and Michael Millgate. Clarendon, 1980.

———. "Compassion." In *The Complete Poems of Thomas Hardy*, edited by James Gibson. Macmillan, 1976, pp. 822–823.

———. *Far from the Madding Crowd*. Penguin, 2003.

———. *Jude the Obscure*. Barnes and Noble, 2003.

———. *The Life and Work of Thomas Hardy*, edited by Michael Millgate. Macmillan, 1984.

———. *The Personal Notebooks of Thomas Hardy*, edited by Richard Taylor. Columbia University Press, 1979.

———. *Thomas Hardy's Public Voice: The Essays, Speeches, and Miscellaneous Prose*, edited by Michael Millgate. Oxford, 2001.

Hayes, T. W. L. "Vegetarianism and Butchers." *Animal World*, vol. 9, no. 111, Dec. 1878, pp. 183–184.

Herbert, Auberon. "The Choices between Personal Freedom and State Protection." In *The Right and Wrong of Compulsion by the State and Other Essays*, edited by Eric Mack. Liberty Fund, 1978, pp. 33–51.

Hobhouse, L. T. *Liberalism and Other Writings*, edited by James Meadowcroft. Cambridge University Press, 2006.
Holland, Mrs. "The Robins' Reply to Their Benefactor (Lord Erskine) at Hampstead." *Animal World*, vol. 1, no. 6, March 1870, p. 103.
Horsell, W. "Vegetarianism Defended." *The Truth-Tester*, Jan. 1848, pp. 63–65.
Hutton, R. H. Review of *Far from the Madding Crowd*, by Thomas Hardy. In *Thomas Hardy: The Critical Heritage*, edited by R. G. Cox. Barnes and Noble, 1970, pp. 21–27.
Huxley, T. H. "A Liberal Education; and Where to Find It." In *Science and Education*. D. Appleton, 1910, pp. 76–110.
Ivens, Alison. "Vegetarianism and Butchers." *Animal World*, vol. 9, no. 109, Oct. 1878, p. 158.
James, Henry. Review of *Far from the Madding Crowd*, by Thomas Hardy. In *Thomas Hardy: The Critical Heritage*, edited by R. G. Cox. Barnes and Noble, 1970, pp. 27–31.
"Jeremy Taylor on Animals." *Animal World*, vol. 2, no. 20, May 1871, p. 118.
Jesse, E. "Cruelties at Port Elizabeth." *Animal World*, vol. 6, no. 65, Feb. 1875, p. 30.
"John Austin Respectfully Invites the Nobility, Gentry, and the Public, to View His Collection of Animals of Opposite Natures Living in One Cage, Which Are Shown on Waterloo and Southwark Bridges." *New Sporting Magazine*, vol. 19, no. 93, Jan. 1839, p. 73.
Kingsley, Charles. *The Water-Babies: A Fairy Tale for a Land-Baby*. T. O. H. P. Burnham, 1864.
Lang, Andrew. Rev. of *Far from the Madding Crowd*, by Thomas Hardy. In *Thomas Hardy: The Critical Heritage*, edited by R. G. Cox. Barnes and Noble, 1970, pp. 35–39.
"Late Royal Patronage of Educational Measures for the Prevention of Cruelty to Animals." *Animal World*, vol. 3, no. 36, Sept. 1872, pp. 194–195.
Lindsay, William Lauder, *Mind in the Lower Animals in Health and Disease*. 2 vols. D. Appleton, 1880.
Locke, John. *Some Thoughts Concerning Education* and *Of the Conduct of the Understanding*, edited by Ruth W. Grant and Nathan Tarcov. Hackett, 1996.
— *Two Treatises of Government*, edited by Peter Laslett. Cambridge University Press, 2004.
Martin, Annie. *Home Life on an Ostrich Farm*. George Philip & Son, 1890.
Marx, Karl, and Frederick Engels. "The Communist Manifesto." In *Karl Marx Selected Writings*, edited by David McLellan. Oxford University Press, 1988, pp. 221–247.
Mayhew, Henry. *Mayhew's Characters*, edited by Peter Quennell. Spring Books, 1967.
Michaels, Leo. "Best Method for Organised Propaganda of Vegetarian Principles." *The Vegetarian*, vol. 2, no. 24, June 15, 1889, pp. 377.
Mill, John Stuart. *Considerations on Representative Government*. In *On Liberty and Other Essays*, edited by John Gray. Oxford University Press, 1998, pp. 203–467.

"Inaugural Address at St. Andrews." In *James and John Stuart Mill on Education*, edited by F. A. Cavenhagh. Cambridge University Press, 1930, pp. 132–198.

On Liberty. In *On Liberty and Other Essays*, edited by John Gray. Oxford University Press, 1998, pp. 1–128.

Principles of Political Economy. Oxford University Press, 2008.

Utilitarianism. In *On Liberty and Other Essays*, edited by John Gray. Oxford University Press, 1998, pp. 129–201.

"The Westminster Election of 1865, 8 July 1865." In *The Collected Works of John Stuart Mill*, vol. 28. 33 vols., edited by John Robson and Bruce Kinzer. University of Toronto Press, 1988, pp. 31–40.

"Occasional Notes." *Animal World*, vol. 2, no. 20, May 1871, p. 123.

"Opinions of the Press on Our Journal." *Animal World*, vol. 1, no. 2, Nov. 1869, pp. 47–48.

"The Ostrich and Its Wings." *Animal World*, vol. 14, no. 162, March 1883, p. 38.

"Ostriches and the Selborne Society." *Animal World*, vol. 17, no. 203, Aug. 1886, pp. 126.

"Ostriches and Their Feathers." *Animal World*, vol. 17, no. 202, July 1886, pp. 99–100.

"Our Jubilee Meeting." *Animal World*, vol. 5, no. 59, Aug. 1874, pp. 114–122.

"Our Object." *Animal World*, vol. 1, no. 1, Oct. 1869, p. 8.

The Parliamentary Debates. Vol. X. Hansard, 1824.

The Parliamentary Debates. Vol. XII. Hansard, 1825.

Poe, Edgar Allan. Rev. of *Barnaby Rudge*, by Charles Dickens. *Graham's Magazine*. Feb. 1, 1842, pp. 124–129.

"A Raven's Appeal from St. Leonards-on-Sea." *Animal World*, vol. 7, no. 77, Feb. 1876, p. 30.

Records of Proceedings in Parliament, Letters and Articles in the "Times" and Other Publications, and of the General Progress of Public Opinion, with Reference to the Prevention of Cruelty to Animals and the Promotion of Their Proper Care and Treatment. 1800–1895. Vol. II: 1823–1826.

"Review of *Far from the Madding Crowd*." *Athenaeum*, Dec. 5, 1874, pp. 747–748. In *Thomas Hardy: The Critical Heritage*, edited by R. G. Cox. Barnes and Noble, 1970, pp. 27–31.

"'Reynard' on Vivisection." *Animal World*, vol. 7, no. 84, Sept. 1876, p. 142.

"Richard Martin." *Animal World*, vol. 2, no. 24, Sept. 1871, pp. 193–196.

Romanes, George. *Animal Intelligence*. D. Appleton, 1906.

S.K.H. "Can Ostrich Feathers Be Had without Cruelty"? *Animal World*, vol. 24, no. 282, March 1893, p. 47.

Salt, Henry. *Animal's Rights: Considered in Relation to Social Progress*. Macmillan, 1894.

"A Plea for Vegetarianism, and Other Essays." The Vegetarian Society, 1886.

"Socialism and Vegetarianism." *The Vegetarian*, vol. 2, no. 27, July 1889, p. 420.

Schreiner, Olive. *From Man to Man*. Academy Press, 1977.

Letter to Betty Molento. Aug. 22, 1898. *The Olive Schreiner Letters Online*. University of Edinburgh and Leeds Beckett University.

Letter to Betty Molento. May 5, 1902. *The Olive Schreiner Letters Online.* University of Edinburgh and Leeds Beckett University.

Letter to Edward Carpenter. Dec. 25, 1892. *The Olive Schreiner Letters Online.* University of Edinburgh and Leeds Beckett University.

Letter to Havelock Ellis. Dec. 25, 1884. *The Olive Schreiner Letters Online.* University of Edinburgh and Leeds Beckett University.

Letter to Havelock Ellis. Dec. 13, 1914. *The Olive Schreiner Letters Online.* University of Edinburgh and Leeds Beckett University.

Letter to John T. Lloyd. Oct. 29, 1892. *The Olive Schreiner Letters Online.* University of Edinburgh and Leeds Beckett University.

Letter to Will Schreiner. July 11, 1905. *The Olive Schreiner Letters Online.* University of Edinburgh and Leeds Beckett University.

"Our Waste Land in Mashonaland." In *Thoughts on South Africa.* T. Fisher, 1923, pp. 393–398.

The Story of an African Farm, edited by Patricia O'Neill. Broadview, 2003.

Thoughts on South Africa. T. Fisher, 1923.

Women and Labor. Dover, 1998.

Sewell, Anna. *Black Beauty.* Penguin, 2008.

"Sheep and Lambs." *Animal World,* vol. 141, no. 12, June 1881, p. 88.

"Sheltering Sheep in Bad Weather." *Animal World,* vol. 137, no. 12, Feb. 1881, p. 25.

Shipman, R. "Flesh Meat Should Be Eschewed." *Animal World,* vol. 11, no. 125, Feb. 1880, p. 30.

Simpson, James. "Address to Vegetarians." *The Truth-Tester,* vol. 2, Aug. 1847, p. 20.

Smiles, Samuel. *Self-Help: With Illustrations of Character and Conduct.* Ticknor and Fields, 1866.

"Society for the Prevention of Cruelty to Animals." *The Times* [London]. June 17, 1824. *The Times Digital Archive.*

Styles, John. *The Animal Creation: Its Claims on Our Humanity Stated and Enforced.* Thomas Ward, 1839.

Thompson, Edward Pett. *The Passions of Animals.* Chapman and Hall, 1851.

"Toby. – A Portrait by Harrison Weir." *Animal World,* vol. 4, no. 49, Oct. 1873, p. 145.

"Toby's Autobiography." *Animal World,* vol. 4, no. 49, Oct. 1873, p. 146.

Trimmer, Sarah. *Fabulous Histories: The History of the Robins.* Grant and Griffith, 1848.

Trollope, Anthony. *Phineas Finn.* Oxford University Press, 2008.

"The Use of Sheep." *The Vegetarian,* vol. 1, no. 25, June 23, 1888, p. 180.

Waterton, Charles. *Essays on Natural History, Chiefly Ornithology.* Longman, Orme, Brown, Green, & Longmans, 1838.

"What Shall I Do to Help the Animals?" *Animal World,* vol. 3, no. 39, Dec. 1872, pp. 241–242.

Youatt, William. *The Obligations and Extent of Humanity to Brutes, Principally Considered with Reference to the Domesticated Animals.* Longman, 1839.

Secondary Sources

Ackroyd, Peter. *Dickens*. Harper Collins, 1990.
Agamben, Giorgio. *Homo Sacer: Sovereign Power and Bare Life*, translated by Daniel Heller-Roazen. Stanford University Press, 1998.
— *The Open: Man and Animal*, translated by Kevin Attell. Stanford University Press, 2004.
Ahuja, Neel. "Postcolonial Critique in a Multispecies World." *PMLA*, vol. 124, no. 2, 2009, pp. 556–563.
Amato, Sarah. *Beastly Possessions: Animals in Victorian Consumer Culture*. University of Toronto Press, 2015.
Anderson, Amanda. *Bleak Liberalism*. University of Chicago Press, 2016.
— *The Powers of Distance: Cosmopolitanism and the Cultivation of Detachment*. Princeton University Press, 2001.
Anderson, Nancy Fix. *The Sporting Life: Victorian Sports and Games*. Praeger, 2010.
Armstrong, Nancy. *Desire and Domestic Fiction: A Political History of the Novel*. Oxford University Press, 1987.
— *How Novels Think: The Limits of Individualism from 1719–1900*. Columbia University Press, 2005.
— "The Occidental Alice." In *Contemporary Literary Criticism: Literary and Cultural Studies*. 4th ed., edited by Robert Con Davis and Ronald Schleifer. Longman, 1998, pp. 537–564.
Armstrong, Philip. "Samuel Butler's Sheep." *Journal of Victorian Culture*, vol. 17, no. 4, 2012, pp. 442–453.
— *Sheep*. Reaktion, 2016.
Aslami, Zarena. *The Dream Life of Citizens: Late Victorian Novels and the Fantasy of the State*. Fordham University Press, 2012.
Atkins, Peter, ed. *Animal Cities: Beastly Urban Histories*. Ashgate, 2012.
Atterton, Peter. "Ethical Cynicism." In *Animal Philosophy: Ethics and Identity*. Continuum, 2004, pp. 51–61.
Auerbach, Nina. "Alice and Wonderland: A Curious Child." *Victorian Studies*, vol. 17, no. 1, 1973, pp. 31–47.
Ballantyne, R. M. *The Settler and the Savage: A Tale of Peace and War in South Africa*. James Nisbet, 1877.
Bargheer, Stefan. "The Fools of the Leisure Class." *European Journal of Sociology*, vol. 47, no. 1, 2006, pp. 3–35.
Beer, Gillian. *Alice in Space: The Sideways Victorian World of Lewis Carroll*. University of Chicago Press, 2016.
— *Darwin's Plots: Evolutionary Narrative in Darwin, George Eliot, and Nineteenth-Century Fiction*. Cambridge University Press, 2000.
Beinart, William, and Lotte Hughes. *Environment and Empire*. Oxford University Press, 2007.
Bennett, Jane. *Vibrant Matter: A Political Ecology of Things*. Duke University Press, 2010.

Berger, Sheila. *Thomas Hardy and Visual Structures: Framing, Disruption, Process.* New York University Press, 1990.

Berkman, Joyce Avrech. *The Healing Imagination of Olive Schreiner: Beyond South African Colonialism.* University of Massachusetts Press, 1989.

Betensky, Carolyn. *Feeling for the Poor: Bourgeois Compassion, Social Action, and the Victorian Novel.* University of Virginia Press, 2010.

Bhabha, Homi. "Of Mimicry and Man: The Ambivalence of Colonial Discourse." *October*, vol. 28, spring 1984, pp. 125–133.

Bivona, Daniel. "Alice the Child-Imperialist and the Games of Wonderland." *Nineteenth-Century Literature*, vol. 41, no. 2, 1986, pp. 143–171.

Blake, Kathleen. *Play, Games, and Sport: The Literary Works of Lewis Carroll.* Cornell University Press, 1974.

Boddice, Rob. "Manliness and the 'Morality of Field Sports': E. A. Freeman and Anthony Trollope, 1869–71." *The Historian*, vol. 70, no. 1, 2008, pp. 1–29.

Boggs, Colleen Glenny. *Animalia Americana: Animal Representations and Biopolitical Subjectivity.* Columbia University Press, 2013.

Boos, Florence S. "The Education Act of 1870: Before and After." *BRANCH: Britain, Representation, and Nineteenth-Century History*, edited by Dino Franco Felluga. Extension of *Romanticism and Victorianism on the Net*.

Braidotti, Rosi. *The Posthuman.* Polity, 2013.

Brantlinger, Patrick. "Did Dickens Have a Philosophy of History? The Case of *Barnaby Rudge*." *Dickens Studies Annual*, vol. 30, 2001, pp. 59–74.

Brooks, Jean R. "The Place of the Animal Kingdom in Thomas Hardy's Works." *The Aligarh Critical Miscellany*, vol. 4, no. 2, 1991, pp. 157–173.

Brown, Nicola. "Introduction: Crying over Little Nell." *19: Interdisciplinary Studies in the Long Nineteenth Century*, vol. 4, 2007.

Buckley, Jerome H. "'Quoth the Raven': The Role of Grip in *Barnaby Rudge*." *Dickens Studies Annual*, vol. 21, 1992, pp. 27–35.

Butt, John, and Kathleen Tillotson. *Dickens at Work.* Methuen, 1957.

Campbell, Michael L. "Thomas Hardy's Attitude toward Animals." *Victorians Institute Journal*, vol. 2, 1973, pp. 61–71.

Campbell, Timothy. "Bios, Immunity, Life: The Thought of Roberto Esposito." *Diacritics*, vol. 36, no. 2, 2006, pp. 2–22.

Carlise, Janice. *John Stuart Mill and the Writing of Character.* University of Georgia Press, 2010.

"On the Second Reform Act, 1867." *BRANCH: Britain, Representation, and Nineteenth-Century History*, edited by Dino Franco Felluga. Extension of *Romanticism and Victorianism on the Net*.

Carney, Bethan. "Introduction: 'Mr Popular Sentiment': Dickens and Feeling." *19: Interdisciplinary Studies in the Long Nineteenth Century*, vol. 14, 2012. DOI: http://doi.org/10.16995/ntn.644.

Chen, Mel Y. *Animacies: Biopolitics, Racial Mattering, and Queer Affect.* Duke University Press, 2012.

Chez, Keridiana. *Victorian Dogs, Victorian Men: Affect and Animals in Nineteenth-Century Literature and Culture.* Ohio State University Press, 2017.

Works Cited

Chrisman, Laura. *Rereading the Imperial Romance: British Imperialism and South African Resistance in Haggard, Schreiner, and Plaatje*. Clarendon, 2000.
Chrulew, Matthew. "Animals as Biopolitical Subjects." In *Foucault and Animals*, edited by Matthew Chrulew and Dinesh Joseph Wadiwel. Brill, 2017, pp. 222–238.
Chrulew, Matthew, and Dinesh Joseph Wadiwel, eds. *Foucault and Animals*. Brill, 2017.
Cochrane, Alasdair. *An Introduction to Animals and Political Theory*. Palgrave, 2010.
Cohen, Jane. *Charles Dickens and His Original Illustrators*. Ohio State University Press, 1980.
Cohen, Morton. *Lewis Carroll: A Biography*. Knopf, 1996.
Cohn, Elisha. *Still Life: Suspended Development in the Victorian Novel*. Oxford University Press, 2016.
Colley, Ann. *Wild Animal Skins in Victorian Britain: Zoos, Collections, Portraits, and Maps*. Ashgate, 2014.
Collini, Stefan. "The Idea of 'Character' in Victorian Political Thought." *Transaction of the Royal Historical Society*, vol. 35, 1985, pp. 29–50.
Cosslett, Tess. *Talking Animals in British Children's Fiction, 1786–1914*. Ashgate, 2006.
Derrida, Jacques. *The Animal That Therefore I Am*, translated by David Wills. Fordham University Press, 2008.
—— *The Beast and the Sovereign*. Vol. 1, edited by Michel Lisse, Marie-Louise Mallet, and Ginette Michaud, translated by Geoffrey Bennington. University of Chicago Press, 2009.
—— "Eating Well, or the Calculation of the Subject: An Interview with Jacques Derrida." In *Who Comes after the Subject?*, edited by Eduardo Cadava, Peter Connor, and Jean-Luc Nancy. Routledge, 1991, pp. 96–119.
Derrida, Jacques, and Elisabeth Roudinesco. *For What Tomorrow . . . A Dialogue*, translated by Jeff Fort. Stanford University Press, 2004.
Donald, Diana. *Picturing Animals in Britain*. Yale University Press, 2007.
Doughty, Robin W. *Feather Fashions and Bird Preservation: A Study in Nature Protection*. University of California Press, 1975.
Dransfield, Scott. "Reading the Gordon Riots in 1841: Social Violence and Moral Management in *Barnaby Rudge*." *Dickens Studies Annual*, vol. 27, 1998, pp. 69–95.
Eley, Geoff. *Forging Democracy: A History of the Left in Europe 1850–2000*. Oxford University Press, 2002.
Esposito, Roberto. *Bíos: Biopolitics and Philosophy*, translated by Timothy Campbell. University of Minnesota Press, 2008.
Feuerstein, Anna. "The Realism of Animal Life: The Seashore, *Adam Bede*, and George Eliot's Animal Alterity." *Victorians Institute Journal*, vol. 44, 2016, pp. 29–55.
—— "Seeing Animals on Egdon Heath: The Democratic Impulse of Thomas Hardy's The Return of the Native." *19: Interdisciplinary Studies in the Long Nineteenth Century*, vol. 26, 2018. DOI: http://doi.org/10.16995/ntn.816.

Flegel, Monica. "'How does your collar suit me?': The Human Animal in the RSPCA's Animal World and Band of Mercy." *Victorian Literature and Culture*, vol. 40, no. 1, 2012, pp. 247–262.

Pets and Domesticity in Victorian Literature and Culture: Animality, Queer Relations, and the Victorian Family. Routledge, 2015.

Foucault, Michel. *The History of Sexuality.* Vol. 1, translated by Robert Hurley. Vintage, 1990.

"Omnes et Singulatim." In *Power: Essential Works of Foucault 1954–1984*, translated by Robert Hurley, edited by James D. Faubion. New Press, 2000, pp. 298–325.

Security, Territory, Population. In *Lectures at the Collège de France 1977–1978*, translated by Graham Burchell, edited by Michel Senellart. Picador, 2009.

Society Must Be Defended. In *Lectures at the Collège de France 1975–1976*, translated by David Macey, edited by Mauro Bertani and Alessandro Fontana. Picador, 2003.

"The Subject and Power." In *Power: Essential Works of Foucault 1954–1984*, translated by Robert Hurley, edited by James D. Faubion. New Press, 2000, pp. 326–348.

Frederickson, Kathleen. *The Ploy of Instinct: Victorian Sciences of Nature and Sexuality in Liberal Governance.* Fordham University Press, 2014.

Freeden, Michael. *The New Liberalism: An Ideology of Social Reform.* Clarendon, 1978.

French, Richard. *Antivivisection and Medical Science in Victorian Society.* Princeton University Press, 1975.

Gandhi, Leela. *Affective Communities: Anticolonial Thought, Fin-de-Siècle Radicalism, and the Politics of Friendship.* Duke University Press, 2006.

Garland, Carina. "Curious Appetites: Food, Desire, Gender, and Subjectivity in Lewis Carroll's Alice Texts." *The Lion and the Unicorn*, vol. 32, 2008, pp. 33–39.

Gaskell, Jeremy. *Who Killed the Great Auk?* Oxford University Press, 2000.

Gates, Barbara. "Greening Victorian Studies." *Victorian Review*, vol. 36, no. 2, fall 2010, pp. 11–14.

Gibson, James, ed. *Thomas Hardy: Interviews and Recollections.* Macmillan, 1999.

Gilbert, Pamela. *The Citizen's Body: Desire, Health, and the Social in Victorian England.* Ohio State University Press, 2007.

Gissing, George. *The Immortal Dickens.* Cecil Palmer. 1925.

Gold, Joseph. *Charles Dickens: Radical Moralist.* University of Minnesota Press, 1972.

Goodlad, Lauren. "'Character Worth Speaking Of': Individuality, John Stuart Mill, and the Critique of Liberalism." *Victorians Institute Journal*, vol. 36, 2008, pp. 7–45.

The Victorian Geopolitical Aesthetic: Realism, Sovereignty, and Transnational Experience. Oxford University Press, 2015.

Victorian Literature and the Victorian State: Character and Governance in a Liberal Society. Johns Hopkins University Press, 2003.

Gordon, Colin. "Governmental Rationality: An Introduction." In *The Foucault Effect: Studies in Governmentality*, edited by Graham Burchell, Colin Gordon, and Peter Miller. University of Chicago Press, 1991, pp. 1–51.
Gray, Beryl. *The Dog in the Dickensian Imagination*. Routledge, 2014.
Guyer, Sara. "The Girl with the Open Mouth: Through the Looking Glass." *Angelaki: Journal of the Theoretical Humanities*, vol. 9, no. 1, 2004, pp. 159–163.
Hadley, Elaine. *Living Liberalism: Practical Citizenship in Mid-Victorian Britain*. University of Chicago Press, 2010.
—. *Melodramatic Tactics: Theatricalized Dissent in the English Marketplace, 1800–1885*. Stanford University Press, 1995.
—. "The Past Is a Foreign Country: The Neo-Conservative Romance with Victorian Liberalism." *The Yale Journal of Criticism*, vol. 10, no. 1, 1997, pp. 7–38.
Hale, Piers. *Political Descent: Malthus, Mutualism, and the Politics of Evolution in Victorian England*. University of Chicago Press, 2014.
Haraway, Donna. *The Companion Species Manifesto: Dogs, People, and Significant Otherness*. Prickly Paradigm, 2003.
—. *Staying with the Trouble: Making Kin in the Chthulucene*. Duke University Press, 2016.
Harrison, Brian. "Animals and the State in Nineteenth-Century England." *The English Historical Review*, vol. 88, no. 349, 1973, pp. 786–820.
Harwood, Dix. *Love for Animals and How It Developed in Great Britain*, edited by Rod Preece and David Fraser. Edwin Mellen, 2002.
"History of the Vegetarian Society." *Vegetarian Society*, www.vegsoc.org/history.
Howell, Philip. *At Home and Astray: The Domestic Dog in Victorian Britain*. University of Virginia Press, 2015.
Jaques, Zoe. *Children's Literature and the Posthuman: Animals, Environment, Cyborg*. Routledge, 2015.
Jones, Lawrence. "George Eliot and Pastoral Tragicomedy in Hardy's 'Far from the Madding Crowd.'" *Studies in Philology*, vol. 77, no. 4, 1980, pp. 402–425.
Joyce, Patrick. *The Rule of Freedom: Liberalism and the Modern City*. Verso, 2003.
Kant, Immanuel. *Lectures on Ethics*, translated by Peter Heath. Cambridge University Press, 1997.
Kean, Hilda. *Animal Rights: Political and Social Change in Britain since 1800*. Reaktion, 1998.
Kenyon-Jones, Christine. *Kindred Brutes: Animals in Romantic-Period Writing*. Ashgate, 2001.
Kete, Kathleen. "Animals and Ideology: The Politics of Animal Protection in Europe." In *Representing Animals*, edited by Nigel Rothfels. Indiana University Press, 2002, pp. 19–34.
—. *The Beast in the Boudoir: Petkeeping in Nineteenth-Century Paris*. University of California Press, 1994.
Kete, Kathleen. ed. *A Cultural History of Animals in the Age of Empire*. Berg, 2007.
Klooper, Dirk. "Boer, Bushman, and Baboon: Human and Animal in Nineteenth-Century and Early Twentieth-Century South African Writings."

Safundi: The Journal of South African and American Studies, vol. 11, 2010, pp. 3–18.

Krebs, Paula M. "Olive Schreiner's Racialization of South Africa." *Victorian Studies*, vol. 40, no. 3, 1997, pp. 427–444.

Kreilkamp, Ivan. "The Ass Got a Verdict: Martin's Act and the Founding of the Society for the Prevention of Cruelty to Animals, 1822." *BRANCH: Britain, Representation and Nineteenth-Century History*, edited by Dino Franco Felluga. Extension of *Romanticism and Victorianism on the Net*.

——. "Dying like a Dog in *Great Expectations*." In *Victorian Animal Dreams: Representations of Animals in Victorian Literature and Culture*, edited by Deborah Denenholz Morse and Martin A. Danahay. Ashgate, 2007, pp. 81–94.

——. "Petted Things: Wuthering Heights and the Animal." *The Yale Journal of Criticism*, vol. 18, no. 1, 2005, pp. 87–110.

——. "Pitying the Sheep in *Far from the Madding Crowd*." *NOVEL: A Forum on Fiction*, vol. 42, no. 3, 2009, pp. 474–481.

Lansbury, Carol. *The Old Brown Dog: Women, Workers, and Vivisection in Edwardian England*. University of Wisconsin Press, 1985.

Ledger, Sally. *Dickens and the Popular Radical Imagination*. Cambridge University Press, 2007.

Lee, Michael Parrish. "Eating Things: Food, Animals, and Other Life Forms in Lewis Carroll's Alice Books." *Nineteenth-Century Literature*, vol. 68, no. 4, 2014, pp. 484–512.

Lee, Paula Young, ed. *Meat, Modernity, and the Rise of the Slaughterhouse*. University of New Hampshire Press, 2008.

Lee, Sanghee. "The Farming Body in Thomas Hardy's *Far from the Madding Crowd*." *Victorian Network*, vol. 6, no. 1, 2015, pp. 93–112.

Leighton, Mary Elizabeth, and Lisa Surridge. "The Empire Bites Back: The Racialized Crocodile of the Nineteenth Century." In *Victorian Animal Dreams: Representations of Animals in Victorian Literature and Culture*, edited by Deborah Denenholz Morse and Martin A. Danahay. Ashgate, 2007, pp. 249–270.

Lerer, Seth. *Children's Literature: A Reader's History, from Aesop to Harry Potter*. University of Chicago Press, 2008.

Levinas, Emmanuel. "The Name of a Dog, or Natural Rights." In *Animal Philosophy: Ethics and Identity*, edited by Peter Atterton and Matthew Calarco. Continuum, 2004, pp. 47–49.

——. *Totality and Infinity: An Essay on Exteriority*, translated by Alphonso Lingis. Duquesne University Press, 1969.

Levine, George. "Hardy and Darwin: An Enchanting Hardy?" In *A Companion to Thomas Hardy*, edited by Keith Wilson. Wiley-Blackwell, 2012, pp. 36–53.

——. *Realism, Ethics and Secularism: Essays on Victorian Literature and Science*. Cambridge University Press, 2008.

Levinson, Brett. "Biopolitics in Balance: Esposito's Response to Foucault." *CR: The New Centennial Review*, vol. 10, no. 2, 2010, pp. 239–262.

Linzey, Andrew, and Priscilla Cohen. "Terms of Discourse." *Journal of Animal Ethics*, vol. 1, no. 1, spring 2011, pp. vii–ix.

Lippit, Akira Mizuta. *Electric Animal: Toward a Rhetoric of Wildlife*. Minneapolis: University of Minnesota Press, 2000.
Lloyd, David, and Paul Thomas. *Culture and the State*. Routledge, 1998.
Lovell-Smith, Rose. "The Animals of Wonderland: Tenniel as Carroll's Reader." *Criticism*, vol. 45, no. 4, 2003, pp. 383–415.
——— "Eggs and Serpents: Natural History Reference in Lewis Carroll's Scene of Alice and the Pigeon." *Children's Literature*, vol. 35, 2007, pp. 27–53.
Lowe, Lisa. *The Intimacies of Four Continents*. Duke University Press, 2015.
MacKenzie, John. *The Empire of Nature: Hunting, Conservation and British Imperialism*. Manchester University Press, 1988.
Mackintosh, Alex. "Foucault's Menagerie: Cock Fighting, Bear Baiting, and the Genealogy of Human–Animal Power." In *Foucault and Animals*, edited by Matthew Chrulew and Dinesh Joseph Wadiwel. Brill, 2017, pp. 161–189.
Macpherson, C. B. *The Political Theory of Possessive Individualism: Hobbes to Locke*. Clarendon, 1962.
Magnum, Theresa. "Narrative Dominion or the Animals Write Back? Animal Genres in Literature and the Arts." In *A Cultural History of Animals in the Age of Empire*, edited by Kathleen Kete. Berg, 2007, pp. 153–173.
Marcus, Steven. *Dickens: from Pickwick to Dombey*. Chatto & Windus, 1965.
Massumi, Brian. *What Animals Teach Us about Politics*. Duke University Press, 2014.
Mayer, Jed. "The Vivisection of the Snark." *Victorian Poetry*, vol. 47, no. 2, 2009, pp. 428–448.
Mazzeno, Laurence, and Ronald Morrison, eds. *Animals in Victorian Literature and Culture*. Palgrave, 2017.
McClintock, Anne. *Imperial Leather: Race, Gender and Sexuality in the Colonial Contest*. Routledge, 1995.
McDonell, Jennifer. "Bull's-Eye, Agency, and the Species Divide in *Oliver Twist*: A Cur's-Eye View." In *Animals in Victorian Literature and Culture*, edited by Larry Mazzeno and Ronald Morrison. Palgrave, 2017, pp. 109–128.
McWilliam, Rohan. "Liberalism Lite?" *Victorian Studies*, vol. 48, no. 1, 2005, pp. 103–111.
Mehta, Uday Singh. *The Anxiety of Freedom: Imagination and Individuality in Locke's Political Thought*. Cornell University Press, 1992.
——— "Liberal Strategies of Exclusion." *Politics and Society*, vol. 18, no. 4, 1990, pp. 425–454.
——— *Liberalism and Empire: A Study in Nineteenth-Century British Liberal Thought*. University of Chicago Press, 1999.
Menely, Tobias. *The Animal Claim: Sensibility and the Creaturely Voice*. University of Chicago Press, 2015.
Miller, J. Hillis. "The Dark World of *Oliver Twist*." In *Modern Critical Views: Charles Dickens*, edited by Harold Bloom. Chelsea House, 1987, pp. 29–69.
——— *Thomas Hardy: Distance and Desire*. Belknap Press, 1970.
Miller, John. *Empire and the Animal Body: Violence, Identity and Ecology in Victorian Adventure Fiction*. Anthem, 2012.

"Postcolonial Ecocriticism and Victorian Studies." *Literature Compass*, vol. 9, 2012, pp. 476–488.

Moore, Grace. "Beastly Criminals and Criminal Beasts: Stray Women and Stray Dogs in *Oliver Twist*." In *Victorian Animal Dreams: Representations of Animals in Victorian Literature and Culture*, edited by Deborah Deneholz Morse and Martin A. Danahay. Ashgate, 2007, pp. 201–214.

Moore, Jason. *Capitalism and the Web of Life*. Verso, 2015.

Moore-Colyer, R. J. "Feathered Women and Persecuted Birds: The Struggle against the Plumage Trade c. 1860–1922." *Rural History*, vol. 11, no. 1, 2000, pp. 57–73.

Moore-Gilbert, Bart. "Olive Schreiner's *Story of an African Farm*: Reconciling Feminism and Anti-Imperialism?" *Women: A Cultural Review*, vol. 14, no. 1, 2003, pp. 85–103.

Morris, Pam. *Imagining Inclusive Society in Nineteenth-Century Novels: The Code of Sincerity in the Public Sphere*. Johns Hopkins University Press, 2004.

Morrison, Ronald. "Dickens, *Household Words*, and the Smithfield Controversy at the Time of the Great Exhibition." In *Animals in Victorian Literature and Culture*, edited by Larry Mazzeno and Ronald Morrison. Palgrave, 2017, pp. 41–63.

"Humanity towards Man, Woman, and the Lower Animals: Thomas Hardy's Jude the Obscure and the Victorian Humane Movement." *Nineteenth-Century Studies*, vol. 12, 1998, pp. 64–82.

Morse, Deborah Deneholz, and Martin Donahay, eds. *Victorian Animal Dreams: Representations of Animals in Victorian Literature and Culture*. Ashgate, 2007.

Morton, Timothy. *The Ecological Thought*. Harvard University Press, 2010.

Shelley and the Revolution in Taste: The Body and the Natural World. Cambridge University Press, 1994.

Moss, Arthur. *Valiant Crusade. The History of the R.S.P.C.A*. Cassell, 1961.

Mouffe, Chantal. *The Return of the Political*. Verso, 1993.

Mushet, David. *The Wrongs of the Animal World*. Hatchard and Son, 1839.

Naas, Michael. *The End of the World and Other Teachable Moments: Jacques Derrida's Final Seminar*. Fordham University Press, 2015.

Nibert, David. *Animal Oppression and Human Violence: Domesecration, Capitalism, and Global Conflict*. Columbia University Press, 2013.

Nixon, Rob. *Dreambirds: The Strange History of the Ostrich in Fashion, Food, and Fortune*. Picador, 1999.

Ortiz-Robles, Mario. "Animal Acts: 1822, 1835, 1849, 1850, 1854, 1876, 1900." *BRANCH: Britain, Representation and Nineteenth-Century History*, edited by Dino France Felluga. Extension of *Romanticism and Victorianism on the Net*.

Osborne, Thomas. "Security and Vitality: Drains, Liberalism and Power in the Nineteenth Century." In *Foucault and Political Reason: Liberalism, Neo-Liberalism and Rationalities of Government*. University of Chicago Press, 1996, pp. 99–121.

Otter, Chris. "Civilizing Slaughter: The Development of the British Public Abattoir, 1850–1910." In *Meat, Modernity, and the Rise of the Slaughterhouse*,

edited by Paula Young Lee. University of New Hampshire Press, 2008, pp. 89–106.
Palmer, Clare. "'Taming the Wild Profusion of Existing Things'? A Study of Foucault, Power, and Human/Animal Relationships." In *Foucault and Animals*, edited by Matthew Chrulew and Dinesh Joseph Wadiwel. Brill, 2017, pp. 107–131.
Pandian, Anand. "Pastoral Power in the Postcolony: On the Biopolitics of the Criminal Animal in South India." *Cultural Anthropology*, vol. 23, no. 1, 2008, pp. 85–117.
Perkins, David. *Romanticism and Animal Rights*. Cambridge University Press, 2003.
Perren, Richard. "Filth and Profit: Impediments to Slaughterhouse Reform in Victorian Britain." In *Meat, Modernity and the Rise of the Slaughterhouse*, edited by Paula Young Lee. University of New Hampshire Press, 2008, pp. 127–150.
The Meat Trade in Britain. Routledge, 1978.
Peterson, Christopher. *Bestial Traces: Race, Sexuality, Animality*. Fordham University Press, 2013.
Pick, Anat. *Creaturely Poetics: Animality and Vulnerability in Literature and Film*. Columbia University Press, 2011.
Plotz, John. *The Crowd: British Literature and Public Politics*. University of California Press, 2000.
Pollock, Mary Sanders. "Ouida's Rhetoric of Empathy: A Case Study in Victorian Anti-Vivisection Narrative." In *Figuring Animals: Essays on Animal Images in Art, Literature, Philosophy, and Popular Culture*, edited by Mary Sanders Pollock and Catherine Rainwater. Palgrave, 2003, pp. 135–159.
Rajamannar, Shefali. *Reading the Animal in the Literature of the British Raj*. Palgrave, 2012.
Reichertz, Ronald. *The Making of the Alice Books: Lewis Carroll's Uses of Earlier Children's Literature*. McGill-Queen's University Press, 1997.
Rice, Thomas J. "The Politics of *Barnaby Rudge*." In *The Changing World of Charles Dickens*, edited by Peter Giddings. Vision, 1983, pp. 51–74.
Richardson, LeAnne. *New Women and Colonial Adventure Fiction in Victorian Britain: Gender, Genre, and Empire*. University of Florida Press, 2006.
Richter, Virginia. *Literature after Darwin: Human Beasts in Western Fiction, 1859–1939*. Palgrave, 2011.
Ritvo, Harriet. *The Animal Estate: The English and Other Creatures in the Victorian Age*. Harvard University Press, 1987.
——. "The Emergence of Modern Pet-Keeping." In *Animals and People Sharing the World*, edited by Andrew N. Rowan. University Press of New England, 1988, pp. 13–31.
Roth, Christine. "The Zoocentric Ecology of Hardy's Poetic Consciousness." In *Victorian Writers and the Environment: Ecocritical Perspectives*, edited by Ronald Morrison and Laurence Mazenno. Routledge, 2016, pp. 79–96.

Rothfels, Nigel. "How the Caged Bird Sings: Animals and Entertainment." In *A Cultural History of Animals in the Age of Empire*, edited by Kathleen Kete. Berg, 2007, pp. 95–112.

Roy, Rohan Deb. "Nonhuman Empires." *Comparative Studies of South Asia, Africa and the Middle East*, vol. 35, no. 1, 2015, pp. 66–75.

Said, Edward. *Culture and Imperialism*. Vintage, 1993.

Samstag, Tony. *For Love of Birds: The Story of the Royal Society for the Protection of Birds, 1889–1988*. Royal Society for the Protection of Birds, 1988.

Santner, Eric. *On Creaturely Life: Rilke, Benjamin, Sebald*. University of Chicago Press, 2006.

Sartori, Andrew. *Liberalism in Empire: An Alternative History*. University of California Press, 2014.

Saudo-Welby, Nathalie. "Learning from Nature: Feminism, Allegory and Ostriches in Olive Schreiner's The Story of an African Farm (1883)." *Cahiers victoriens et édouardiens* (85), 2017.

Scheckner, Peter. "Chartism, Class, and Social Struggle: A Study of Charles Dickens." *Midwest Quarterly*, vol. 29, no. 1, 1987, pp. 93–112.

Shevelow, Kathryn. *For the Love of Animals: The Rise of the Animal Protection Movement*. Henry Holt, 2008.

Shires, Linda M. "Narrative, Gender, and Power in 'Far from the Madding Crowd.'" *NOVEL: A Forum on Fiction*, vol. 24, no. 2, 1991, pp. 162–177.

Shukin, Nicole. *Animal Capital: Rendering Life in Biopolitical Times*. University of Minnesota Press, 2009.

———. "Tense Animals: On Other Species of Pastoral Power." *CR: The New Centennial Review*, vol. 11, no. 2, 2011, pp. 143–167.

Shuman, Cathy. *Pedagogical Economies: The Examination and the Victorian Literary Man*. Stanford University Press, 2000.

Sivasundaram, Sujit. "Imperial Transgressions: The Animal and Human in the Idea of Race." *Comparative Studies of South Asia, Africa and the Middle East*, vol. 35, no. 1, 2015, pp. 156–172.

Sonstroem, David. "Fettered Fancy in 'Hard Times.'" *PMLA*, vol. 84, no. 3, 1969, pp. 520–529.

Spencer, Colin. *The Heretic's Feast: A History of Vegetarianism*. University Press of New England, 1995.

Spillman, Deborah Shapple. *British Colonial Realism in Africa: Inalienable Objects, Contested Domains*. Palgrave, 2012.

Spivak, Gayatri. "Can the Subaltern Speak?" In *Colonial Discourse and Post-Colonial Theory: A Reader*, edited by Patrick Williams and Laura Chrisman. Columbia University Press, 1993, pp. 66–111.

Squires, Michael. *The Pastoral Novel: Studies in George Eliot, Thomas Hardy, and D. H. Lawrence*. University of Virginia Press, 1974.

Stein, Sarah. *Plumes: Ostrich Feathers, Jews, and a Lost World of Global Commerce*. Yale University Press, 2008.

Stevens, Valerie. "Human–Animal 'Mother-Love' in Novels by Olive Schreiner." *English Literature in Transition, 1880–1920*, vol. 61, no. 2, 2018, pp. 147–171.

Straley, Jessica. "Of Beasts and Boys: Kingsley, Spencer, and the Theory of Recapitulation." *Victorian Studies*, vol. 49, no. 4, 2007, pp. 583–609.
Stuart, Barbara L. "The Centaur in *Barnaby Rudge*." *Dickens Quarterly*, vol. 8, no. 1, 1991, pp. 29–37.
Stuart, Tristram. *The Bloodless Revolution: A Cultural History of Vegetarianism from 1600 to Modern Times*. Norton, 2006.
Sumpter, Caroline. "On Suffering and Sympathy: Jude the Obscure, Evolution, and Ethics." *Victorian Studies*, vol. 53, no. 4, 2011, pp. 665–687.
Swabe, Joanna. *Animals, Disease and Human Society: Human–Animal Relations and the Rise of Veterinary Medicine*. Routledge, 1999.
Thompson, Dorothy. *The Chartists: Popular Politics in the Industrial Revolution*. Pantheon, 1984.
— *The Dignity of Chartism*, edited by Stephen Roberts. Verso, 2015.
Tucker, Herbert F. "In the Event of a Second Reform." *BRANCH: Britain, Representation, and Nineteenth-Century History*, edited by Dino Franco Felluga. Extension of *Romanticism and Victorianism on the Net*.
Turner, Beatrice. "'Which is to be master?' Language as Power in *Alice in Wonderland* and *Through the Looking-Glass*." *Children's Literature Association Quarterly*, vol. 35, no. 3, 2010, pp. 243–254.
Turner, James. *Reckoning with the Beast: Animals, Pain, and Humanity in the Victorian Mind*. Johns Hopkins University Press, 1980.
Vernon, James. "What Was Liberalism, and Who Was Its Subject? Or, Will the Real Liberal Subject Please Stand Up?" *Victorian Studies*, vol. 53, no. 3, 2011, pp. 303–310.
Viswanathan, Gauri. *Masks of Conquest: Literary Study and British Rule in India*. Columbia University Press, 1989.
Watt, Ian. *The Rise of the Novel*. University of California Press, 2001.
Welker, Robert Henry. *Birds and Men: American Birds in Science, Art, Literature, and Conservation 1800–1900*. Atheneum, 1966.
West, Anna. "'Rot the genuine': Moral Responsibility and *Far from the Madding Crowd*'s Cancelled Fragment." *Journal of Victorian Culture*, vol. 21, no. 3, 2016, pp. 387–404.
— *Thomas Hardy and Animals*. Cambridge University Press, 2017.
Willett, Cynthia. *Interspecies Ethics*. Columbia University Press, 2014.
Williams, Carolyn. "Melodrama." In *The Cambridge History of Victorian Literature*, edited by Kate Flint. Cambridge University Press, 2012, pp. 193–219.
— "Stupidity and Stupefaction: *Barnaby Rudge* and the Mute Figure of Melodrama." *Dickens Studies Annual*, vol. 46, 2015, pp. 357–376.
Winter, Sarah. "Mental Culture: Liberal Pedagogy and the Emergence of Ethnographic Knowledge." *Victorian Studies*, vol. 41, no. 3, 1998, pp. 427–454.
— "On the Morant Bay Rebellion in Jamaica and the Governor Eyre-George William Gordon Controversy." *BRANCH: Britain, Representation, and Nineteenth-Century History*, edited by Dino Franco Felluga. Extension of *Romanticism and Victorianism on the Net*.

Wolfe, Cary. *Before the Law: Humans and Other Animals in a Biopolitical Frame.* University of Chicago Press, 2013.

"Human, All Too Human: 'Animal Studies' and the Humanities." *PMLA*, vol. 124, no. 2, 2000, pp. 564–575.

Wolfe, Patrick. *Settler Colonialism and the Transformation of Anthropology: The Politics and Poetics of an Ethnographic Event.* Cassell, 1999.

Woloch, Alex. *The One vs. the Many: Minor Characters and the Space of the Protagonist in the Novel.* Princeton University Press, 2003.

Woods, Rebecca J. H. "From Colonial Animal to Imperial Edible: Building an Empire of Sheep in New Zealand, ca. 1880–1900." *Comparative Studies of South Asia, Africa and the Middle East*, vol. 35, no. 1, 2015, pp. 117–136.

Woodward, Wendy. *The Animal Gaze: Animal Subjectivities in Southern African Narratives.* Wits University Press, 2008.

Young, Robert. *Colonial Desire: Hybridity in Theory, Culture and Race.* Routledge, 1995.

Zipes, Jack, ed. *Victorian Fairy Tales: The Revolt of the Fairies and Elves.* Routledge, 1987.

Index

Act to Prevent the Cruel and Improper Treatment of Cattle (1822), 45, 48, 95
adventure novels, 9, 212
alterity, 15, 98, 109, 130, 133, 135, 142, 144, 152, 214, 228; animal, 8, 111, 124–126, 129–130, 132, 138, 209; definition of, 22; Jacques Derrida on, 20, 22, 109, 148, 154; and the realist novel, 9
animal autobiography, 9, 80–82
animal character, 6, 9, 34, 60–61, 65, 71, 73, 78, 80–83, 98–102, 108, 116; in *Barnaby Rudge*, 125–128; and birds, 53–54, 59; and cats, 79–80; in *Oliver Twist*, 120–121; and ostriches, 207–208; and ravens, 122
animal epistemology, 72, 99; in *Hard Times*, 109–112; in *The Story of an African Farm*, 214
animal politics, 4, 9, 19, 26–28, 89–91, 136, 165, 167, 226, 228; in *Alice's Adventures in Wonderland*, 146, 148, 154–155, 157, 159; in *Barnaby Rudge*, 124, 126, 130; of Charles Dickens, 98, 100, 103–108, 122; in *Hard Times*, 109, 111; of Thomas Hardy, 176, 182, 197; of Brian Massumi, 4; in *Oliver Twist*, 113, 116; of Olive Schreiner, 199–202, 211, 219, 224–226; in *The Story of an African Farm*, 220
animal studies, 18–21, 203, 227
animal training, 101–102, 126; as education, 80, 82, 101, 146
animality, 4, 57, 83, 98, 101, 113, 201–202, 213–214; in *Barnaby Rudge*, 26, 123–125, 129, 131–132; Mel Chen on, 3, 5; Jacques Derrida on, 20, 46; in liberal pedagogy, 140; Brian Massumi on, 4; and racism, 220–222; in *The Story of an African Farm*, 28, 215, 217; and the working class, 105–106, 130
anthropomorphism, 8–9, 23
anti-cruelty legislation, 34–36, 45, 48–51; wild bird legislation, 51–62. *See also* Lord Thomas Erskine; Richard Martin

anti-vivisection, 51, 78; Lewis Carroll on, 158; Thomas Hardy on, 177

Ballantyne, R.M., *The Settler and the Savage*, 209
Bentham, Jeremy, 16, 70
biopolitics, 6, 45, 60, 112, 167, 169–170, 175, 187; affirmative, 182, 195. *See also* biopower; Michel Foucault; realism, biopolitical
biopower, 6, 17, 44–45, 52, 164, 167, 169–170, 172, 182, 184, 187–190, 202, 227. *See also* biopolitics; Michel Foucault
birds, 32–33, 80; in *Barnaby Rudge*, 121–133; character of, 55–58; in *Jude the Obscure*, 180; Olive Schreiner on, 199, 219, 226; ravens, 121–123; wild bird legislation, 51–62. *See also* ostriches
Boers, 199, 204, 208, 212, 220–223
Bray, Cara, *Our Duty to Animals*, 163, 172–174

capitalism, 84, 97, 103, 107, 120, 167, 189, 225; and animal welfare, 71, 74; and anti-cruelty legislation, 51, 53; and biopolitics, 170; Charles Dickens's critique of, 103–107, 111–112; Thomas Hardy's critique of, 178–180, 187–188, 193–196; and ostrich farming, 205, 207–211; and the RSPCA, 25, 86, 175; and social reform novels, 97; and vegetarianism, 85, 87
Carlyle, Thomas, 124; *Chartism*, 95, 130
Carroll, Lewis, 147; *Alice's Adventures in Wonderland*, 27, 136–137, 146–159; "Popular Fallacies about Vivisection", 158–159; *Through the Looking Glass*, 159
cats, 80; in *Alice's Adventures in Wonderland*, 150–151, 157; and anti-cruelty legislation, 21, 49; cat shows, 79–80; and feminism, 151
Cattle Diseases Prevention Act (1866), 168
cattle industry reform, 28, 167–175, 191
Chartism, 95, 106, 123–124, 131–132
children's literature, 9, 27, 134–141, 147, 152, 159

247

Council of Justice to Animals, 178
Coutts, Angela Burdett, 141
creature(s), 9–10; liberal, 10, 35, 60, 66, 70, 75, 82, 164, 207

Darwin, Charles, 14, 22, 180–181, 196
democracy, 18, 26, 163, 228; in *Alice's Adventures in Wonderland*, 155–158; animals and, 2, 19, 50, 77, 82, 102–103, 182, 195–196; in *Barnaby Rudge*, 124–125, 130–133; and liberal education, 27, 142–145; and the realist novel, 7, 99. *See also* Chartism; minor characters
Derrida, Jacques: on animal rights, 34–35, 57, 73, 195; *The Animal That Therefore I Am*, 20–22, 154; *The Beast and the Sovereign*, 4, 46; carnophallogocentrism, 43, 57, 66, 159; "Eating Well", 109, 148–149
detachment, 71–72, 74
Dickens, Charles, 25, 97–99, 104–105, 107–108; and animal welfare, 103; *Barnaby Rudge*, 26–27, 121–133; on Chartism, 123; and dogs, 104; "From the Raven in the Happy Family", 99, 101–103; *Great Expectations*, 104, 107; *Hard Times*, 26, 108–112, 134–135; "The Heart of Mid-London", 103; *Oliver Twist*, 26, 103, 112–121; "Perfect Felicity in a Bird's Eye View", 99–101; on Smithfield Market, 103–104; social reform novel, 97
Disraeli, Benjamin, *Sybil*, 106
dogs, 14, 103; Charles Dickens and, 104; dog carts, 95; in *Far from the Madding Crowd*, 185–188, 194, 196; in *Hard Times*, 108, 111–112; loyal, 33, 80, 96, 111–112, 116–121; in *Oliver Twist*, 113–114, 116–121; and rabies, 60; in *The Story of an African Farm*, 215
domestication, 39; as subjection, 70–72
domesticity, 157, 223; and empire (ostriches), 204–207, 209–211; as subjection, 176
Douglass, Arthur, *Ostrich Farming in South Africa*, 205, 217
Drummond, William, 3; *The Rights of Animals*, 69–74, 117

ecology, 51–53, 167, 181–182, 195–197
education, 27, 110, 127, 133, 135–138, 145–146, 164, 213; in *Alice's Adventures in Wonderland*, 27, 147–158; Lewis Carroll on, 147; and the RSPCA, 65, 75–76, 141–142
Eliot, George, 174, 212; *Felix Holt, the Radical*, 163
Engels, Friedrich, *The Conditions of the Working Class in England*, 105

Erskine, Lord Thomas; 1809 anti-cruelty speech, 36–42; Cruelty to Animals Bill, 37, 42–44; "The Liberated Robins", 31–33, 61

Fariman, Frank, *Principles of Socialism Made Plain*, 89–90
Foucault, Michel, 11, 41–42, 52, 105; and animal studies, 17–18; the subject, 17, 74. *See also* biopolitics; biopower; governmentality; pastoral power
freedom, 40–41, 44, 48, 101, 113–114, 118–121, 129; and birds, 32–34, 52–53, 58–59, 61, 81; Thomas Hardy on, 176–177

Gaskell, Elizabeth, 124; *Mary Barton*, 97, 106
Gordon Riots, 26, 123
governmentality, 12, 14–15, 52, 82, 96–102, 104–108, 155, 159; and animal welfare, 65–67, 88; and anti-cruelty legislation, 24, 35–36, 41, 44–45, 48, 58, 60–61; in *Barnaby Rudge*, 124, 129, 131; definition of, 5, 38; education as, 143; in *Hard Times*, 109–111; in *Oliver Twist*, 116, 120

Happy Family (John Austin), The, 99, 102
Hardy, Thomas, 165–167; and animal welfare, 175–182; "Bags of Meat", 178–179; "Compassion", 178; *Far from the Madding Crowd*, 28, 166–167, 182–194; *Jude the Obscure*, 178, 180–181; and the RSPCA, 178
Herbert, Auberon, 53–55, 58–59, 172
Hobhouse, L.T., 2, 58
homo economicus, 7, 39–40, 139, 164, 171–172, 175, 193
Humanitarian League, 89, 168, 175

imperialism: and animals, 199; and hunting, 219–220; J. S. Mill on, 202; and racism, 220–225; Olive Schreiner's critique of, 213–214, 219, 225–226

Kingsley, Charles, 124; *The Water-Babies*, 136, 139

laissez-faire, 48, 58–59
Landseer, Edward, 96, 116, 118
liberal cognition, 3, 11, 15, 136, 143, 152; and animals, 3, 6, 148, 195
liberalism: and anti-cruelty legislation, 12; bleak liberalism, 11, 97, 123; definition of, 2, 11; and empire, 11–12, 143–144, 202–203, 225–226; individualism, 2–3, 6–7, 9, 19, 39,

125, 193–195, 204–205; moral character, 2, 9, 72–73, 96–97, 108, 113, 120, 124, 130, 133; opinion, 3, 11, 76–79, 102, 151–152
Locke, John, 3, 9, 15–16, 34, 39–40, 70, 142; *Second Treatise*, 139; *Some Thoughts Concerning Education*, 12, 27, 67, 135–141
London Vegetarian Society, 25, 66, 84, 174; best essay prize, 90; *The Vegetarian*, 87

Martin, Annie, *Home Life on an Ostrich Farm*, 207–208, 219
Martin, Richard, 45–47, 49–50, 78
meerkats, 198–199, 208
Metropolis Buildings Act (1844), 170
Mill, John Stuart, 16–17; 1865 speech at Westminster, 165; and anti-cruelty legislation, 16, 58; *Considerations on Representative Government*, 163; and democracy, 144–146; and education, 103, 142–144; *On Liberty*, 9–10, 152; *Principles of Political Economy*, 164, 202
minor characters, 98, 108, 196; animals as, 7–8, 107; Grip as (*Barnaby Rudge*), 124, 131–132

New Poor Law, 26, 112–113, 115

ostriches, 28, 202, 208–211; in *From Man to Man*, 219; ostrich character, 207–208; ostrich farming, 204–207, 223; plumage trade, 205–207; in *The Settler and the Savage*, 209; in *The Story of an African Farm*, 215–218

pastoral power, 2, 6, 17–18, 164–165, 172, 190, 202; in *Alice's Adventures in Wonderland*, 137, 153–154, 158–160; and animal welfare, 63–65, 68–75; and anti-cruelty legislation, 39, 44–49; and Charles Dickens, 98–99, 107, 112–121, 126–128; and Thomas Hardy, 167, 183–185, 187–188; and the London Vegetarian Society, 87; and Olive Schreiner, 199–200, 215; and the Vegetarian Society, 87
paternalism, 97, 106, 136, 138, 175
Peel, Sir Robert, 48
pet-keeping, 20, 89, 139, 157, 215, 222, 227
political community (multi-species), 2, 16–19, 23–24, 33–36, 48, 65–66, 70–72, 74–76, 82–83, 88, 91, 99, 174–176, 182, 194, 199
posthumanism, 15, 21–24, 51
Prevention of Cruelty to Animals Act, 49, 95
property, 59, 65, 89, 141, 193, 203; animals as, 3, 15–16, 32, 123–124, 127–128, 137, 139, 151, 157, 164, 178; and anti-cruelty legislation, 12, 36–40, 49, 52–53; and the liberal subject, 2, 43, 136

Public Health Act (1875), 168, 172
Pultney, Sir William, 12

realism, 5, 8; biopolitical realism, 166–167, 184, 191, 193; Olive Schreiner, 211–212
Reform Act (1832), 96
Reform Act (1867), 50, 143
Royal Society for the Prevention of Cruelty to Animals (RSPCA), 21, 24–25, 49, 55, 65–69, 76, 88, 115, 141; *Animal World*, 25, 31–33, 49, 55–57, 85, 87, 117, 141, 146, 206–207; *Band of Mercy*, 49, 141; best essay prize, 63, 69–70, 74–75, 90; and cattle industry reform, 167–168, 172–175, 191; Marx and Engels on, 105; and religion, 63, 65, 67, 69–70; and vegetarianism, 84–87. *See also* Society for the Prevention of Cruelty to Animals

Salt, Henry, 89; on pet-keeping, 89; "Socialism and Vegetarianism", 88
Schreiner, Olive, 28, 201–202, 213–214, 220–226; and animals, 199–200; *From Man to Man*, 218–219, 224; *The Story of an African Farm*, 28, 211–213, 215–218, 221, 226; *Thoughts on South Africa*, 198, 200, 212, 220; *Trooper Peter Halket of Mashonaland*, 213; *Women and Labor*, 218–220
settler-colonialism, 201–202, 218, 223, 226
Sewell, Anna, *Black Beauty*, 8–9, 41
sheep, 27, 45, 48, 163, 166–167; and cattle industry reform, 167, 172; in *Far from the Madding Crowd*, 183–194; and Thomas Hardy, 165–166; J. S. Mill on, 17; and pastoral power, 47, 65, 68–69, 164; working class as, 163–165
slaughterhouses, 85, 91, 178; and cattle-industry reform, 167–173.
Smiles, Samuel, 156; *Self-Help*, 73, 82
Smithfield Market, 96, 103–104, 168
Society for the Prevention of Cruelty to Animals (SPCA), 5, 96; formation of, 67. *See also* Royal Society for the Prevention of Cruelty to Animals
South Africa. *See* imperialism; Olive Schreiner; settler-colonialism
sovereignty, 6, 36–37, 39–40, 42, 48, 50–51, 54, 57, 61, 64–65, 73, 89–90
speciesism, 54, 170, 175, 177, 195, 211, 221, 223, 228; and governmentality, 131; and imperialism, 201, 203, 219, 221–222, 225
Styles, John, *The Animal Creation*, 63–65, 72–74, 117

Trimmer, Sarah, *History of the Robins*, 136, 138
Trollope, Anthony, *Phineas Finn*, 42

Vegetarian Society, 25, 66, 83–87, 167
vegetarianism: and radical politics, 85; and socialism, 88–90. *See also* London Vegetarian Society; Royal Society for the Prevention of Cruelty to Animals, vegetarianism; Vegetarian Society

Windham, William, 42–43

Youatt, William, *The Obligation and Extent of Humanity to Brutes*, 69–72

CAMBRIDGE STUDIES IN NINETEENTH-CENTURY LITERATURE
AND CULTURE

General editor
GILLIAN BEER, *University of Cambridge*

Titles published
1. *The Sickroom in Victorian Fiction: The Art of Being Ill*
   MIRIAM BAILIN, *Washington University*
2. *Muscular Christianity: Embodying the Victorian Age* edited by
   DONALD E. HALL, *California State University, Northridge*
3. *Victorian Masculinities: Manhood and Masculine Poetics in Early
   Victorian Literature and Art*
   HERBERT SUSSMAN, *Northeastern University, Boston*
4. *Byron and the Victorians*
   ANDREW ELFENBEIN, *University of Minnesota*
5. *Literature in the Marketplace: Nineteenth-Century British Publishing
   and the Circulation of Books* edited by
   JOHN O. JORDAN, *University of California, Santa Cruz* and Robert L. Patten,
   Rice University, Houston
6. *Victorian Photography, Painting and Poetry*
   LINDSAY SMITH, *University of Sussex*
7. *Charlotte Brontë and Victorian Psychology*
   SALLY SHUTTLEWORTH, *University of Sheffield*
8. *The Gothic Body: Sexuality, Materialism and Degeneration at the Fin de Siècle*
   KELLY HURLEY, *University of Colorado at Boulder*
9. *Rereading Walter Pater*
   WILLIAM F. SHUTER, *Eastern Michigan University*
10. *Remaking Queen Victoria* edited by
    MARGARET HOMANS, *Yale University* and Adrienne Munich, *State University
    of New York, Stony Brook*
11. *Disease, Desire, and the Body in Victorian Women's Popular Novels*
    PAMELA K. GILBERT, *University of Florida*
12. *Realism, Representation, and the Arts in Nineteenth-Century Literature*
    ALISON BYERLY, *Middlebury College, Vermont*
13. *Literary Culture and the Pacific*
    VANESSA SMITH, *University of Sydney*

14. *Professional Domesticity in the Victorian Novel: Women, Work and Home*
    MONICA F. COHEN

15. *Victorian Renovations of the Novel: Narrative Annexes and the Boundaries of Representation*
    SUZANNE KEEN, *Washington and Lee University, Virginia*

16. *Actresses on the Victorian Stage: Feminine Performance and the Galatea Myth*
    GAIL MARSHALL, *University of Leeds*

17. *Death and the Mother from Dickens to Freud: Victorian Fiction and the Anxiety of Origin*
    CAROLYN DEVER, *Vanderbilt University, Tennessee*

18. *Ancestry and Narrative in Nineteenth-Century British Literature: Blood Relations from Edgeworth to Hardy*
    SOPHIE GILMARTIN, *Royal Holloway, University of London*

19. *Dickens, Novel Reading, and the Victorian Popular Theatre*
    DEBORAH VLOCK

20. *After Dickens: Reading, Adaptation and Performance*
    JOHN GLAVIN, *Georgetown University, Washington, DC*

21. *Victorian Women Writers and the Woman Question* edited by
    NICOLA DIANE THOMPSON, *Kingston University, London*

22. *Rhythm and Will in Victorian Poetry*
    MATTHEW CAMPBELL, *University of Sheffield*

23. *Gender, Race, and the Writing of Empire: Public Discourse and the Boer War*
    PAULA M. KREBS, *Wheaton College, Massachusetts*

24. *Ruskin's God*
    MICHAEL WHEELER, *University of Southampton*

25. *Dickens and the Daughter of the House*
    HILARY M. SCHOR, *University of Southern California*

26. *Detective Fiction and the Rise of Forensic Science*
    RONALD R. THOMAS, *Trinity College, Hartford, Connecticut*

27. *Testimony and Advocacy in Victorian Law, Literature, and Theology*
    JAN-MELISSA SCHRAMM, *Trinity Hall, Cambridge*

28. *Victorian Writing about Risk: Imagining a Safe England in a Dangerous World*
    ELAINE FREEDGOOD, *University of Pennsylvania*

29. *Physiognomy and the Meaning of Expression in Nineteenth-Century Culture*
    LUCY HARTLEY, *University of Southampton*

30. *The Victorian Parlour: A Cultural Study*
THAD LOGAN, *Rice University, Houston*

31. *Aestheticism and Sexual Parody 1840–1940*
DENNIS DENISOFF, *Ryerson University, Toronto*

32. *Literature, Technology and Magical Thinking, 1880–1920*
PAMELA THURSCHWELL, *University College London*

33. *Fairies in Nineteenth-Century Art and Literature*
NICOLA BOWN, *Birkbeck, University of London*

34. *George Eliot and the British Empire*
NANCY HENRY *The State University of New York, Binghamton*

35. *Women's Poetry and Religion in Victorian England: Jewish Identity and Christian Culture*
CYNTHIA SCHEINBERG, *Mills College, California*

36. *Victorian Literature and the Anorexic Body*
ANNA KRUGOVOY SILVER, *Mercer University, Georgia*

37. *Eavesdropping in the Novel from Austen to Proust*
ANN GAYLIN, *Yale University*

38. *Missionary Writing and Empire, 1800–1860*
ANNA JOHNSTON, *University of Tasmania*

39. *London and the Culture of Homosexuality, 1885–1914*
MATT COOK, *Keele University*

40. *Fiction, Famine, and the Rise of Economics in Victorian Britain and Ireland*
GORDON BIGELOW, *Rhodes College, Tennessee*

41. *Gender and the Victorian Periodical*
HILARY FRASER, *Birkbeck, University of London* Judith Johnston and Stephanie Green, *University of Western Australia*

42. *The Victorian Supernatural* edited by
NICOLA BOWN, *Birkbeck College, London* Carolyn Burdett, *London Metropolitan University* and Pamela Thurschwell, *University College London*

43. *The Indian Mutiny and the British Imagination*
GAUTAM CHAKRAVARTY, *University of Delhi*

44. *The Revolution in Popular Literature: Print, Politics and the People*
IAN HAYWOOD, *Roehampton University of Surrey*

45. *Science in the Nineteenth-Century Periodical: Reading the Magazine of Nature*
GEOFFREY CANTOR, *University of Leeds* Gowan Dawson, *University of Leicester*

Graeme Gooday, *University of Leeds* Richard Noakes, *University of Cambridge* Sally Shuttleworth, *University of Sheffield* and Jonathan R. Topham, *University of Leeds*

46. *Literature and Medicine in Nineteenth-Century Britain from Mary Shelley to George Eliot*
JANIS MCLARREN CALDWELL, *Wake Forest University*

47. *The Child Writer from Austen to Woolf* edited by
CHRISTINE ALEXANDER, *University of New South Wales* and Juliet McMaster, *University of Alberta*

48. *From Dickens to Dracula: Gothic, Economics, and Victorian Fiction*
GAIL TURLEY HOUSTON, *University of New Mexico*

49. *Voice and the Victorian Storyteller*
IVAN KREILKAMP, *University of Indiana*

50. *Charles Darwin and Victorian Visual Culture*
JONATHAN SMITH, *University of Michigan-Dearborn*

51. *Catholicism, Sexual Deviance, and Victorian Gothic Culture*
PATRICK R. O'MALLEY, *Georgetown University*

52. *Epic and Empire in Nineteenth-Century Britain*
SIMON DENTITH, *University of Gloucestershire*

53. *Victorian Honeymoons: Journeys to the Conjugal*
HELENA MICHIE, *Rice University*

54. *The Jewess in Nineteenth-Century British Literary Culture*
NADIA VALMAN, *University of Southampton*

55. *Ireland, India and Nationalism in Nineteenth-Century Literature*
JULIA WRIGHT, *Dalhousie University*

56. *Dickens and the Popular Radical Imagination*
SALLY LEDGER, *Birkbeck, University of London*

57. *Darwin, Literature and Victorian Respectability*
GOWAN DAWSON, *University of Leicester*

58. *'Michael Field': Poetry, Aestheticism and the Fin de Siècle*
MARION THAIN, *University of Birmingham*

59. *Colonies, Cults and Evolution: Literature, Science and Culture in Nineteenth-Century Writing*
DAVID AMIGONI, *Keele University*

60. *Realism, Photography and Nineteenth-Century Fiction*
DANIEL A. NOVAK, *Louisiana State University*

61. *Caribbean Culture and British Fiction in the Atlantic World, 1780–1870*
    TIM WATSON, University of Miami

62. *The Poetry of Chartism: Aesthetics, Politics, History*
    MICHAEL SANDERS, University of Manchester

63. *Literature and Dance in Nineteenth-Century Britain: Jane Austen to the New Woman*
    CHERYL WILSON, Indiana University

64. *Shakespeare and Victorian Women*
    GAIL MARSHALL, Oxford Brookes University

65. *The Tragi-Comedy of Victorian Fatherhood*
    VALERIE SANDERS, University of Hull

66. *Darwin and the Memory of the Human: Evolution, Savages, and South America*
    CANNON SCHMITT, University of Toronto

67. *From Sketch to Novel: The Development of Victorian Fiction*
    AMANPAL GARCHA, Ohio State University

68. *The Crimean War and the British Imagination*
    STEFANIE MARKOVITS, Yale University

69. *Shock, Memory and the Unconscious in Victorian Fiction*
    JILL L. MATUS, University of Toronto

70. *Sensation and Modernity in the 1860s*
    NICHOLAS DALY, University College Dublin

71. *Ghost-Seers, Detectives, and Spiritualists: Theories of Vision in Victorian Literature and Science*
    SRDJAN SMAJIĆ, Furman University

72. *Satire in an Age of Realism*
    AARON MATZ, Scripps College, California

73. *Thinking About Other People in Nineteenth-Century British Writing*
    ADELA PINCH, University of Michigan

74. *Tuberculosis and the Victorian Literary Imagination*
    KATHERINE BYRNE, University of Ulster, Coleraine

75. *Urban Realism and the Cosmopolitan Imagination in the Nineteenth Century: Visible City, Invisible World*
    TANYA AGATHOCLEOUS, Hunter College, City University of New York

76. *Women, Literature, and the Domesticated Landscape: England's Disciples of Flora, 1780–1870*
    JUDITH W. PAGE, University of Florida Elise L. Smith, Millsaps College, Mississippi

77. *Time and the Moment in Victorian Literature and Society*
    SUE ZEMKA, *University of Colorado*

78. *Popular Fiction and Brain Science in the Late Nineteenth Century*
    ANNE STILES, *Washington State University*

79. *Picturing Reform in Victorian Britain*
    JANICE CARLISLE, *Yale University*

80. *Atonement and Self-Sacrifice in Nineteenth-Century Narrative*
    JAN-MELISSA SCHRAMM, *University of Cambridge*

81. *The Silver Fork Novel: Fashionable Fiction in the Age of Reform*
    EDWARD COPELAND, *Pomona College, California*

82. *Oscar Wilde and Ancient Greece*
    IAIN ROSS, *Colchester Royal Grammar School*

83. *The Poetry of Victorian Scientists: Style, Science and Nonsense*
    DANIEL BROWN, *University of Southampton*

84. *Moral Authority, Men of Science, and the Victorian Novel*
    ANNE DEWITT, *Princeton Writing Program*

85. *China and the Victorian Imagination: Empires Entwined*
    ROSS G. FORMAN, *University of Warwick*

86. *Dickens's Style*
    DANIEL TYLER, *University of Oxford*

87. *The Formation of the Victorian Literary Profession*
    RICHARD SALMON, *University of Leeds*

88. *Before George Eliot: Marian Evans and the Periodical Press*
    FIONNUALA DILLANE, *University College Dublin*

89. *The Victorian Novel and the Space of Art: Fictional Form on Display*
    DEHN GILMORE, *California Institute of Technology*

90. *George Eliot and Money: Economics, Ethics and Literature*
    DERMOT COLEMAN, *Independent Scholar*

91. *Masculinity and the New Imperialism: Rewriting Manhood in British Popular Literature, 1870–1914*
    BRADLEY DEANE, *University of Minnesota*

92. *Evolution and Victorian Culture* edited by
    BERNARD LIGHTMAN, *York University, Toronto* and Bennett Zon, *University of Durham*

93. *Victorian Literature, Energy, and the Ecological Imagination*
    ALLEN MACDUFFIE, *University of Texas, Austin*

94. Popular Literature, Authorship and the Occult in Late Victorian
   Britain
   ANDREW MCCANN, *Dartmouth College, New Hampshire*

95. Women Writing Art History in the Nineteenth Century: Looking
   Like a Woman
   HILARY FRASER, *Birkbeck, University of London*

96. Relics of Death in Victorian Literature and Culture
   DEBORAH LUTZ, *Long Island University, C. W. Post Campus*

97. The Demographic Imagination and the Nineteenth-Century City:
   Paris, London, New York
   NICHOLAS DALY, *University College Dublin*

98. Dickens and the Business of Death
   CLAIRE WOOD, *University of York*

99. Translation as Transformation in Victorian Poetry
   ANNMARIE DRURY, *Queens College, City University of New York*

100. The Bigamy Plot: Sensation and Convention in the Victorian Novel
   MAIA MCALEAVEY, *Boston College, Massachusetts*

101. English Fiction and the Evolution of Language, 1850–1914
   WILL ABBERLEY, *University of Oxford*

102. The Racial Hand in the Victorian Imagination
   AVIVA BRIEFEL, *Bowdoin College, Maine*

103. Evolution and Imagination in Victorian Children's Literature
   JESSICA STRALEY, *University of Utah*

104. Writing Arctic Disaster: Authorship and Exploration
   ADRIANA CRACIUN, *University of California, Riverside*

105. Science, Fiction, and the Fin-de-Siècle Periodical Press
   WILL TATTERSDILL, *University of Birmingham*

106. Democratising Beauty in Nineteenth-Century Britain: Art and the Politics
   of Public Life
   LUCY HARTLEY, *University of Michigan*

107. Everyday Words and the Character of Prose in Nineteenth-Century Britain
   JONATHAN FARINA, *Seton Hall University, New Jersey*

108. Gerard Manley Hopkins and the Poetry of Religious Experience
   MARTIN DUBOIS, *University of Newcastle upon Tyne*

109. Blindness and Writing: From Wordsworth to Gissing
   HEATHER TILLEY, *Birkbeck College, University of London*

110. *An Underground History of Early Victorian Fiction: Chartism, Radical Print Culture, and the Social Problem Novel*
GREGORY VARGO, *New York University*

111. *Automatism and Creative Acts in the Age of New Psychology*
LINDA M. AUSTIN, *Oklahoma State University*

112. *Idleness and Aesthetic Consciousness, 1815–1900*
RICHARD ADELMAN, *University of Sussex*

113. *Poetry, Media, and the Material Body: Autopoetics in Nineteenth-Century Britain*
ASHELY MILLER, *Albion College, Michigan*

114. *Malaria and Victorian Fictions of Empire*
JESSICA HOWELL, *Texas A&M University*

115. *The Brontës and the Idea of the Human*
ALEXANDRA LEWIS, *University of Aberdeen*

116. *The Political Lives of Victorian Animals: Liberal Creatures in Literature and Culture*
ANNA FEUERSTEIN, *University of Hawai'i-Manoa*

Printed in the United States
by Baker & Taylor Publisher Services